ONLINE BRANDING FOR MARKETING SUCCESS

BRANDING.COM

DEBORAH KANIA

NTC Business Books
NTC/Contemporary Publishing Group

ΛΛ AMERICAN MARKETING ASSOCIATION

Library of Congress Cataloging-in-Publication Data

Kania, Deborah, 1963–
    Branding.com : online branding for marketing success / Deborah Kania.
        p.   cm. (American Marketing Association)
    Includes bibliographical references and index.
    ISBN 0-658-00307-0
      1. Internet marketing.   2. Brand name products—Marketing.
    I. Title: Branding dot com.   II. American Marketing Association.
    III. Title.
    HF5415.1265.K36   2000
    658.8'27—dc21   00-30477
                                                 CIP

Cover and interior design by Monica Baziuk

Published by NTC Business Books (in conjunction with the American Marketing
Association)
A division of The McGraw-Hill Companies
4255 West Touhy Avenue, Lincolnwood (Chicago), Illinois 60712-1975 U.S.A.
Copyright © 2001 by Deborah Kania
Printed in the United States of America
International Standard Book Number: 0-658-00307-0
01 02 03 04 05 06 LB 20 19 18 17 16 15 14 13 12 11 10 9 8 7 6 5 4 3 2 1

[Contents]

CHAPTER 7

Online Advertising and Promotion   *173*

CHAPTER 8

The Website: as Brand Experience   *205*

CHAPTER 9

Branding's Tech Future   *243*

[Preface   ]

I was first introduced to the Internet in 1993. Back then it was a text-based interface that was kind of neat, but not too exciting for this marketer. It allowed the eleven-person software company I worked for to provide technical and marketing support to customers. Then, two short years later, I was reintroduced to the Internet. This time, text *and* pictures! To a marketer this was an epiphany. To my further amazement, I could click on things and would be whisked away to another website and to another part of the world altogether.

It didn't take long for many people—marketers especially—to catch on to this new communications tool. Up went the Web pages, the banner ads, the hyperlinks, the e-mail addresses, the graphics, and the ideas. Everyone was experimenting, trying to figure out how to use the Web. It was much like a small child trying to learn how to ride a bike, but in this case, no one was there to teach us marketers how to ride. We were all trying to figure it out at the same time. Businesses, customers, advertisers, ad agencies, interactive agencies, advertising and Web technology companies feverishly experimented with this new medium, sometimes with wonder and other times with frustration. I look back on those times fondly. I look forward to the future of Internet marketing with the same fondness. Every day I eagerly await the next person who comes up with another great idea for marketing on the Web.

So just why did I write this book? It was an idea I couldn't resist. After a couple of events prompted me to think about the idea of this book, I could not stop thinking about it.

The first of these events was the debate among marketers about the Web. The question: To brand or not to brand? Some would say that the Web is the best vehicle for direct-response marketing. Others would say that the Web is a great tool for branding, but they couldn't prove it quite yet. It was something they knew in their marketing gut. The direct-response force seemed to be pulling all marketers toward creating and measuring campaigns with the almighty click-through. The problem arose when the click-through rate plummeted. The responses from the advertising agency and service companies? "Don't worry about click-through; the Web gives you brand exposure, too." For marketers this is a problem, because no one could provide any brand-marketing performance measures at the time. What they could do was create other advertising and marketing formats that could increase click-through again. It worked, but for brand marketers without direct-response objectives, this wasn't good enough. Luckily, progress is being made to give online marketers the tools to measure the Web against brand-marketing objectives and calculate return on investment for branding.

The other event that prompted me to take on this project was my reading an article about branding and the Internet. The article quoted a marketer from a major consumer goods company as saying that the company would not do much marketing on the Internet until there was higher-speed access and the quality of sound and video improved. There are two important rebuttals to this objection. First, waiting can be a dangerous proposition if you have competition. Second, if you have worked with the Web for some time, you know that it has many unique features that can be effective *today* for branding. Among those features are interactivity, personalization, community, e-mail, utilities, and other applications.

The Internet is a moving target, and the act of writing a book about Internet marketing is much like trying to hit a moving target. The purpose of this book is to discuss the impact of the Internet on marketing and, in particular, brand marketing. This book covers the past, present, and future of online branding. It is a 360-degree view of the new medium and its place in the brand-marketing mix. I have interviewed researchers, analysts, marketers at both dot-com and traditional-brand companies, Web designers and developers, and industry experts in marketing and the Internet. I talked to people at advertising agencies, interactive agencies, online ad software companies, and online ad service companies.

I take a nostalgic look at the previous century of branding and what may be coming in the next century. I review the short history of the Internet and predictions for its growth and adoption by people and businesses around the world. Next, I take a look at the electronic marketplace, where many significant changes are taking place in the exchange of goods and services, media consumption, and consumer behavior. You also get a brief look at generational marketing concepts from Yankelovich and Partners and author Don Tapscott. This discussion shows how the coming generations exhibit different media and buying habits. I discuss the brand-marketing principles and the impact of the online medium on these long-standing principles. I share some firsthand insights from marketers regarding their experience with the Web medium. I discuss what it takes to build the online brand—for both dot-com and traditional brands—and the importance of establishing trust when building relationships between customers and the brand via the Web. Next, there is an in-depth discussion about the Web media channel, including the current state and future of online advertising and promotions. Then I discuss the role of websites as the ultimate vehicle for building a brand experience. Finally, you will get a peek at some key technology advances and innovations that will extend branding beyond the PC, take the brand further into the organization, and allow brand marketers to delve deeper into the customer's mind. Also, I address online privacy, which is an important part of every marketer's job. Besides introducing the subject, I offer some resources to help you understand the challenge of online privacy.

A special companion website, www.brandingbook.com, is available for *Branding.com* readers. It features resources and articles for further exploration of online branding. It will contain up-to-date material that will keep you moving along with the speed of Internet brand marketing.

Although I wrote this book, it belongs to everyone who gave time and knowledge to make it what it is. Therefore, this book also belongs to my family, friends, and colleagues who supported me during this project. I hope they understand the depth of my gratitude for their acts of encouragement.

Good luck with your online branding efforts.

[Traditional Branding Is Dead. Long Live Branding!]

>> ALL OF US IN THE PRACTICE OF BUILDING AND NURTURING BRANDS HAVE BEEN VERY LUCKY FOR THE LAST FIFTY YEARS. BASICALLY, WE HAVE FAILED TO IMPROVE PRODUCTIVITY OR ACCOUNTABILITY AND WE'VE GOTTEN AWAY WITH IT. BUT OUR TIME IS ABOUT TO RUN OUT. THE VILLAIN OR THE WHITE KNIGHT, DEPENDING ON YOUR POINT OF VIEW, IS THE INTERNET.>>

-- PETER SEALEY, PH.D., ADJUNCT PROFESSOR OF MARKETING, UNIVERSITY OF CALIFORNIA

The practice of brand marketing is about 100 years old. With the introduction of each medium—newspapers, magazines, radio, and television—brand-marketing practices had to adapt. For the most part, marketers used these traditional media to carry out similar branding tactics: delivering single messages to a mass audience. The Internet is a new communications vehicle that is changing brand marketing in significant ways.

The Internet is a roller-coaster ride for marketers—very exciting and very scary. One thing for sure is that the Internet is unlike any ride brand managers have taken before. Many marketers quickly realized that taking this ride requires considerable bravery in order to truly take advantage of the World Wide Web's uniqueness.

At the same time, this new adventure is important. The coming generation of consumers, known as Generation Y or the Net Generation, has grown up totally digital, using computers, video games, and the Internet as everyday technology. The Net Generation has sophisticated expectations regarding what can be produced on the Web. Virtual brand experience and interactivity are the language of this generation. This language is new for most brand marketers.

New Media, New Customer

Electronic media, including the Internet, are known as the *new media*. The Internet provides brand-marketing programs with some unique characteristics, such as two-way communications via e-mail and online chat, hyperlinks, and real-time access to databases for product information and customer information. With the new media, marketers have to consider new customer needs and behaviors. In traditional brand advertising, the customer is passive, receiving a single message broadcast in one direction. The Internet has transformed branding from these unidirectional messages into an electronic dialogue with the customer.

According to Jim Kelly, chairman and CEO of United Parcel Service (UPS), the Internet is "the new age of technology-driven consumerism." The Internet is changing the relationship between companies and customers. From product-centered mass production to customer-centered personal solutions and services, the change in the relationship dynamic has turned brand marketing into something altogether new: Customers first, brand second. In the early days of modern branding, the marketer created marketing messages that were received by a mass market. In the age of direct marketing, marketers identified segments within the market and tailored marketing messages to each segment. In the age of Internet marketing, the brand can mean something different and personal to each individual customer. Websites are database driven; customers can receive relevant marketing messages and product recommendations via personalized applications.

Along with this new branding dynamic, the Internet gives the online audience an unprecedented level of choice and control over the marketing messaging. Unlike the passive reception of TV and radio commercials, the interactive nature of the Web requires the customer to click on marketing messages. Online customers must seek out a website. The brand marketer's challenge, then, is to get customers to remember the brand or website and then take action and visit the site. This challenge is balanced by the targeting capabilities of Web applications. Brand marketers can efficiently reach target customers and present the brand at the right time, at the right place, to the right person to get results.

Some marketing professionals say the Web is the best direct-response vehicle ever invented. Customers can go online, see something they would like to buy, and take immediate and impulsive action. Other marketers have already recognized that the Internet also has huge branding potential. Whereas the combination of audio and video once made TV the ultimate branding vehicle, the Web allows people to interact in a deeper way with a brand than in any other medium. With advances in formats, described in Chapter 7, the online medium will become a more flexible and powerful branding tool.

A brand manager today can take advantage of many techniques and technologies to accomplish brand objectives. Studies have already shown that the Web can increase brand awareness, with some online advertising campaigns achieving the same recall rate as TV commercials. Although Web surfers often ignore static Web banner ads, other online advertising formats, such as rich media, are increasing marketers' online brand impact. For building brand loyalty, the unique communication capabilities of the Web are unmatched. One-to-one marketing on a website or via e-mail encourages customers to spend time inputting information to personalize their online shopping and brand experience. This level of personal investment will increase customer visits and purchases, and thus loyalty. In addition to generating frequent customer visits and purchases, this customer information gives brand managers better insight into their customers' needs, preferences, and behavior. Brand managers obtain detailed customer data in addition to data from focus group research and other studies traditionally used to create marketing messages and benefits. As described in Chapter 7, marketers can use online research tools not only to measure the number of clicks on an ad or website, but to gauge brand impact and return on investment (ROI) for the online medium. For example, marketers can use online intercept surveys to measure brand awareness, preference, and loyalty.

The Internet Brings Much Change, Yet Basic Principles Remain the Same

Marketing practitioners are in agreement on one thing: Although brand marketing is accomplished differently on the Internet than in other media, the basic brand-marketing principles are the same. Increasing brand awareness is key for any organization, whether it advertises on the Web or uses traditional media. However, building brand awareness with an Internet audience can be more challenging than with other media. Similarly, the brand promise remains the same on the Web, although it may be communicated in a more interactive and experiential way. Nike's website (www.nike.com) features related websites that provide in-depth interactive experiences and e-commerce with Nike. For example, at a dedicated microsite users were able to keep updated on Nike-sponsored Lance Armstrong's progress as he moved toward winning his second consecutive Tour de France in 2000. The site included daily updates during the event, Armstrong's video journal, his training regimen, and Nike cycling clothing. The benefit of this type of brand interaction is that Web users will spend a few or several minutes or maybe hours interacting with a website, which can make a long-lasting impression of the brand in the customer's mind as well as encourage purchases on the site or at retail locations. In contrast, Nike magazine and TV ads don't allow customers to experience the brand in such an interactive way.

Another unchanged principle is that brand positioning and differentiation are key components of successful brand programs. In fact, positioning messages are even more important to communicate on the Web, because competitors' websites are just a couple of clicks away, vying for your customers with traditional frequent-buyer programs, loyalty programs, and customer service. Given the online customer's easy access to competition and a brief attention span, marketers more than ever must distinguish their brand from the competition.

Thus, a related brand-marketing principle is to cultivate perceived quality. A customer judges a brand's quality each time the customer experiences the brand. Like television commercials, product packaging, and customer service representatives, websites are responsible for communicating and exhibiting brand quality.

The remaining question among marketers boils down to this: *how* to use the Web to meet brand objectives. Specifically, where does the Web fit in the overall media mix? As marketers have done with traditional media, they must find the optimum place for the Web in their overall media mix. Many industry professionals feel that this process of optimization will be much shorter with the Web than with other media, corresponding to the steep adoption curve of the Internet itself. So far, although the Web is changing brand-marketing processes and practices, it is also a successful vehicle for many traditional branding techniques, such as sweepstakes, couponing and sampling, sponsorships, and loyalty programs. These electronic versions of offline brand-marketing methods have already become popular with online customers.

Brand-marketing principles dictate that the right media mix is one that supports the brand objectives. In their early days, dot-com companies like Yahoo! and Amazon.com spent nearly 100 percent of their marketing budgets on the Internet. Now, with more sophisticated brand strategies, they are scooping up time and space on TV, radio, print, direct mail, outdoor, and other traditional media to accomplish their objectives. These dot-com companies need to establish brand awareness and credibility with the masses, just as the traditional brands like Hershey's and Hallmark have done all of these years.

So where does the Web fit? Online media and websites can build brand awareness, preference, and loyalty. The next frontier for Internet marketers is media and channel integration. Integrating offline messages with online media and vice versa is important for consistent communications. Marketers also need to ensure that their website works in conjunction with other distribution channels such as retail outlets, call centers, reseller/distribution partners, the sales force, and their other commerce channels. No matter which way the customer wants to interact with the company, the company should be available to the customer.

The Net Frontier

For some brands, the Internet is a huge opportunity to find new customers—locally or globally. For other brands, it is just a niche market opportunity, at least for the time being. Either way, technology has created an information-rich selling environment that challenges such traditional marketing practices as using TV to implant words and emotions inside the customer's mind. With the Internet, the customer has instant and far-reaching access to information about the brand and product—and those of competitors.

For marketers the Internet has opened a frontier full of opportunity. Not only does it reach customers at their computers, it has helped build momentum for wireless devices and interactive TV. Marketers can send messages to handheld computers, cellular phones, and other portable devices. Consumers will not be able to escape advertising in the future. It will follow them everywhere they take their pager or cell phone. Interactive TV, for many years considered a possibility, has become a reality, thanks to the Internet. In the very near future, marketers will be able to advertise brands one-to-one over the television. The TV ads can be chosen and customized for delivery to each individual viewer.

The frontier of Web marketing is still largely unexplored. In contrast to TV, which has been around several decades, the Web has been available to marketers for less than ten years, and the Internet is still evolving quickly. The marketing pioneers who explore the Net frontier will therefore encounter many surprises. After all, just as other transforming technologies such as electric power, the printing press, and automobiles changed society in many unforeseen ways, the Internet is sure to bring change beyond what our minds can imagine.

Under these circumstances, branding strategy is not for people who are timid or prefer the comfort of known territory. For those involved in online marketing since its earliest days, as well as those who are new to the Internet, the good and the bad news is that the pace of change will not be slowing down any time soon. Marketers who relish excitement, creativity, and adventure will prosper in this turbulent environment. By adapting new practices to the old marketing principles, and by combining experimentation with responsiveness to new information, these marketers will find a good home for their brands online.

CHAPTER <1>

[A New Chapter in Marketing History]

>> THE INTERNET IS THIS BIG, HUGE HURRICANE. THE
ONLY CONSTANT IN THAT STORM IS THE CUSTOMERS. >>

-- JEFFREY P. BEZOS, FOUNDER OF AMAZON.COM

One hundred years ago, no one could have predicted how brand marketing would evolve over the course of the century. Who would have envisioned putting a company logo on blimps or T-shirts, or showing a scantily clad clothing model on a billboard? Could anyone have fathomed the concept of on-hold telephone advertising, or even telemarketing? In 1945 television viewers would gather around to watch their favorite programs sponsored by their favorite brands. Those viewers couldn't have known that in about forty years they would be able to watch a TV infomercial starring the brand itself and be able to dial a toll-free number to get the product shipped right to their doorstep the next day.

Now consumers have a new information, entertainment, and shopping device, the personal computer. This technology would have been unimaginable to those 1940s-era television viewers, or even their counterparts in the 1960s. Marketers of that time never dreamed of the ability to "click to buy." The Internet has brought a new opportunity and challenge to marketers. And we can only begin to imagine what will happen in the next hundred years.

Marketers feel confident with the traditional media vehicles, including newspapers, television, and direct mail. However, the Internet inspires excitement and uneasiness rather than confidence among many marketers. As marketers try to figure out how to maximize the online medium now—and fast, they think, "If we don't, our competitors will." Of course, this is difficult, since the technology, media, and methods are changing constantly and quickly. Just when marketers thought they had mastered Web banner advertising, they were introduced to affiliate marketing, interstitial pop-up ads, and e-mail marketing. The Internet is a *disruption medium*. In other words, it is completely different from what came before it—so different that projecting its evolution is impossible. Furthermore, what marketers know about maximizing TV advertising, telemarketing, or direct mail does not always apply to the Web.

The prospect of using the Web may be overwhelming, but the Web is an important medium in the marketer's toolbox. Brand managers have to figure out how to make their website and online advertising work as individual media, as well as in their role as part of the entire media mix. For some companies, the website also functions as a distribution channel, so that online marketing encompasses the whole spectrum of marketing strategy. To tackle these challenges and opportunities, it is helpful to understand how marketing got to this point—the Interactive Age—and what it might look like in the future.

100 Years of Branding in a Nutshell

Successful brands elicit well-known and favorable associations. Thinking of some popular brands from the past century brings to mind a few words and phrases:

- *Fondness*—Disney (introduced in 1923), Spam (1937), Pillsbury "Poppin' Fresh" (1965)

- *Nostalgia*—Campbell's Soup (1897), Harley-Davidson (1903), Burma Shave (1925), *Life* magazine (1936)

- *Time-tested*—Nestlé (1867), Levi Strauss (1873), Ivory soap (1879), Coca-Cola (1893), Hershey's (1894), Goodyear (1898), Ford (1903), United Parcel Service (1907)

- *Slice of life*—Sears (1893), Kraft (1903)
- *Innovative*—3M (1902), IBM (1924), Hewlett-Packard (1938), Xerox (1961), Microsoft (1975), Apple (1977)
- *Unconventional*—Virgin (late 1960s), L'eggs (1971), Starbucks (1971 and 1984), Nike (1972), Body Shop (1976), MTV (1981), Dell (1984)

With dot-com brands, the oldest date back only to about 1994. They are too young for anyone to guess which will succeed. It will be interesting to see if Yahoo!, eBay, Amazon.com, Excite, America Online (AOL), and other Net brands are able to sustain themselves for the next 100 years.

Like many traditional brands, dot-com brands will have to continue redefining themselves with the ebb and flow of markets and cultures until the Internet stabilizes. Already some have done so. For example, Amazon.com used to be thought of as the world's largest bookstore. Now it promises "Earth's Biggest Selection" of a variety of products, including books, CDs, electronics, games, toys, and online auctions. Amazon's brand positioning changed in just a few short years. Some dot-com brands have already changed their names in their very short history, in order to broaden the appeal of their brand, product offerings, and audience. Such a repositioning has typically been in response to the Internet's shift from a niche-marketing tool to a mass-marketing vehicle. Here is a sample of changes in brand names among dot-com companies:

Original Dot-Com Name	*Current Dot-Com Name*
Software.net	Beyond.com
The Mining Company (www.miningco.com)	About.com
Computer Literacy Bookstore	Fatbrain.com
1800Batteries.com	iGo

The new brand names allow these companies to tap into emotions that can be associated with the brand. The new names are not product focused—they are benefit focused. For sites such as iGo the new name allowed the company to expand beyond a specific product, batteries, to a broader offering: batteries and any type of product for mobile devices such as cell phones and personal digital assistants (PDAs). The Mining Company, a site where people help other people find what they need on the Internet, was renamed About.com in 1999 "to reflect its breadth of content, services, and ease of use."

>> A Brief Look at the History of Media

There would be no advertising, other than word-of-mouth advertising, if it weren't for the invention of paper by the Chinese in 1275 and Johannes Gutenberg's Bible project in 1452 using the printing press. Here are additional milestones in media history:

1631	The first classified advertisements appeared in a French newspaper.
1704	A Boston newspaper printed advertising.
1841	The first ad agency was born in the United States.
1919	The short-wave radio was invented.
1922	A commercial radio broadcast cost $100.
1928	Television sets were put into three homes.
1939	Regular TV broadcasts began.
1954	Regular color television broadcasts began.
1963	Zip codes were introduced.
1971	Intel built the microprocessor.
1972	The early video game Pong was introduced.
1994	The Internet became available to private industry and the public at large.

The different media—newspapers, magazines, radio, television, and the Internet—have attracted audiences by offering more than older media could. In *The Internet Advertising Report*, Mary Meeker identifies highlights of this evolution:

Typically, new media have done some key things "better" than older media. For example, newspapers were better than town criers because the information was recorded; magazines were better than newspapers because they focused on national issues (and had cool pictures); radio was better than magazines because it was live and timely; television was better than radio because it was live, timely, and had cool pictures; and we contend that the Internet is better than television because it provides live, timely, viewable and often storable information and entertainment when users want it, with the powerful addition of interactivity.

The expanding capabilities of media have enlarged the ways advertisers can communicate. Advertisers can choose the most timely media (newspapers, radio, television, the Internet) or those that target specific groups (certain magazines, radio stations). They can craft emotional appeals with strong visuals (magazines, television) or acting (radio, television). And they can directly involve their audience in the communication, perhaps even stimulating an immediate purchase (the Internet).

Although each new medium has presented advances with respect to visual and audio communications, each medium has its weaknesses as well as strengths. The Web, to cite just one example, lacks some of television's ability to draw on the audience's emotions with sound and moving visuals. Some marketers are therefore waiting to leverage the Web until it improves the delivery of audio and video. Now that the Web has begun to deliver TV-quality sound and video, it seems likely that in a few years, consumers will avail themselves of interactive Net content and interactive buying. For marketers, adoption of this technology will make the Internet the most complete brand-advertising vehicle.

>> A Few Milestones of Modern Advertising

The beginning of modern advertising can be tracked back to the first handbill advertisements in the 1400s in England. England's first newspaper advertisement appeared in a London newspaper in 1650.

The first newspaper advertisement in America was an ad in a Boston newspaper in 1704.

The first advertising agency in America was opened by Volney Palmer in Philadelphia, Pennsylvania, in 1843. Until the late 1880s, advertisements were made up of text and engraved illustrations. Then came the invention of photography. Many people consider the first Ivory soap ads in 1882 to be a milestone in brand advertising. Ivory's famous ad campaign featured the slogan "99 and $^{44}/_{100}$% Pure," brand positioning that continues in today's Ivory soap advertisements. In the 1890s, Sears & Roebuck began mailing its famous catalog enabling people to purchase clothing, household items, and even the house itself. The 1920s brought full-color magazine advertisements. Also in that decade, radio emerged as a popular mass-advertising vehicle. The radio soap opera was born, and people would surround the radio to hear the next installment of *Betty and Bob* sponsored by Gold Medal flour.

After World War II came television advertising, which has since become the most popular vehicle for brand advertising. By 1952, more than 20 million U.S. households had a television. Magazines remained a popular advertising vehicle, with advertisers going into great detail extolling the virtues of their products. But magazine advertising changed in 1959 with the famous "Think Small" Volkswagen magazine ad, which relied on simplified visuals and copy.

As branding messages became simplified, the number of media outlets began to expand. In the 1970s and 1980s, there was an explosion of specialty magazines and direct marketing. The introduction of cable TV advertising and growth in the number of radio stations gave customers hundreds of choices. Advertisers began to fine tune advertising and target market segments. Media and the marketplace had become fragmented, requiring advertising that was far different from the mass advertising typical early in the twentieth century. At the end of the century, nearly every ad—TV, radio, magazine, and Web—was punctuated with a ".com." Today, spending for online advertising continues to grow rapidly as marketers and customers are becoming comfortable with the Web.

The Internet Phenomenon

The Internet reached fifty million users in just *five* years, far faster than it took other media to reach an audience of that size. According to Morgan Stanley Technology Research, radio attracted fifty million listeners in thirty-eight years, television took thirteen years, and cable TV reached fifty million in ten years.

The Internet caught on fast, and its influence continues to expand. Even among those who have not yet logged on to the Internet, the media coverage (and hype) has brought awareness of the Internet into the mainstream.

>> *Internet and Web Histories*
The Internet is the huge, interlaced network of computers reaching across all borders. It began in the 1960s with ARPANET, the network of the Pentagon-sponsored Advanced Research Projects Agency. The Internet now comprises more than 30,000 independent networks and continues to grow at an exponential pace. According to Network Solutions, it took four years to register the first million Web domain names, but only three months to grow from four million to five million domain names!

Most people access the Internet with a personal computer (PC), so the success of that technology made the Internet's expansion possible. The launch of the Apple II computer in the late 1970s introduced consumers to the idea of personal computing. In 1981 IBM introduced the IBM Personal Computer (IBM PC) and sold 671,537 units in the United States that year.

Since then, prices have fallen while capabilities have expanded. Today U.S. households are using over 100 million PCs. Close to 400 million are in use globally, about two-thirds of them in North America, Europe, and Japan.

In the United States the majority of PC owners have Internet access. Other consumers are logging on at schools and public libraries. The Internet is finding its way to other computerized devices as well, including handheld computers and wireless phones. A growing number of households view Internet content and do online buying with their televisions.

Many consumers were drawn to the Internet by the multimedia content of the World Wide Web. But this content was out of most people's reach without a browser that would allow users to easily pinpoint websites of interest from the awesome volumes of information scattered throughout cyberspace. Tim Berners-Lee, a consultant with CERN (the European Laboratory for Particle Physics in Geneva, Switzerland), led development of the Mosaic browser. Mosaic, precursor to Netscape Navigator, was launched in 1993, and the Web was opened to the public in 1994. Soon millions of people were discovering the riches of cyberspace. Today a variety of user-friendly Web browsers and search engines are available free or for a small cost. Along with their development, the number of websites has ballooned from about 1,000 commercial sites in 1994 to millions at the end of the 1990s. All signs are that the number will continue growing for years to come.

>> Electronic-Commerce Market

The participants in electronic commerce come from the total population of Internet users. Globally, that population has grown from the tens of millions in the mid-1990s to the hundreds of millions today.

EXHIBIT 1.1

Projected Internet Population, 2005 (in millions)

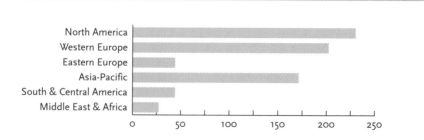

>> Computer Industry Almanac, *August 1999.*

According to an August 1999 forecast by the *Computer Industry Almanac*, the Internet population in 2005 will number more than 700 million adults and children worldwide. Exhibit 1.1 details how that population is expected to be distributed by region.

Within this population, electronic commerce is already booming. Online consumers are using the Internet to purchase everything from low-consideration items such as books and toothpaste to high-consideration products such as automobiles and homes. In the business-to-business market, buyers use the Internet to purchase everything from computer supplies to an entire computer network.

Recent trends support forecasts that global e-commerce will surpass $1 trillion by 2003. Online spending already neared the trillion-dollar mark in 1999. So far, much of that spending is by U.S. customers (74 percent in 1998, according to IDC Research). Within the United States, business-to-business e-commerce outweighs consumer spending online by a margin of almost two to one. Chapter 2 provides more detail about the online customer and the e-marketplace.

>> *The Birth of Online Advertising*

Most people recognize the birth of online advertising as the introduction of the Web banner advertisement created by *Wired* magazine in 1994. Exhibit 1.2 shows one of the early *Wired* banner ads.

The novelty of clicking on a banner initially delighted users. Being able to view an ad, click on it, go to the company's website, and then make a purchase was very exciting for both advertiser and buyer. The result was a compressed AIDA (awareness, interest, desire, action) cycle. At that time, banner ads were small and static. Now online ads can be as large as a Web page and even comprise multiple Web pages. Banner ads also allow a user to interact and transact right within the banner without being taken to a website. In addition, many other ad formats are available on the Web, and e-mail has emerged as a significant marketing vehicle.

With all these possibilities, spending for Internet advertising is increasing at a rate much like the Internet's population growth rate. According to eStats, companies spent $175 million for online advertising in 1996 and $650 million in 1997. According to Jupiter Communications, online advertising spending was expected to reach $4.4 billion in 2000 and $11.3 billion in 2003. (For more background about online advertising, see Chapter 6.)

Brand Impact

The Internet has quickened the speed of establishing a brand. Networked communications, where word-of-mouth (or word-of-e-mail) advertising spreads like wildfire across telecommunications connections, give companies unprecedented market reach and speed to market. One look at what Amazon.com has accomplished can convince anyone of that. According to Interbrand, Amazon.com is number fifty-seven among the top sixty brands in the world, just below Procter & Gamble's Pampers brand of diapers (introduced in 1961); Amazon.com came to market in July 1995. Because the Internet has reached more U.S. households more quickly than other media such as radio and TV, brands can reach a large audience more rapidly and economically. Brands have immediate access to a global market. Also, the cycle time for brand advertising to be produced and distributed online is much shorter than the production cycle for offline media. Online advertising campaigns can be created and launch within hours and days, versus weeks and months with TV, magazines, and other media.

The Internet has also transformed competitive positioning. The Internet marketplace is up for grabs. The dot-com start-up brands are

EXHIBIT 1.2

Early *Wired* Banner Advertisement

challenging the long-time offline brands. Even established offline brands become challenger brands because they don't automatically have the number-one brand in their category on the Internet. The established brands, number one in their offline marketplace, must fight new dot-com start-ups and their other offline competitors (with less offline marketshare) who are making swift moves to grab the attention of the online audience. In his book *Eating the Big Fish* (Wiley, 1999), author Adam Morgan defines *challenger brands* as brands with the potential to successfully challenge brands in the number-one spot (the *establishment brands*). The Internet has produced dot-com challenger brands such as E*Trade, CD Now, Autobytel.com, Yahoo!, CNET, eBay, the Motley Fool, PlasticsNet.com, and Gloss.com. These new entrants into the market are challenging traditional brands for the consumer's top-of-mind awareness—not only on the Web but also in traditional channels and media. The obvious example is the online competition between Amazon.com and Barnes & Noble as well as with other booksellers. In studies of online brand awareness, Amazon.com ranks higher than Barnes & Noble (www.bn.com).

In addition, marketers with traditional brands have been creating new online brands, such as Ziff-Davis's ZDNet, Hearst Corporation's HomeArts, and Amway's Quixtar. Some brands, such as Disney and CBS, have forged tight cobranding partnerships (Disney's Go.com and CBS SportsLine, respectively), while others have acquired websites. Other traditional brands are creating differently positioned versions of their offline brands, such as the *New York Times* website. Some, including Egghead.com, have completely shut down the traditional retail stores to become solely dot-com companies. Other companies, like Microsoft, have created a veritable dot-com conglomerate through their own sites or acquisitions—Microsoft Expedia, Microsoft CarPoint, the Microsoft Network (MSN), MSN Sidewalk, MSN Slate, etc. Finally, Internet service providers and traditional media companies have merged to deliver entertainment, news, content, and online shopping.

Amidst all this change, the long-term brand impact is still unknown. According to Fred Siegel, Excite@Home's senior vice president of marketing, "There are no strong brands on the Net at this point. There is strong awareness of names online, but it hasn't translated to brand preference or loyalty. It is still all up for grabs."

As brand marketers know, a lasting connection with the customer requires much more than a name and a logo. Customers must know the brand so well that they can recite in their own words what the brand means—brand attributes, brand promise, value proposition, etc. But as shown in Exhibit 1.3, a majority of respondents to a survey could not name a single website in many product categories.

The Web requires brands to challenge themselves. Marketers should think of any brand—the 100-year-old staple brand or the newbie Web-born brand—as a challenger in the new medium. This mindset ensures that brand strategies and programs will truly leverage the idiosyncrasies of a unique medium. For an example of a company that is already doing this, read the lessons learned by Hewlett-Packard on page 15.

EXHIBIT 1.3

Brand Unawareness: Percent of Respondents Not Naming a Website

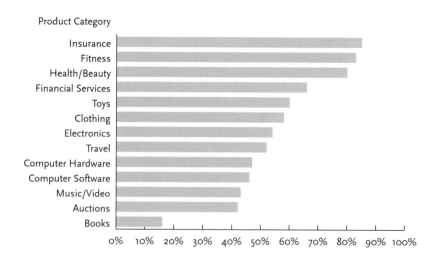

>> Courtesy of e-commerce/Harris Interactive, April 1999.

>> *Traditional Brand Advantages and Challenges*

Incumbent brands have the initial advantage over new entrants to a market. With traditional brands, marketers have spent many dollars and invested many years to establish brand awareness and build equity. Thus, well-known offline brands have the familiarity advantage when Web users surf the Internet and see companies and logos they are familiar with. If this familiarity is positive, it instantly connects the online user with the brand's online presence.

Seeing this advantage, dot-coms have tried to get to the Web first in their category and to generate plenty of advertising and publicity along the way. The objective is to become well known both online and offline. Thus, traditional and dot-com businesses alike have tried to enjoy the status of being the "traditional" brand.

So far, traditional brand advantages have generated a good dose of consumer awareness online. In the top online shopping categories identified in Exhibit 1.4, a majority of the brands mentioned are also well known in the offline world. That Amazon.com is known for books comes as no surprise, because it was first in creating the online book-selling model. Similarly, eBay, which was mentioned most often for auctions, was responsible for creating the consumer online auction. In other product categories, offline winners dominate brand awareness online. These categories include computer software (Microsoft, Egghead—originally a bricks-and-mortar retailer), clothing (Gap, Lands' End), and health and beauty (Avon).

Traditional brands cannot, however, rest on their laurels when they build their online presence.

In some e-commerce categories, traditional retailers are struggling to compete with online upstarts. For example, eToys is challenging retailer Toys "R" Us, and E*Trade is challenging well-known financial services company Charles Schwab. In most product categories, traditional brands have gained a whole new set of competitors that didn't exist prior to the Internet.

Furthermore, the online audience behaves differently and has different expectations when interacting with a brand on the Web rather than in other channels such as a store or catalog, or in other media, such as magazines, TV, or radio. Online consumers are on a mission, seeking information or solutions to their needs. They want marketing that helps them learn more about a product or service. Since online users have so much more control over the marketing they receive online, marketers will have to work harder to entice users to stop their info-seeking mission and spend time with marketing information. Currently, a majority of the top e-commerce websites are dot-com companies, which were online significantly earlier than other retailers. Still, their first-mover advantages are being challenged by well-known catalog and bricks-and-mortar companies with considerable brand equity to bring to the Internet. A notable example is Volvo (see page 18).

EXHIBIT 1.4

Online Brands Mentioned by Survey Respondents

Product Category	Brand
Books	Amazon
Auctions	eBay
Music/video	Amazon
Computer hardware	Dell, Gateway
Computer software	Microsoft, Egghead
Travel	Travelocity, Priceline
Clothing	Gap, Lands' End
Financial services	Schwab, E*Trade
Toys	eToys, Toys"R"Us
Health/beauty	Avon
Electronics	No winner
Fitness	No winner

>> *Courtesy of e-commerce/Harris Interactive, April 1999.*

>> Hewlett-Packard Thinks Strategically

Hewlett-Packard has been quick to appreciate the power of the Web, both as an advertising medium and as a marketing channel. Ian Ryder, HP's director of Global Brand Management, also recognizes some of the pitfalls that await unwary marketers, so he navigates them carefully.

One of those pitfalls is failure to acknowledge the extent to which the online experience empowers customers. Ryder points out that the Internet customer can easily gather information and control the selling process. Consequently, he says, "Brand is more important as a point of differentiation." The customers who consistently return to a website and buy a company's product will be those who have a close and positive relationship with the company's brand.

How can you create such a relationship in the seemingly cold and indifferent world of cyberspace? Ryder maintains that advertisers can make an emotional impact in *any* medium if they do their job well. As an analogy, he points out that although print is a two-dimensional medium, perfume and fashion companies have long been using print advertising to send compelling messages.

Another pitfall for online marketers is lack of preparation for the global marketplace. Ryder explains, "Like it or not, if you don't participate [on the Web], then you are missing out on a fast-developing, key channel to market, and if you do participate, then you are putting yourself into a global marketplace instantly." In contrast to other media, a website automatically grants the advertiser a global presence. To succeed on that scale requires a careful strategy. Ryder advises coupling broad standards (such as a navigational framework) with localization of the site for different geographic areas. For example, he explains, "You will not see much success from a website in Poland which is only in English." The solution again is to create a consistent and favorable experience that supports the marketer's branding strategy: "The essential thing to bear in mind is that the total customer experience, from in-country direct or indirect brand contacts, must be consistent—and consistent with what the customer expects and wants."

(continued)

The essence of meeting this challenge, concludes Ryder, is that providing a positive total customer experience on the Internet requires a masterful blend of branding, business strategy, and technology. And what of the company that doesn't bring these talents together? Ryder predicts it "will sooner or later be seen in the obituary pages of the financial press!" >>

>> *Dot-Com Brand Advantages and Challenges*

Dot-com brands have the advantage of originating in a high-tech context. Dot-com businesses started out with an intimate knowledge of Internet technology and the online audience. Since these brands were born on the Web, they are marketed by people who typically know the magic of the interactive dialogue and experience that bring together the user and the brand. As a result, many dot-com websites that lack high levels of brand awareness have accrued high preference and loyalty ratings.

In general, however, awareness is strongly correlated with preference. For example, in Exhibit 1.5, the clothing sites that had the highest unaided recall among survey respondents were also the ones respondents most preferred. The survey, conducted by IntelliQuest, found this awareness-preference correlation across all of the product categories studied.

Along with awareness, brand trust is extremely important for increasing customers' loyalty to brands. Brand marketers invest much time and money establishing a close and lasting relationship with customers. The trust relationship comes from the brand delivering on its promises. Brand trust also comes from a customer-brand relationship that is positive, consistent, and dependable. On the Web, brand trust is of critical importance. Issues surrounding privacy and security have made the online audience skeptical of any e-commerce or marketing website, particularly ones that they have never heard of before.

To meet this challenge, Web brands must add other dimensions— familiarity and security—when building the trusting brand relation-

EXHIBIT 1.5

Consumers Like What They Know: Recall and Preference Rates for Clothing Websites

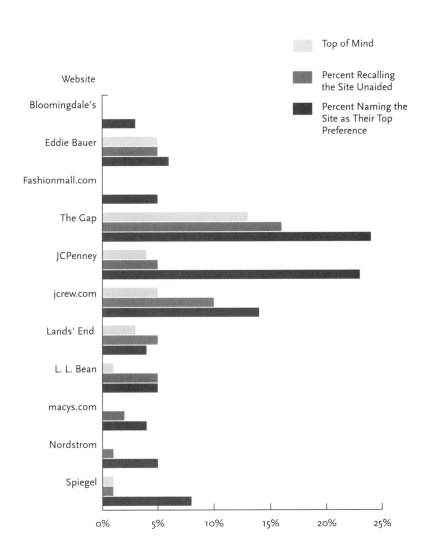

>> IntelliQuest consumer e-branding study, First Quarter 1999.

>> MVBMS Drives Volvo's Brand Online

Messner Vetere Berger McNamee Schmetterer/EURO RSCG, Volvo's U.S. advertising agency, has been helping Volvo with its brand for more than nine years. Several years ago, Volvo began to redesign its cars to make them more interesting to look at and more fun to drive—supplementing the brand's reputation for safe automobiles.

At the same time, the Web became a viable channel for car buying. Volvo leveraged the Web as a medium for making its brand "hipper." According to Ron Berger, chief executive of MVBMS, "The Web is contemporary, and any brand that is online has the association of being forward-thinking and contemporary." Volvo became one of the first automobile manufacturers to host a website (www.volvocars.com). The website created by MVBMS was designed to bring offline communications to the online audience. The demographics of the Web audience (above-average income and education) played to Volvo's new brand strengths.

Volvo conducted its first online advertising campaign in 1996 to test whether the online medium could generate sales leads. The campaign's objective was to get prospective car buyers to the website to schedule a test drive and answer a fifteen-item questionnaire for lead qualification. Overall, Volvo expected about 400 respondents for the entire campaign. Within an hour of the campaign, the company received 100 leads.

MVBMS's experience with Volvo reflects its own commitment to learn what online advertising can do for brands. According to Frank D'Angelo, director of interactive services at MVBMS, "We didn't know what to expect from the online medium, but we didn't want to pigeonhole it either. Instead, we experimented with it to gain a holistic understanding of what the online medium is capable of accomplishing." Although television may be a greater tool for emotional appeals, D'Angelo insists that a website can tell a story that also appeals to the emotions and senses. Eventually, however, he expects the two media to join forces: "Interactive TV is the future. It brings the best of both worlds, the emotional abilities of TV and the interactive, targeting, and call-to-action capabilities of the Web." >>

ship. Familiarity with a company or brand produces feelings of higher trust (unless a person has a negative perception of a brand). In a joint research study conducted by Cheskin Research and Sapient responses indicated a strong correlation between familiarity and trust. However, many dot-com brands have not yet achieved the level of familiarity necessary to achieve trust. The most interesting finding of the study was that there was not a strong correlation between site usage and trust—familiarity was clearly a more important indicator of trust. This presents a disadvantage to any brand that does not have a high degree of familiarity within its market. To increase awareness, many dot-com brands have increased their overall marketing budgets significantly and have shifted a majority of the media mix to traditional offline media such as radio, TV, and outdoor advertising. For example, fatbrain.com once dedicated over 80 percent of its marketing budget to online efforts but in 1999 spent 66 percent in offline marketing efforts such as magazine advertising. Two online brands, eBay and Garden.com, have created their own print magazines for newsstand and subscription distribution. According to Competitive Media Research, total dot-com spending on offline advertising between January and September 1999 almost tripled from the same period in 1998.

To develop brand trust on the Internet, traditional offline brands and online brands also must address the issue of security and privacy. The online audience expects that websites will protect personal data, provide for secure payment, and maintain the privacy of online communications. Therefore, along with a secure connection for transmitting credit card information, users want a highly visible privacy policy that informs them how their personal data will be used by the company. Because of the potential for abuse, as frequently reported by the news media, consumers are on high alert. The Cheskin/Sapient study mentioned earlier found that the use of certain language (text describing site's security, safe shopping guarantee, and the words *Visa* and *MasterCard*) and seals of approval (TRUSTe, VeriSign, MasterCard, Visa, American Express, Netscape Key) increased the feelings of trust among online buyers who responded to the survey. Aside from the

---

>> CompuBank Builds Awareness and Trust

CompuBank, launched on the Internet in 1998, was one of the first virtual banks. Customers can manage their bank accounts online and get cash from an automated-teller machine, but they cannot walk into the bank—there are no physical locations. Not only does CompuBank have the challenge of establishing itself as a household name, it must convince people to trust the whole new concept of using a virtual bank. As acceptance of online banking grows, traditional banks are going online at an aggressive rate. The customer mindset is beginning to shift to the Net banking model, but CompuBank has to compete with traditional institutions.

Building brand loyalty under these circumstances calls for superior marketing. Jonathan Lack, executive vice president at CompuBank, says, "We focused on two key areas: first getting trusted third-party endorsements, second charging no or less fees than bricks-and-mortar banks. This is a huge advantage, since traditional banks are coming under fire for the enormous fees."

To present a stable image yet also create a whole new model for banking, CompuBank uses an affiliate marketing program, something that works well for popular consumer goods. According to Lack, half of CompuBank's customers come from affiliates." Also, CompuBank features a rewards program. For every purchase made with the CompuBank check card, the customer receives one ClickMile from ClickRewards. This strategy is unusual for a bank, but as many marketers have already experienced, the Web establishes no rules. Marketers keep inventing new rules as they figure out how to optimize the online channel. >>

---

privacy and security issues, Jupiter Communications has identified these key components of building trust in the minds of online consumers: strong offline brand, word-of-mouth referrals, branded products, good online experience, quality of the website, and quantity of information on the site.

Message and Media Impact

The Internet's impact on brand messaging and media is so substantial as to call for a paradigm shift in the way we regard these elements of marketing strategy. Traditional brand message and media have largely called for a unidirectional broadcast out to the masses—singular messages that are largely untargeted and sent in one direction from advertiser to audience. Although direct-marketing techniques made it possible to tackle market segments and niches with semi-tailored messages, the Web offers bidirectional communications—dialogue that is targeted and in some cases personalized to an individual customer in a one-to-one manner. Before the Web, markets were already fragmented, with highly targeted direct mail, specialized magazines, and hundreds of cable TV channels. The Web takes this even further in permitting messages to be communicated to the smallest of target markets very cost-effectively. For many companies, the Web expands the available market by making global reach economical.

Along with dialogue, the Internet encourages networked communications. For marketers, networked communications enables building virtual communities where a brand can host a community of customers with common desires, interests, and concerns.

These unique capabilities of the Web change many notions of messaging and media used in other channels and communications vehicles. In earlier Web days, it seemed that the equivalent of an online brochure worked, but the minimum requirement today and into the future is a total interactive Web *experience*.

As the Web is shaking brand organizations to the core, marketers are wondering what will work: "Will my current brand messages work on the Web?" and "Should we change our messages, our brand, or even our name?" For example, 1-800-Flowers changed its name to 1-800-Flowers.com—seemingly a simple change. In contrast, Hearst Communications is known offline by the names of its individual magazines—*Good Housekeeping*, *Redbook*, and *Cosmopolitan*. It created an online brand using Women.com (and HomeArts) as an umbrella brand for its magazines, instead of making each magazine its own stand-alone brand.

Some dot-com brand names seem to be have been chosen to describe benefits, feelings, lifestyle, and emotions rather than what the company does or the name of the founder. For example, here is a sampling of dot-com brand names alongside some traditional brand names:

Dot-Com Brands	Traditional Brands
About.com	Nestlé
More.com	Levi's
Beyond.com	Kodak
Go.com	Disney
Uproar.com	Volkswagen
Yahoo!	AT&T
Fool.com	IBM
Streamline.com	Intel
Google	Louis Vuitton
Spree.com	Swatch
Monster.com	Apple
Gloss.com	Calvin Klein
Fatbrain.com	Microsoft

Besides influencing one of the most valuable brand assets, the brand name, the Web has challenged the current state of brand marketing in all facets. In particular, the Web has had a tremendous impact on brand messaging in both online and offline media. The Web has been known as an irreverent, in-your-face, break-all-the-rules, anarchist, freedom-minded community and medium. It is not unusual to see messages online that exhibit these attributes. Now dot-com brands have brought these bold styles of messages to television, radio, and print. Monster.com, in its Super Bowl 1999 ads, featured kids talking about their career goals in a sarcastic way that mocked current corporate recruiting and career development. And E*Trade used the slogan "Bucking conventional financial services" to bring unconventional messages to TV. Under this influence, traditional offline brands have presented messages differently, especially if they are going after the Net Generation audience. (For more about the Net Generation, see Chapter 3).

Future Media and Channels

The leading penetration of Internet users is in the United States, with an estimated one-third of U.S. households having Internet access in 2000. Though the most common access to the Internet is by PC, already there are new places to place brand messages: Internet boxes (e.g., WebTV), cable set-top boxes, game machines, interactive satellite set-top boxes, electronic book devices, and wireless/smart handheld devices like palm-sized computers, cellular phones, and Web phones. The wireless-device industry is just beginning to explode and promises great growth and opportunity. According to IDC, shipments of consumer information appliances will surpass home PC shipments in the United States in 2001.

Already, Yahoo! is making content from its site and its partners downloadable to handheld computers and other wireless devices (mobile.yahoo.com). In addition to Web news and content, maps, applications, and other services, brands will be able to push out their advertising to owners of these devices. Also, United Parcel Service allows customers to track packages using a Palm VII device. (See Chapter 9 for an in-depth discussion about information appliances, smart handhelds, and other devices.)

Books and items traditionally bought through mail-order catalogs can be naturally extended to the Net, but who would have thought that consumers would purchase a new car or new home via the Internet? In 1995 a static banner ad was quite novel. Now there are interactive online ads and in-banner tracking. What's next? "If anyone tells you they know what is coming in the future, they are blowing smoke," says Anne Benvenuto, senior vice president of Autobytel.com. "We are lucky if we can predict what is going to happen in the next six months."

In a *Business Week* article (October 4, 1999), Robert Hof echoes her opinion:

> *Out of this primordial technological swamp called the Internet are emerging new companies, business models, corporate structures— even new industries. It's a time of such tumult and confusion that no one can agree on what's happening now, much less on what's coming*

next. In the five years since the World Wide Web made the Internet usable by mere mortals, everything we thought we knew about business seems questionable.

There is much we cannot predict, but in terms of marketing, we have already learned one important lesson about the online medium and channel: The most significant change is that the Internet puts the customer, rather than the product or service, at the center of the branding process.

TOP-OF-MIND THOUGHTS

From hot-metal type to rich-media banners, who could have imagined? In one sense we are light-years away from the beginning of modern advertising. At the same time, the Web can bring us back to that highly personal service provided by local merchants before the Industrial Age. With the Web, advertising can be sliced, diced, and served up in hundreds of ways—to the point of sending a single highly personalized message to each customer, even if there are millions of them. This capability also brings complexity, so the Web may make some nostalgic marketers yearn for the simpler times of mass advertising. A more positive response is to learn how to cope.

>> Establish familiarity and trust. These are the two elements necessary for establishing the online brand.

>> Marketers should keep an open mind when it comes to building their online brand and using the online medium for brand marketing. The Web medium is still nascent and changing in a way that demands flexibility in creative and in the execution of brand campaigns.

>> Think "customer-centric." Customers, not products, are at the center of the new marketing universe—not just online, but also in other media and distribution channels.

CHAPTER <2>

[The E-Marketplace]

>> WE'RE SEEING THE WAY WE DO BUSINESS CHANGE
BEFORE OUR VERY EYES. BUT THE QUESTION REMAINS, WILL WE
HARNESS THE POWER OF E-COMMERCE TO HELP ESTABLISH OUR
CUSTOMERS' BUYING PATTERNS, INTEGRATE OUR SUPPLY CHAINS,
AND PROVIDE BETTER CUSTOMER SERVICE? OR WILL WE STAND
STILL, SHOCKED BY FEAR OF THE UNKNOWN AND COMFORTABLE WITH
THE STATUS QUO, WHILE OUR COMPETITORS TRANSFORM THEIR
BUSINESS MODELS TO FORGE LASTING ELECTRONIC CONNECTIONS
TO OUR CUSTOMERS? >>

-- JIM KELLY, CHAIRMAN AND CEO,
UNITED PARCEL SERVICE

Now that we have entered the next millennium, it is a great time to reflect on the future marketplace, the electronic marketplace (e-marketplace). Undoubtedly, the Internet has changed the exchange of goods and services in the marketplace. Shoppers quickly accepted the Internet as a place to gather information about goods and services. Almost as quickly, they have branched out to the act of online buying, moving from information gathering to comparison shopping, from product selection to payment. From the comfort of their homes, Internet users can shop till their cursors drop. The convenience of researching and/or buying products online is unprecedented. Internet users are conveniently purchasing groceries, framed artwork, sofas, golf clubs, kayaks, toys, skis, chocolate, alcoholic beverages, houseplants, and even trees.

There will not be many limitations to what online consumers or business customers can buy online in the twenty-first century. At first, the typical online consumer purchases were low-risk, low-priced items such as books and music CDs. Now consumers use the Internet to buy just about any product or service, including travel, homes, automobiles, and other highly considered purchases. For most items, buyers won't even be limited by their availability to receive purchases, thanks to what Tom Frey, senior researcher of the DaVinci Institute, calls "the Mailbox of the Millennium." These new mailboxes are about the size of small refrigerators. They can be refrigerated as well as attached to the owner's house to blend in with the architecture. Parcels delivered to such a mega-mailbox are protected and secure, and the box holds almost any product, no matter how oversized, irregularly shaped, or perishable.

The marks of the e-marketplace are networked communications, online communities, interactivity, virtual experiences, one-to-one communications, and the blurring of channels. Ultimately, companies and brands leverage the Web by allowing online customers to experience the brand using Web technologies and incredibly deep, complex, and sophisticated databases. No longer is the brand's logo enough to forge the iron-clad loyal brand relationship on the Internet. For online consumers, brand loyalty will develop from relationships.

The business-to-business marketplace is changing as dramatically as the retail marketplace. In the Web's early days, businesses created simple and brief websites that were essentially electronic versions of their corporate and product brochures. Now corporate websites allow business customers to place orders, access account information, receive custom pricing, and use other applications that speed up the business process, reduce communications costs, and increase customer loyalty.

Networked Communications

As a vast global network, the Internet gives buyers and sellers unprecedented reach and access to people, products, services, and information. Sellers, buyers, and users of products can communicate directly with one another. Shoppers compare notes, sellers supply product information, and everyone keeps track of the latest business and consumer trends. This is *networked communication*, and it makes the e-marketplace unlike any other market. With networked communications, marketers encounter the thrilling and perhaps terrifying combination of two-way communication, global markets, virtual communities, new distribution channels, and faster cycle times.

>> *Real-Time, Two-Way Communication*

In the traditional mass marketplace, customers were many steps away from the brand. For many consumer goods, the brand manufacturer would sell to a distributor, who would sell to a retailer, who would sell to consumers. If consumers wanted to provide feedback, they usually directed their comments to the store; some might call or write to a manufacturer's customer service department.

With the Web, in contrast, the manufacturer invites customers to participate in an ongoing dialogue. Customers have an open invitation to visit the website, explore its contents, and react to what is there. As they visit, customers provide feedback, either consciously (by sending e-mail) or unconsciously (by clicking on items at a site that gathers data about users' online behavior). Many websites try to maintain a dialogue by providing content of interest, inviting comments, and personalizing future content according to the information gathered from the user.

>> *Global Opportunities (and Competition)*

The Internet erases borders between countries, creating a global marketplace. By establishing an Internet presence, marketers are communicating with people in every country and offering products around the world, to anyone who should happen to find their websites. Likewise, customers can look for sellers on every continent. A search for information about books, machine tools, or adventure vacations may turn up suppliers in Brazil or Britain, not just in the shopper's own backyard.

This immediate access to other countries presents marketers with both an opportunity and a challenge. The opportunity comes from the almost instant access to worldwide markets. Companies can roll out a new product in international markets faster and at less cost than using traditional channels and media to enter these markets. However, companies that go online must do their homework, quickly acquiring knowledge of the legal, trade, and cultural aspects of each market. (Of course, they can use the Internet to gather that knowledge much more quickly.) Another challenge, mentioned previously, is that the e-marketplace gives customers easy access to the marketer's global competition.

>> Virtual Communities

Networked communications spawns virtual communities large and small through bulletin boards, newsgroups, forums, discussion groups, and chat. In virtual villages and virtual product user groups, people can easily share ideas with each other or with the company. As people's reach is expanding because of the Internet, these micro-communities make the world feel smaller. Virtual communities let people gather from all over the world to trade thoughts about their common interests.

From the marketer's perspective, virtual communities essentially "wire" word-of-mouth advertising. This development can help or hurt companies to a much greater extent than before and much more quickly. If a customer is displeased with a product or service, he or she can instantly e-mail a scathing account to several people, who in turn can forward that message. In this manner, word-of-mouth communications can speed around the world with a few mouse clicks.

>> New Distribution Channels

Woe to the brand that is the subject of a nasty rumor! But favorable word-of-mouth is a priceless opportunity. Networked communication has created new channels of distribution. Among these are *infomediaries*, vast networks of affiliates and cobranding partnerships (msn.com and sciquest.com, for example). News organizations have added e-commerce elements to their websites. Alternatively, in addition to supplying product information, online retailers are becoming in-depth resources for content. WebRx.com has an "Info Center" for many of its shopping areas to educate consumers while they shop for health and beauty products. This shortens the consideration-to-purchase cycle but also blurs the line between information and advertising.

>> Shorter Cycle Times

Networked communication speeds up the communication cycles involved with product development, advertising and promotions, purchasing, order processing, and customer service. For example, e-mail has increased the speed and removed the distance barrier of transmitting information between sender and recipient. Without communication delays, companies can introduce products much faster, and customers can provide immediate feedback. The brand marketer's product development cycle also shortens. Marketers speed up the process of product development, testing, and introduction by using e-mail, file transfer, and electronic meetings. The customer feedback process shortens considerably when customers use websites, e-mail, and online chat.

>> Super-Empowered Customers

Networked communication has created the *super-empowered customer*. Such a customer not only can surf sites and gather information independently, he or she can e-mail twenty-five friends in an instant to seek their opinion or experience with a particular company or brand. Web users can also participate in a chat with other people interested in the same products and brands. With these tools, customers can easily find not only the companies they are looking for, but also their competitors, located just a click away. The search is even easier with comparative shopping services such as CompareNet and *bots* such as MySimon. Bots are software applications that search the Internet for data and evaluate the data according to the user's criteria. For example, shopping bots scour the Net for comparative pricing and other information on the behalf of a Web user. In sum, comparative shopping is much easier than before—especially when all companies are using the online medium to leverage the customer self-service model and provide all the information the customer needs to make a purchase decision.

With super-empowered customers, brand strength comes into play more than ever before. When a shopping bot provides the user with a list of online vendors offering similar prices, all but the most price-sensitive buyers typically select the shopping sites they are familiar with and trust. The growing proliferation of online shopping services therefore requires marketers to generate brand awareness and brand preference within the online audience. Fortunately for marketers, the concept of brand strength and its protection against price competition are nothing new.

Brands in the E-Marketplace

There is incredible power in network communication if marketers leverage it in a way that strengthens brand loyalty. The key to leveraging network communication is to embrace it. By using the networked community to increase favorable perceptions of the brand and develop brand relationships, marketers build brand loyalty.

There are degrees of brand loyalty—from no loyalty, where the customer easily switches to another brand based on price promotions, to extreme loyalty by customers who are so delighted that they become advocates or friends of the brand. A loyal customer base protects the brand from price pressure, reduces marketing costs, increases time to respond to competitive threats, and enhances marketing's effectiveness in attracting customers. Many say that acquiring a customer costs five to six times more than selling to an existing customer. The benefits of brand loyalty thus flow right to the bottom line.

>> *Loyalty to Strong Brands*

Although networked communication can make it tougher for a brand to establish a strong position online, creating a strong brand is essential in the e-marketplace. Online customers gravitate to brands they know and trust. Also, a strong brand offers protection against discounting and other forms of competition. Many offline brands have the initial advantage of familiarity and loyalty when they move their business online. But even dot-coms can build strength by applying the basics of brand marketing:

- *Brand awareness*—Establish awareness of brand name and brand characteristics in the brand's marketplace in order to enhance familiarity and liking. To consider a brand, customers must be aware of it.

- *Perceived quality*—Create a perception of quality in the mind of the buyer. More important than an objective measure of the brand's quality is the customer's perception. If a product is of superb quality but the customer perceives the brand as inferior, the customer won't buy it. Thus, successful brand marketers concentrate on what their customers observe and care about.

- *Brand associations*—Provide a meaning of the brand to the customer. This meaning comes from the brand's association with images, experiences, characters, celebrities, personalities, customers, benefits, prices, and whatever else differentiates the brand and forms the bond between the customer and brand.

These principles hold true for marketers on the Internet. Some specific marketing tactics utilize the unique capabilities of the Web to increase brand awareness, create favorable perceptions, and build positive brand associations.

>> 1-800-Flowers.com Connects with Customers

By Internet standards, 1-800-Flowers.com is an online retail veteran. The company entered into its first agreement with an online service, CompuServe, in 1992, signed a deal with America Online in 1994, and launched its own website in 1995. It continues to sign deals with major portals for the brand exposure, as a blocking move against competition, and, of course, to generate more sales.

One of the company's biggest brand moves was changing its name, adding ".com" at the end of 1-800-Flowers. "We wanted to communicate to the marketplace that we have expanded our offering beyond the telephone to include the Web," explains Donna Iucolano, vice president of interactive services. Other strategic changes at 1-800-Flowers.com involve the product mix, which has expanded to include other gift items including gourmet food baskets. "The challenge to extending our product line is the potential dilution of the brand, but we added products that were natural extensions of the gifting services we already provide," says Iucolano.

The brand strategy at 1-800-Flowers.com focuses on the core brand attributes of quality and convenience. In support of convenience, 1-800-Flowers.com has, like many marketers, created an affiliate program that allows other websites to sell the company's products. But unlike the open, "come one, come all" approach many marketers take toward signing up affiliates, 1-800-Flowers.com carefully evaluates and continually monitors all affiliates to ensure they exhibit the high level of quality that its customers expect.

On its website (www.1800flowers.com), 1-800-Flowers.com is striving to provide the same level of convenience it has mastered over the telephone and at its retail stores. Staff members respond to all e-mails within just an hour or two. "We are very responsive to e-mail in order to give our customers the same level of convenience and service they expect from our call center representatives. Online buying is still new, and there are still a lot of barriers to remove to make the experience pain free for our customers," says Ken Young, the company's public relations director. Besides e-mail, the website provides many different ways for customers to interact with 1-800-Flowers.com, including real-time online chat with customer service representatives. With a planned "click to talk" feature on the site, customers can actually talk with a representative while on the site. Building on 1-800-Flowers.com's history of advising customers on their gifting needs over the phone, the Web-based chat and voice interaction will help the company continue to provide expert advice and assistance in the e-marketplace. >>

>> Loyalty from Strong Relationships

Beyond awareness of and positive associations with a brand name, brand loyalty arises from a favorable brand relationship. Currently, there is a lot of brand awareness online, but little measurable brand preference and loyalty. However, the Web is the perfect medium to facilitate relationships with customers. Because it provides two-way communications, interactivity, and personalization, marketers can use the Web to maximize their brand's relationship with each customer. By enabling economical communications with customer segments and individual customers, the Web helps marketers build customer-focused brands.

Long gone are the days of guessing what customers want or need. Customers can go online to communicate their needs, desires, and concerns directly with the company. Companies that heed these communications can create for each customer a value proposition optimized for that customer. By using the Web to build and maintain individual customer profiles, companies can present products and solutions that particular customers will be more willing to buy and will be more satisfied with. This personalized approach generates repeat Web visits and purchases—and offline buying and communications as well.

An example of a company that leverages these relationship-building capabilities is Furniture.com. Its website features many services that give online customers a personalized shopping experience:

- Real-time online chats offer users quick answers from a design consultant.

- The My Selections function allows customers to store details of furniture selections in a database for future reference.

- By clicking on Personal Shopper, the online customer can contact a design consultant (a real human being), who recommends products that match the customer's needs and posts the recommendations online for the customer to review.

- Using the personalized Room Planner, customers can organize a virtual room with their existing furniture and any new furniture they are thinking of ordering from Furniture.com.

- Customers can order a fabric swatch from the website, and Furniture.com will send it to the customer free of charge.

Besides fostering interactions with individual customers, marketers can leverage the Internet's virtual communities to form stronger relationships between their brands and groups of customers. The Web brings together people to form communities, using technologies such as e-mail, real-time online chat, and discussion boards. According to John Hagel and Arthur Armstrong, authors of *Net Gain*, virtual communities shift the balance of power from companies to customers. Companies that organize, sponsor, and facilitate a community of customers have a chance to build a higher degree of customer loyalty and gain the resulting economic returns.

There are many examples of brands facilitating affinity groups using online community technologies such as discussion forums and online chat. The more of themselves that customers invest in these company, brand, or affinity groups, the more they will do business with these companies or brands. A famous offline example of successfully building a loyal customer following through affinity groups is that of Harley-Davidson motorcycles. In 1983, the company formed the Harley Owners Group (HOG) to get Harley owners more involved in the sport of riding motorcycles. It is now the largest factory-sponsored motorcycle club in the world. Some Harley-Davidson owners are so loyal that they gather for rides and parties, and some customers even tattoo the brand's logo on their arm. With this example, it is hard to call these folks Harley-Davidson "customers"—they are Harley-Davidson *advocates*. Further, these staunch supporters of the brand prove to be extremely loyal and enthusiastically provide word-of-mouth referrals to other people.

Micro Markets and Virtual Communities

Even without the impact of the Internet, today's marketplace is highly fragmented. Moving beyond classification criteria such as gender, age, income, ethnicity, and race, marketers can segment their total market in terms of detailed demographics (e.g., by zip code and profession), psychographics (values, lifestyle, and personality), and other criteria. Pinpointing specific customer segments can produce substantial economic benefits. A marketer can cost-efficiently match specific marketing messages and offers to specific target markets within the brand's overall market. Through individually addressable media, including Web databases and e-mail, marketers can even send a single personalized marketing message to a single prospect or customer.

From a marketing standpoint, the Internet is a collection of thousands and hundreds of thousands of micro markets. Many of these take the form of communities united according to many common characteristics—geography, age, gender, product use, recreational interest, art enjoyment, ethnicity, religion, education, economic status, technology adoption, life situations, product or brand interests . . . and the list goes on. The old days of mass production and advertising may look attractively simple compared to the sophistication and complexity of marketing on the Internet. However, the benefits of targeting market segments and establishing online communities are economically attractive. In the long run, one-to-one marketing can bring attractive returns if marketers are patient enough to look beyond short-term results.

>> *Fragmented Media and Markets*

In the nineteenth century and early twentieth century, fewer products were marketed, markets were broadly segmented, and marketing messages traveled via a few media vehicles. As marketing evolved in the twentieth century, it spread to new media, including cable TV, satellite TV, special-interest magazines, catalogs, targeted direct mail, and the Internet. As the variety of media increased, so did the number and volume of marketing messages. An individual American consumer once received a few hundred advertising messages each day; that number had grown to a few thousand messages today.

Who is delivering all those messages? Just take a look at the extent of media in the United States, according to Morgan Stanley:

- About 54 million newspapers circulate daily in the United States.

- Over 10,000 magazines are being published in the United States, with an average of over 600 new magazines introduced per year between 1988 and 1995.

- About 11,550 U.S. radio stations broadcast every day.

- There are about 1,200 broadcast television stations in the United States (compared to 17 experimental TV stations in 1937).

- Cable TV was introduced around 1948. In 1995, there were about 64 million cable subscribers in the United States, accounting for 11 percent of television advertising spending.

That represents only the basics. U.S. media also include direct mail, satellite TV, telemarketing, the Internet and PC, wireless devices, kiosks, high-tech billboards, interactive TV, and even TV screens in elevators.

To see how the proliferation of media creates fragmentation, consider women's print magazines. Conde Nast's women's magazines include four different fashion/beauty magazines, *Vogue*, *Glamour*, *Mademoiselle*, and *Allure*. Also, Conde Nast has a life-stage magazine, *Bride's*; a health-beauty hybrid magazine, *Self*; and a fitness magazine, *Women's Sports & Fitness*. This is just one publisher's selection of several magazines targeted at specific segments within the market for women's magazines.

The Internet is even more fragmented. There were more than 56.2 million Internet hosts in August 1999 (up from 43.2 million in January 1999), according to Network Wizards and Matrix Information and Directory Services (MIDS). Of these hosts, about 33 percent (18 million) have the ".com" domain. And because Web publishing is so economical, just about anyone can create a website that serves a niche interest based on many classifications, including lifestyles and life stages. On the Internet there are thousands of websites dedicated to women's interests and issues, as specific as *Women & Billiards Online Magazine*. The Internet is one of the best examples of a fragmented medium as well as a fragmented marketplace.

>> Common Interests

One of the greatest strengths of the Internet is that it enables community building. Fundamentally, online communities are similar to the over-the-fence discussions by neighbors or the affinity group gatherings used by traditional brands in an attempt to create an unbreakable connection with the brand. Also, a customer can associate with the company in a personal way by communicating directly with company representatives via the Web and e-mail.

As people log on to the Internet in search of others with common interests, brands can build relationships by facilitating the creation of online communities. Building a community online can take either of two basic forms:

- *Customer community*—The website may bring together a community of customers to interact with one another by sharing their experience with a company or brand. This effort need not be directed and highly commercial. The website can simply offer a forum for affinity groups to share their related experiences. The halo effect from a brand's online community strengthens the connection between the customer and the brand.

- *Company/brand community*—A company may establish a community of company or industry representatives with whom customers can interact. For example, the company may offer a service in which Web users can get expert information and advice from the company directly and personally. With simple applications such as online chat, the company may offer scheduled or real-time chat sessions between customers and customer service representatives, company officials, or credible industry experts.

People will form communities with or without the company involved. A company or brand should strongly consider stepping in to foster the community building as a host. Communities can take on a life of their own. When properly designed and managed, online communities can become highly valuable and even indispensable to customers.

Traditionally, brands create a brand personality as a substitute for a personal endorsement so a customer can identify or associate with the brand. On the Web, brands can create electronic forums for discussions in which actual customers represent and reflect the personalities of the brands. Discussions among customers or between customer and company can produce a much stronger association than a print ad using a model or actor to represent the target audience.

Garden.com, a website that sells garden plants and gardening products, created a special community Web model. Its efforts build on the essence of gardening as a social activity in which enthusiastic gardeners share ideas and secrets with one another. Garden.com has a large community area on its website, offering twenty-four-hour live chat for customers, celebrity chats, Garden Doctor e-mail, weekly member quizzes, and Gardener's Forum (see Exhibit 2.1). According to Dionn Schaffner, vice president of marketing at Garden.com, "Our community gives our customers a sense that we are all in this together. We are virtually there to help gardening enthusiasts and gardeners." Schaffner says the Garden.com website fosters relationships by providing the means for gardeners to talk with experts or one another. This experience increases customer satisfaction by enabling customers to make better product choices, and their satisfaction, in turn, fosters loyalty to the Garden.com brand.

The evidence so far indicates that online communities contribute to increasing repeat visits and the average time a customer spends at a website—which could be many minutes or hours instead of the few seconds spent viewing a television advertisement. According to a 1999 study by Forrester Research, about 10 percent of respondents return to a website because of chat groups and bulletin board systems (BBSs). A survey by Activmedia found that 62 percent of respondents considered the Internet a positive experience for meeting peers and exchanging views. In an NFO Interactive survey of online shoppers, 35 percent said they would buy more online if they could interact with an e-commerce salesperson in real time. As the evidence shows the importance of online communities for building brand relationships and a better online shopping experience, marketers like Garden.com are making community a key component of their websites.

EXHIBIT 2.1

Web Page for Garden.com's Online Community

>> *Courtesy of Garden.com.*

>>   **Relationships Feed Growth at Garden.com**

Garden.com, a gardening content and commerce website, didn't just create a
website to sell trees, shrubs, and plants; it created a whole distribution network of independent nurseries across the United States. It is a gardening
company that cannot exist without the Internet, and it leverages the Net to
deliver a whole new value proposition.

Garden.com spent two and a half years quietly and patiently creating the
infrastructure and brand in order to change how gardening products are purchased. The company first did a branding study of the gardening industry and
found there were no dominant brands. Then it created systems behind the
scenes to ensure delivery of the brand promise for critical things like making
sure plants don't die after being purchased and planted. Those systems
include website tools that help customers select the right product for their
garden's location and attributes, such as sunny or shady. Garden.com also
ensures that their nursery partners meet quality standards. "Building a brand
is a holistic process beyond advertising," states Lisa Sharples, chief marketing officer and founder of Garden.com. "Brands must create the best possible
experience, because news travels fast on the Internet when customers have
bad experiences online."

Garden.com uses both online and offline media to promote the brand.
The company created a magazine, *Garden Escape*, not to become a publisher,
but to serve as a customer acquisition vehicle. The demographic of the magazine reader is different from Garden.com's online customer, and the magazine encourages more people with gardening interests to become users and
customers of the website. The magazine, which is tightly integrated with the
website, is a way for Garden.com to begin communicating with prospective
customers until they are ready to make a transition to the website.

At the heart of the Garden.com brand is community. "Community is a
natural fit for our audience," explains Sharples, who likens the website to "an
online version of the traditional garden tea, party, or over-the-fence discussion between neighbors." In this role, Sharples believes, a website can have a
relationship as intimate as that of a good neighbor who willingly trades ideas

and opinions. To that end, Garden.com's products and services are selected for their ability to contribute to relationships with customers. According to Dionn Schaffner, vice president of marketing at Garden.com, "The community model lets our customers know that we are in this with them and are there to help them with gardening experts, our customer service, and their own community within our site. This creates a powerful and lasting bond." >>

Merchants of the High-Tech Kind

The Web can be the closest equivalent to in-person sales calls or selling in the retail store environment. Before the Industrial Age, there was a lot of personal selling by butchers, bakers, and candlestick makers. Then came the Industrial Age, with its mass production and mass communications. The Information Age has since offered access to a lot of information, but no personal interactions. It seems that only a premium retailer like Nordstrom's has been able to give highly personal service in the traditional bricks-and-mortar retail environment. In the Interactive Age, however, we can return to the roots of merchant selling. With the personalization and real-time communication capabilities of websites, a consumer or a business customer can get a highly personal sales and service experience. With advances in computer technology and bandwidth, websites can create a close approximation of the real-life selling environment, with virtual retail using virtual reality Web applications.

The Web technology at a minimum can handle most of the steps in the purchase cycle for most goods and services. For example, in the case of buying an automobile, buyers can use an automobile website such as Autobytel.com to research alternatives, obtain financing, and find a local dealership. Most of the buying experience is completed online, with exception of the test drive and picking up the vehicle from the dealer's lot.

The goal of any online brand engaged in e-commerce is to make the online shopping experience as good as or better than the real-world retail experience. For online brands that do not sell online, the goal is to give the customer an online experience that makes a personal connection, prompting a purchase at the next opportunity to buy the brand. Also, customers will expect integration with the distribution channel. If a customer buys something online, can he or she return it to the store? If a customer has a question and calls the customer service phone center, will the service representative recognize the customer? Providing this level of integration is a huge opportunity, but it is very difficult to do well. It requires some resources and skills—particularly database marketing skills—beyond those required by the traditional brand-marketing model.

>> One-to-One Marketing, Sales, and Service

Although the adoption of Web technologies for one-to-one communications is still in its early stages, it is growing rapidly. Many leading e-commerce websites have one-to-one features. According to IDC, about 75 percent of top Web merchants use personalization and mass customization. Here are some well-known examples:

- Amazon.com uses information it has gathered from a customer's prior purchases and preferences to recommend books, music, and other products. It also makes recommendations based on other Amazon.com customers who have similar purchase patterns (www.amazon.com).

- With Dell's product configuration tool, people who are buying a computer on the Dell website can customize the features of the computer, including hard-drive space and memory, software, promotions, printers, scanners, and accessories. Dell's Premier Pages allows companies to create preconfigured systems that can be quickly built based on the computing environment (www.dell.com).

- At 1-800-flowers.com, customer service representatives are available to help Web customers at any point in the ordering process (www.1800flowers.com).

- Chemdex's personalized solutions for scientists include personal favorites for easy reordering, real-time order status, and streamlined creation of multisupplier orders (www.chemdex.com).

- American Airlines has put many services on its website, including frequent-flier account management, personalized travel planning, and personalized seat selection when booking flights. Customers can store user-profile information on preferred destinations, seating preference, companion travelers, frequent-flier rewards status, and billing (www.aa.com).

- With a Palm VII wireless handheld device, UPS customers can track packages and use a locator to find the nearest package drop-off location. My UPS is a service that allows customers to register and store billing and shipping information, features a personal address book for up to 300 names, and offers quick shipping and supply ordering based on previous orders (www.ups.com).

- At Lands' End's website, women can build 3-D virtual models based on physical measurements and physical features such as hair color, hair style, skin tone, and face shape. Women can then try on virtual outfits that Lands' End recommends based on their personal model or try on other outfits. The model can be rotated for front, side, and back views (www.landsend.com).

Even companies that don't actually sell products online are using one-to-one Web systems. For example, Kraft Foods has created the Kraft Interactive Kitchen, which offers users personalized tools to help them with meal preparation. These tools include Your Recipe Box, Your Shopping List, Simple Meal-Planner, Make It Now (recipe suggestions based on what is in the user's refrigerator and cupboard), and Party Planner. Other brands that don't sell online but provide useful and entertaining one-to-one Web features include the following:

- Tylenol's website features information about Tylenol pain reliever products and health information and also Tylenol Care

Cards, which are electronic greeting cards that can be personalized (www.tylenol.com).

- Maybelline's site features an interactive tool that allows site visitors to create a new beauty look by choosing skin tone, hair color, etc., and then recommends the Maybelline products that can be used to create the look. The site also features beauty and makeup application tips (www.maybelline.com).

- The Pampers Parenting Institute website provides information about Pampers products, parenting advice, and "Ask the Expert." The site also features a personalized monthly e-mail newsletter that provides customized information to registered users by following along in the growth and development of their children from the third trimester of pregnancy to age two and a half (www.pampers.com).

One-to-one Web systems can be created to give the customer something of value—useful, indispensable, entertaining, informational, and convenient. For marketers, the major benefit of using personalization on a company's website is the increased propensity for an online customer to buy. In a Fletcher Research report, 68 percent of Web users in the United Kingdom who personalized a website made an online purchase—versus 28 percent of Web users who did not use personalization features on websites. Thus, one-to-one systems such as personalization on websites benefit both customers and brands:

Benefits to Customers	*Benefits to the Brand/Company*
Choice	Customer loyalty
Time savings	Competitive advantage
Personalized service	Lower marketing costs
Convenience	Identification of most profitable customers
	Additional revenue from premium personalized services
	Adaptation and continual improvement of products and customer service

In "Words from the Wise" on pages 46–47, marketing expert Martha Rogers provides more ideas for one-to-one marketing.

>> *Virtual Retailing*

One of the biggest challenges for companies is enabling customers to experience the brand online. For many products, it is difficult to let customers touch, feel, get advice, or try before they buy from the Web. With the obvious constraints of current Internet connection speeds, it is difficult to showcase products online. In the case of automobiles, there are 3-D virtual online car tours, but you can't test-drive the car online. Of course, anything involving senses such as taste or smell cannot (yet) be demonstrated online. They can be simulated with text and visual cues, but they cannot come close to the real thing.

In spite of these limitations, creative marketers have developed ways to provide representations of their brands. Like traditional retailers, they dispense product advice and samples. In addition, some online retailers are creating virtual experiences by coupling data provided by customers with their own product data. A sample of virtual retail experiences on websites follows:

- *Product demonstration*—To help online buyers get a real-world experience of a product, or at least closer to reality, many companies have created applications using interactivity, 3-D modeling, or virtual reality that demonstrate the product. Autobytel.com's 3D Virtual Showroom shows users three-dimensional views of cars from the inside and outside. Users can also change colors and options and even see how the vehicle looks in the daytime and at night (www.autobytel.com). Sharper Image presents products online in a similar fashion to their famous in-store product demonstrations, in which shoppers can touch and test products (www.sharperimage.com). The Body Shop's Virtual Makeover shows users makeup options on different models (www.bodyshop.com). Century 21's 360-degree virtual home tours use the iPIX technology to show a complete 360-degree view of each room, from side to side and top to bottom (www.century21.com). IKEA lets users experience IKEA

>> Martha Rogers on Building Brand Relationships
One Customer at a Time

Martha Rogers, Ph.D., is a partner in the management consulting and training firm Peppers and Rogers Group, and coauthor of the international bestsellers The One to One Future *(Currency/Doubleday, 1993) and* Enterprise One to One *(Currency/Doubleday, 1997). She and coauthor Don Peppers also wrote* The One to One Fieldbook *(Currency/Doubleday, 1999) with Peppers and Rogers Group president Bob Dorf, and* The One to One Manager *(Currency/Doubleday, 1999). Visit the Peppers and Rogers Group website at www.1to1.com.*

Deborah Kania: *How does one-to-one marketing change the customer's relationship with a brand?*

Martha Rogers: In the Industrial Age, brands were created as a substitute for relationships. Mass marketers visualized their task in terms of selling a single product to as many consumers as possible. Advertising a brand name and focusing consumer demand on a mass-produced product became increasingly cost-efficient, primarily because of the extraordinary communications efficiency of mass media.

Today, a combination of customer tracking, interactive dialogue, and mass customization capabilities allows companies to create one-to-one relationships with individual customers. The concept of one-to-one marketing, or treating different customers differently, was prohibitively expensive and nearly inconceivable to the traditional marketer just a few years ago.

D.K.: *What can a company do to leverage one-to-one marketing to increase loyalty?*

M.R.: In the Interactive Age, companies can make their customers more loyal and more profitable by establishing *learning relationships* with them. Learning relationships get smarter and smarter with every new interaction. Customers tell the one-to-one enterprise about their needs, and the enterprise customizes its product or service to meet the need. With each interaction and customization, the enterprise gets better at fitting its product or service to individual customers. Now, even if a competitor offers the same type of customization and interaction, customers won't be able to get the same level of convenience until they first reteach the competitor what they already spent time and energy teaching the one-to-one enterprise.

There are four key implementation tasks required to launch an effective one-to-one initiative:

1. *Identify customers.* It is critical to know each customer in as much detail as possible across all contact points, through all media, across every product line, at every location, and in every division.

2. *Differentiate customers.* Customers are different in two different ways: they represent different levels of value, and they have different needs. The enterprise must differentiate individual customers to prioritize efforts with valuable customers and to tailor its behavior based on individual needs.

3. *Interact with customers.* The enterprise must be able to interact with customers across a variety of media. Every interaction should take place in the context of all previous interactions. Conversations should pick up where the last one left off, regardless of time or medium.

4. *Customize for customers.* To lock a customer into a learning relationship, the enterprise must adapt some aspect of its behavior to meet a customer's individually expressed need, whether that means customizing a manufactured product or tailoring the services that surround a product.

D.K.: *What role does the one-to-one relationship play in brand loyalty in the competitive Internet marketplace?*

M.R.: The Web epitomizes the very essence of capabilities needed for one-to-one marketing—it is an immediate and highly cost-efficient interactive channel. As companies can now create and leverage relationships with customers, the role of brand must change to reflect the relationship. In the one-to-one enterprise, a familiar and trusted brand will help establish a connection to a customer, but it is the relationship that will protect profit margins and keep a customer loyal to the firm over competitive brands. >>

furniture before they buy it. The IKEA online assembly guides allow customers who have purchased furniture or are thinking about buying an item to view a step-by-step interactive demo showing how to put the furniture together (www.ikea.com).

- *Product advice*—Many people look to a company's sales and service associates who work in a store or call center to help them make a decision about a purchase, especially if that purchase is a high-ticket item such as a car or needs a specific type of care such as plants. Garden.com's Plant Finder tool allows buyers to choose the right plants for the right geographic location and area of their yard or garden. The interactive Design a Garden tool, featuring the Landscape Planner, has predesigned garden templates, or users can design their own personalized garden (www.garden.com).

- *Sampling*—Sampling and trial uses have been an effective branding technique for a very long time. The Web can facilitate samples and trials for any type of product or service. CD Now provides sound-clip music samples to allow buyers to listen to the music before they purchase the CD (www.cdnow.com). Hallmark has done very well increasing traffic, site registration, and purchasing using free electronic greetings, and it features free card coupons on its website to increase trial in Hallmark retail stores (www.hallmark.com). Furniture.com allows Web visitors to order fabric swatches for the furniture they are interested in purchasing (www.furniture.com). Noxzema's Fitskin.com website lets users request free samples of its Skin Fitness moisturizing lotion (www.fitskin.com).

Internet Channels

As consumers and businesses continue adopting the Internet as a way to purchase goods and services, it won't take long before this marketing channel is widely viewed as a necessity. Forrester Research forecasts that by 2003, 37 percent of all U.S. sales for computing and electronics equipment will occur in the e-marketplace. Online sales will claim smaller but still significant shares in other industries. In the energy industry, for example, 12 percent of sales will be online in 2003, and online purchases of telecommunications, financial services, and retail sales each will account for 5 or 6 percent of U.S. sales in the respective industry.

Even when the percentages are small, they represent significant dollar volumes. According to the Forrester data, online U.S. sales of computing and electronics equipment are expected to grow from $52.8 billion in 1999 to almost eight times that amount, or $410.3 billion, in 2003. Growth forecast for other industries over the same period ranges from a sixfold increase for retailing ($18.2 billion to $108 billion) to a whopping sixteen times greater online sales in 2003 for the energy industry (rising to $170 billion in 2003 from $11 billion in 1999).

The ability to order with one click makes it almost too easy to buy consumer goods and services on the Web. Brands that do not actually sell on their own sites are leveraging relationships with online retailers as well as influencing offline purchases, capturing inquiries, creating coupons, gathering customer profile data, driving in-store purchases, and more. Although many consumers were initially worried about typing in their credit card numbers, online retailing in the United States has caught on and is becoming a regular practice in most wired households. Online spending is much less in other areas of the world, but it is growing in some areas as fast as in the United States (see Exhibit 2.2). Consequently, IDC estimates that global e-commerce spending by consumers will reach $1.3 trillion in 2003.

That spending comes from a growing number of households. Forrester Research estimates that more than seventeen million households shopped online in 1999 and about forty-nine million will do so in 2004. The average online spending by each of those households was $1,167 in 1999 and will be $3,738 in 2004, according to Forrester. A survey of online households by Odyssey L.P. found that almost half had made an online purchase during the preceding six months. Among those households, the mean number of purchases was 3.7. A study by Greenfield Online reported that 39 percent of respondents with access to the Internet spend less time at the mall or local store. Online buyers in the Greenfield study most often reported purchasing books, CDs, computer software, computer hardware, and airline tickets.

At this point, the list of what *cannot* be sold or facilitated by the Web is much shorter than the list of what consumers are buying. Early on, marketers thought consumers would buy only low-risk items online. In fact, consumers are entrusting websites with their financial transactions, making major furniture purchases, getting groceries delivered to their door, planning a relocation, renting an apartment, . . . anything imaginable.

>> *Business-to-Business E-Commerce*

Business-to-business (B2B) e-commerce has exceeded direct-to-consumer online sales, and it is growing at least as fast. According to the Yankee Group in a 1999 report, U.S. B2B e-commerce will achieve a compound annual growth rate of 41 percent over five years. Exhibit 2.3 illustrates the pattern of growth forecast for selected industries.

Channel Changing and Media Blurring

The Internet is simultaneously creating channels and tearing down channels. Many wholesalers and retailers worried that brands that traditionally used distribution channels would sell directly to customers, a practice known as *disintermediation*. This has in fact happened with some brands. For example, although Procter & Gamble has kept its traditional offline grocery and mass merchant channel intact for Tide, visitors to Tide.com can find online retailers offering its detergent. Although Procter & Gamble doesn't sell directly to consumers online, its traditional distribution partners feel threatened by the Internet, and they have put pressure on P&G. Procter & Gamble has embraced the Internet as a viable media outlet and channel, yet it has to balance the need for cooperation with its traditional retailers with the opportunity presented by Net retailers. Similarly, many airlines, including

American Airlines, sell tickets directly to online customers, and this has presented a huge challenge to offline travel agents. And when office furniture giant Herman Miller introduced HMStore.com, the company received considerable negative feedback from its traditional distribution channel.

As in the case of Tide, not all online selling is through direct channels. Another Internet phenomenon is the emergence of new intermediaries, including *infomediaries*. These Web-born companies are

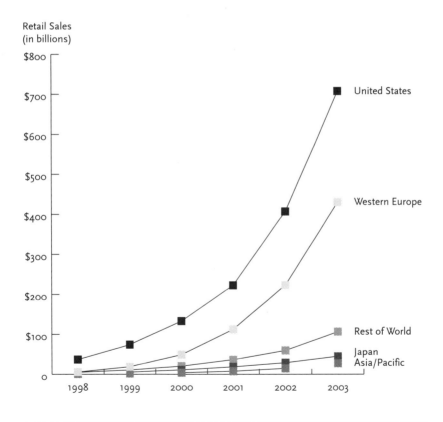

EXHIBIT 2.2

Business-to-Consumer E-Commerce on the Rise

>> *IDC.*

portals or e-commerce sites that aggregate a selection of goods and services in vertical or horizontal markets. For example, to serve the market for scientific products, SciQuest.com matches product seekers with vendors. The vendor-buyer matchmaking applications at SciQuest.com include auctions, customized purchasing, and information for buyers and sellers of scientific and laboratory supplies.

Along with changes in distribution practices, the Internet has shaken up the media world by blurring the lines between advertising

EXHIBIT 2.3

Business-to-Business E-Commerce in the United States

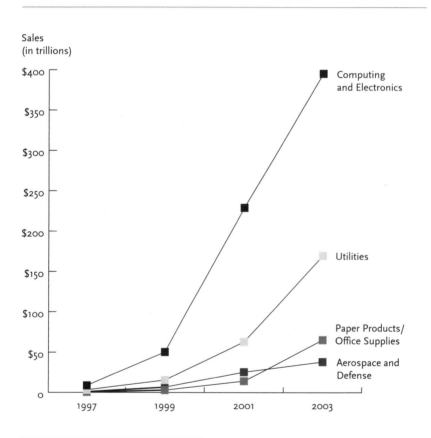

Sales
(in trillions)

>> *Forrester Research.*

and editorial. Traditional publishers and content providers have set up websites at which their customers can buy goods and services directly from advertisers. For example, *USA Today*'s website places its USA Today Marketplace, offering e-commerce features, directly alongside news and editorial. Conversely, some online retailers have become content providers. In addition to product and use information, retailers provide editorial content from credible outside information sources or in-house staff. For instance, PlanetRx.com, the online pharmacy, offers a feature called Health eCenters, which contain in-depth articles about various health topics. Associated with every article topic are recommendations for products from vitamins to sunscreens. Brand marketers must consider the delicate balance between editorial and advertising. For the content to be credible to customers, it must be separate from commerce.

Finally, marketers are leveraging the Internet's dual role as channel and medium by using *affiliate marketing*. This approach involves placing messages with hypertext links to the marketer's website at relevant places on other affiliate websites. Whenever a Web user clicks on the message, the marketer pays a commission to the affiliate. Amazon.com, a master of this technique, places ads for books or CDs whose content is related to what is displayed on the affiliate website. Whenever someone clicks on an ad and buys from Amazon.com, Amazon.com pays the affiliate that displayed the ad. Through this strategy, marketers like Amazon.com have created an online distribution channel of thousands or hundreds of thousands of sites, from really tiny websites to large cobranded alliances.

Affiliate marketing truly leverages the networked communication model and is a highly economical way to create a distribution channel. One reason is that creating electronic communications is relatively cheap, with no expensive paper or CD-ROM sales kits to mail out. Also, it is very quick and easy to enable affiliates to start selling. Affiliate marketing is typically a pay-for-performance model, where the commission is a percentage of the online sale. Finally, with affiliate marketing, the advertising investment is less than other online and offline media.

E-Marketplace Challenges

Along with these novel approaches to marketing come some online challenges. The primary challenges of the e-marketplace involve its limitations in providing sensory experiences and direct human contact.

In the real-world marketplace, customers can use their senses to experience brand attributes. Appealing to the senses of sound, touch, taste, smell, and sight can be a challenge on the Web. Yet, as traditional brand marketers know, appealing to senses and emotions is critical to achieving brand awareness, preference, and loyalty. Some products can be experienced only in real life, so customers may need to experience them offline before they come to buy online. For example, consumers might prefer to test food, fragrances, automobiles, apparel, and homes offline and then complete their transactions online. This challenge presents a strong argument that brand marketers should integrate various media and channels to achieve strong cross-media continuity, in order to ensure the first and subsequent purchases. To meet this challenge, marketers will have to leverage text, graphics, photography, sound, animation, 3-D graphics, community, and other Web features.

The Web also lacks real-life interpersonal interactions. Although the Net facilitates personal communications via e-mail and online chat, it lacks the ability to perform in-person product demonstrations and face-to-face communications. The traditional in-person selling process can be superior to the Web selling environment, because it gives customers a chance to engage in personal, interactive dialogue with companies. Salespeople in in-person selling situations can monitor a prospect's voice inflection as well as body language and modify the selling process accordingly, which may lead to better sales results and relationships. Companies can overcome this challenge by designing their websites to be the best simulation of a sales agent—to be as good as the in-person selling process. Companies can use one-to-one product recommendations and cross-selling, coupled with real-time customer service using online text, chat, e-mail, and voice chat. Websites can even offer "live selling" by using products such as Cisco WebLine, which enables a company salesperson or service representative to browse along with the customer, Web page by Web page, helping with the customer's purchase or service needs.

TOP–OF–MIND THOUGHTS

With networked communications, the e-marketplace replaces the traditional brand marketing model of a single, one-way broadcast communication with many personalized dialogues between companies and their customers. A strong brand transcends any medium, including the Internet. Web applications are available for brand marketers to ensure their brands are successful in the e-marketplace.

>> Branding is as important in the online marketplace as it is in the offline marketplace. Branding arguably is even more critical online as a way to forge loyal customer relationships when networked communication puts the competition just a few clicks away.

>> With traditional brand marketing, the challenge has been to build a loyal, long-term customer base. The Web enables brand marketers to keep track of customers by using Web databases and to keep in touch with customers through e-mail and participation in virtual communities. These practices enhance the brand's ability to build loyalty one customer at a time.

>> Customers may consider the Web too technical and impersonal. The challenge for brand marketers in the e-marketplace is to build websites and online advertising that tap into human emotions and behavior. Virtual communities, personalized communications, virtual retailing, interactive sound and audio applications, and real-time online sales and service can make the online buying experience more personal.

CHAPTER <3>

[The E-Customer]

>> IT'S THE INTERSECTION OF A TECHNOLOGY
REVOLUTION WITH A DEMOGRAPHIC REVOLUTION THAT IS
BEGINNING TO CHANGE EVERY INSTITUTION IN SOCIETY. >>

-- DON TAPSCOTT, AUTHOR OF GROWING UP DIGITAL

Understanding the customer is the keystone of all marketing efforts. Customer demographics, psychographics, behavior, and attitudes give key insights that help marketers define their customers' wants and needs. The Internet gives marketers greater ability to capture this information than ever before.

Early on in the adoption of the Internet, users tended to be technically savvy, highly educated, well paid, and male. Now and into the future, the demographics of online consumers and businesspeople more closely match the makeup of the offline marketplace. The Web marketplace is also looking more global, with Europe, Asia/Pacific, and other regions growing fast enough to rival the U.S. online market in a few short years. As these people welcome the Internet into their daily lives, Web surfing is replacing some of the time spent on other activities, including watching television, making phone calls, and reading magazines.

Although e-customers still watch prime-time TV, read magazines, flip through catalogs, and listen to the radio, their expectations from these media are limited to entertainment and passive information;

they expect something different from the Internet. In general, customers' motivations for using the Internet center on information, utility, entertainment, shopping, and community. More particularly, Internet motivation, needs, and behavior vary across generations. The older Net user goes online for news and shopping, while the younger user goes online to have fun, play online games, and shop. Furthermore, as we saw in the previous chapter, the Internet customer is a super-empowered customer. Online customers are in control. They have access to information that makes them more educated about their purchases. They choose to visit a website and interact in a community, and more important, they interact with marketing messages only if they make the effort to accept and spend time with those messages. To accept marketing messages and buy from a website, a customer expects information, choice, control, trust, and speed. Customers have been more vocal about their needs and requirements on the Internet than with any other media. This can be the marketer's bane—or benefit.

Profile of the Net User

The mainstreaming of the Net has changed the *who* and the *why* of the Web. The who of the Web now represents both genders, all generations, and every geographic region. The why of the Web is the changing motivation for going online. In 1995 gathering and sharing information were the primary motivators, but in 2000 Web users expect online shopping, gaming, trading, instant messaging, transacting, interacting, and participating in communities in a highly dynamic environment.

>> Demographics

Not only consumers but also business users of the Internet are becoming more representative of the mainstream population. Initially only the largest businesses went online. Now the highest growth area for online penetration is small and midsize businesses. Among consumers, the United States has the greatest penetration of online access of any nation, but other countries are gaining. For example, Iceland, Finland, and Sweden have the highest per capita Internet usage. In the future, the biggest shift will be diversity—in types of consumers and types of companies that will be represented online.

Usage by gender varies according to region of the world. In the United States, where Internet use is becoming routine, the gender distribution of online purchasing is comparable to the overall population distribution. Males represent about half of the U.S. population and about half of online buyers. In regions where Internet use is still moving into the mainstream, a larger share of the online population is male. Exhibit 3.1 details the gender split of online users forecast for 2001.

EXHIBIT 3.1

Worldwide Internet Use by Gender

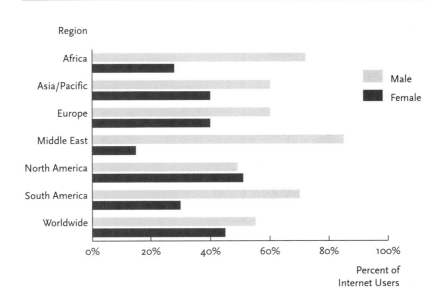

>> *Computer Economics.*

Currently the income of the online user is generally higher than that of the overall population. In an IntelliQuest study titled "World-wise Internet/Online Tracking Service" (WWITS), the majority of U.S. respondents reported incomes of $50,000 or more. A 2000 survey of Internet use in selected countries by Ernst & Young found compara-ble average annual household incomes among online customers. As shown in Exhibit 3.2, average incomes ranged from $36,300 for Ital-ian Internet shoppers to $64,600 for their U.K. counterparts.

With regard to age, Internet users continue to be relatively young. In its WWITS survey of U.S. Internet users, IntelliQuest categorized respondents by age and determined that the U.S. Internet population has an overrepresentation of young adults (see Exhibit 3.3).

Roper Starch Worldwide found that the younger people are, the more likely they are to use the Internet. As shown in Exhibit 3.4, this pattern holds true both in the United States and worldwide.

Internet users in the United States have been and still are rela-tively highly educated, but the mix is changing to make small move-ments in the direction of the general population. For example, *The State of the Net* found that 51 percent of U.S. Internet users had a col-

EXHIBIT 3.2

Average Income Levels of Internet Users

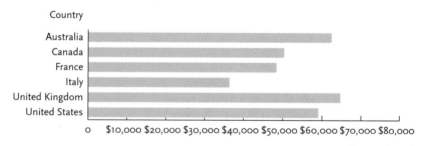

Country

Average Annual
Household Income

>> S. M. Shern, "Global Online Retailing," Ernst & Young, 2000.

EXHIBIT 3.3

U.S. Adults by Age Group: Online and Overall

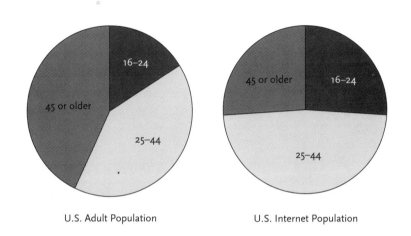

U.S. Adult Population   U.S. Internet Population

>> IntelliQuest, "Worldwide Internet/Online Tracking Service," Second Quarter 1999.

EXHIBIT 3.4

What Ages Go Online?

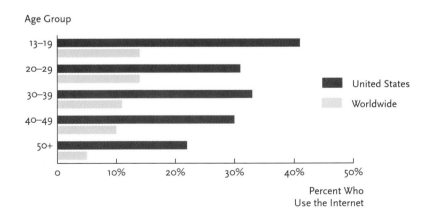

>> Roper Starch Worldwide.

lege education in 1994 and 42 percent did in 1997, compared to 21 percent of the overall U.S. population. A year later, IntelliQuest found that the U.S. Internet population even more closely resembled the overall population in terms of educational background. As shown in Exhibit 3.5, 34 percent of U.S. Internet users reported being college graduates.

Most U.S. Internet users, according to the IntelliQuest study, were employed (62 percent full-time, 8 percent part-time) in 1999. An addi-

EXHIBIT 3.5

Educational Levels for Internet Users and Nonusers

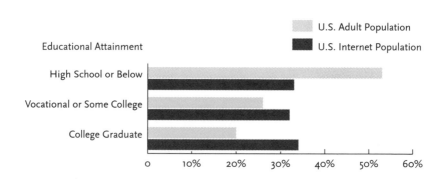

>> IntelliQuest, "Worldwide Internet/Online Tracking Service," Second Quarter 1999.

EXHIBIT 3.6

Percent of U.S. Households Using the Internet by Race/Origin

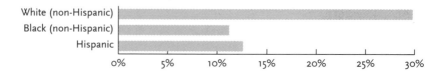

>> U.S. Department of Commerce, "Falling Through the Net: Defining the Digital Divide."

tional 15 percent were full-time students. Among the employed Internet users in the survey, almost half held professional or managerial positions:

Job Title	Percent of Internet Users
Professional staff	19%
Middle management	17%
Upper management	12%
Clerical/support staff/office manager	9%
Laborer	7%
Service staff	7%
Technical staff	7%
Sales representative	5%
Consultant	2%
Other	15%

The U.S. Internet population is beginning to become more ethnically diverse. According to a U.S. Department of Commerce report titled "Falling Through the Net: Defining the Digital Divide," all the major ethnic groups of the United States have a presence on the Web. Exhibit 3.6 details the distribution of Internet households by racial and ethnic groups.

>> Psychographics

Internet users are an active group. Perhaps because of their relative youth, Web users participated in a variety of recreational activities at a higher rate than the overall U.S. population, according to a Media-Mark Research survey of 25,000 U.S. adults. Exhibit 3.7 details these rates.

A survey by Scarborough Research found a similar level of activity. More than half of online buyers had traveled outside of the United States recently, and more than one-third were members of a frequent-flier program. About one-fourth of the online buyers were members

EXHIBIT 3.7

Recreational Activities of Web Users and the U.S. Population

Activity	Participation Rate (in percent)	
	U.S. Population	U.S. Web Users
Owning a valid passport	20.32	29.63
Renting a car (personal use)	14.04	21.20
Renting a car (business use)	9.47	15.86
Driving a sport utility vehicle	8.45	13.21
In-line skating	4.56	7.44
Mountain biking	3.86	6.07
Downhill skiing	3.68	6.55
Water skiing	2.36	3.86

>> *MediaMark.*

of health clubs, one-third had eaten at fast-food restaurants ten or more times in the past three months, three-fourths used ATMs regularly, and 64 percent used mobile phones.

>> *Connections and Computers*

Internet users' hardware limits what marketers can do. In particular, households and businesses use a variety of connections that download information at different speeds. For users with high-speed access, marketers can use sound and video in some online advertising formats and within websites. However, many households are still using modems that operate at 28.8 kilobytes (KB) per second or slower, a pace at which all but the simplest text and graphics seem to download at a crawl.

By 2003, the dominant connection technology in the United States will still be analog (i.e., narrowband). However, the penetration of broadband, which is faster than the maximum one megabyte (MB) per second of narrowband access, will increase significantly. According to the Gartner Group, by 2003 U.S. Internet access will look like this:

Type of Internet Connection	*Percent of U.S. Households*
Analog modem (up to 56 KB/sec.)	63%
Cable modem	14%
xDSL	12%*
ISDN	8%**
Hybrid satellite	3%

* Digital Subscriber Lines, which use sophisticated technology to pack data to be carried over copper telephone wires to attain higher access speeds.

** Integrated Services Digital Network, a standard for sending voice, video, and data over digital or normal telephone wires.

Worldwide, according to International Data Corporation (IDC), analog modems represented almost 90 percent of Internet access in 1999 (see Exhibit 3.8). By 2002, more consumers will have faster con-

EXHIBIT 3.8

How Users Go Online: Worldwide Install Base

Non-PC Net Access Device (in millions)	1999	2000	2003
Interactive cable set-top boxes	1.0	6.0	28
Interactive satellite set-top boxes	0.5	2.5	12
Game machines	0.8	1.5	7
Internet boxes (WebTV)	0.8	1.5	4

Type of PC Internet Connection Worldwide (in millions)	1999	2000	2002
Analog modem	69.39	79.53	93.53
Cable modem	2.10	4.25	10.76
DSL	0.35	1.10	6.20
ISDN	8.99	14.87	28.61
Wireless	0.15	0.25	0.90

>> *Gartner Group; International Data Corporation.*

nections, but analog modems will still be used by 67 percent of online consumers worldwide.

Consumers also are accessing the Internet with devices other than the personal computer. Cahners In-Stat forecasts rapid growth in the install base of non-PC access devices in the United States, as shown in the top half of Exhibit 3.8.

Internet access is not limited by household technology, however. In the United States, in 1997 about three-fourths of users accessed from home, but less than half did so exclusively. Many U.S. users logged on to the Internet from computers at work or school, instead of or in addition to using the Internet at home. Exhibit 3.9 details the usage rates.

>> *Media Consumption*

As Internet usage has grown, it has supplanted other activities, including media use. Over the past few years, a variety of studies have found that Internet users spend less time on other activities when they obtain Internet access. In 1997 Find/SVP reported that many Internet users said they were spending less time watching television, making

EXHIBIT 3.9

Where Users Log On: Internet Access by Location

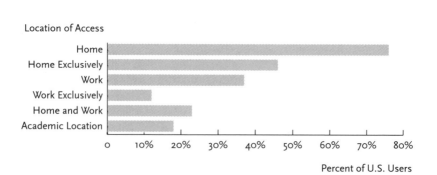

telephone calls, watching videotapes, reading newspapers and magazines, and listening to the radio. A 1998 study by Georgia Tech's Graphic, Visualization & Usability (GVU) Center found similar Internet displacement of other media consumption. According to a 1999 study by Nielsen Media Research and AOL, households with Internet access watched 13 percent less television than households that were not online. The decline in television watching varied by time slot:

- Between 4:30 P.M. and 6:30 P.M., Monday through Friday: 17 percent lower
- Between 6:00 P.M. and 8:00 P.M., Monday through Friday: 14 percent lower
- Between 8:00 P.M. and 11:00 P.M., Monday through Friday: 6 percent lower

An interesting habit of some Internet users is their simultaneous use of the Internet while watching television. An NPD Research study showed that among people who were able to use their computer and TV at the same time, 86 percent watched TV while surfing the Internet. Likewise, Cyber Dialogue found that many U.S. adult Net users spend several hours using the Internet while watching TV each week. To brand marketers this means that they should determine what the media consumption mix is for customers. Since Internet use is still growing, marketers will have to continue to monitor Internet usage by its market(s) in order to continue to refine the media mix.

>> Online User Behavior

The Internet is playing a significant role in online households. According to the IntelliQuest WWITS study, U.S. Internet users in 1999 spent an average of 14.0 hours per week online. Of that time, users devoted 4.7 hours to business purposes, 6.5 hours to personal purposes, and 3.7 hours to school or other purposes. According to Nielsen//NetRatings, here is what monthly Internet usage looked like among U.S. users during July 2000:

	Home	*Work*
Number of sessions	18	37
Number of unique sites visited	10	28
Time spent per site	57:02	43:17
Time spent online	9:40:53	20:08:54
Duration of average session	0:31:32	0:32:25
Duration of average page view	0:00:50	0:00:54

Much like other media such as TV and radio, marketers have very little time to get the attention of an online user. Also, the average number of unique sites visited from home in the month was ten, which means that online consumers tend to visit a few sites, and most of these are likely to be the same ones they visit regularly. The marketer's challenge is to make his or her site one of those frequently visited.

A key feature keeping Internet users online is the variety of activities available on the Web. Web users not only can find information, but also can converse online via chat, read a favorite magazine or local newspaper, post a classified ad for the whole world to see, keep track of up-to-the minute weather reports, book an airline flight, buy favorite CDs, play games against a computer or other online users, participate in an auction, move funds from a savings account to a checking account, purchase stocks, enter sweepstakes and contests, receive all kinds of e-mail (useful or spam), watch webcasts or online TV broadcasts, listen to favorite radio stations, and more.

When consumers are online, they behave differently than they do when in a store. Information gathering online replaces physical product inspection and impulse buying offline. However, impulse buying does take place online, and the behavior will grow as people become more comfortable with online shopping.

<<*Favorite Online Activities*>> People tend to go online, with a directed purpose such as seeking information. Spending time on the Web is a not a passive activity like watching television. Users decide

where to go and what to respond to when they get there. In sum, the Web is the premier interactive medium.

Marketers therefore need to be where their target customers want to go, near the Internet activities that grab these users' attention. IntelliQuest's WWITS study ranked activities according to the percentage of U.S. Internet users who attempted each activity:

Activity	Percent of U.S. Users
Send or receive e-mail	89%
Obtain hobby or personal-interest information	85%
Obtain general news	70%
Obtain travel information	62%
Visit website with audio content	62%
Access information about events	61%
Check weather reports	61%
Obtain information for business or work	60%
Attach a file to e-mail	58%
Obtain information on medical or health topics	58%
Download software	57%
Visit websites with video content	56%
Look up addresses or telephone numbers	53%
Obtain information for school	51%
Obtain sports information	48%
Visit sites that allow customized content	43%
Participate in chat rooms or forums	40%
Monitor stocks or other investments	36%
Play interactive games	34%
Conduct banking transactions or pay bills	16%
Place or receive an Internet-based phone call	14%

The same IntelliQuest study also measured which types of websites were visited most often by U.S. Internet users. As shown in Exhibit 3.10, users varied in terms of their interests, with the most popular topics being sports, travel, news, and education.

Researchers are beginning to compare U.S. online behavior with that of users in other countries. Comparing users in the United Kingdom, United States, Germany, and France, PricewaterhouseCoopers found that e-mail was the primary reason for U.S. households' Internet use. Among U.K. Web users, e-mail and research were of equal importance to U.K. Web users, and research was the primary reason that users from Germany and France went online. Compared to users from the other three countries, people in Germany were the most likely to access the Internet primarily for online banking.

EXHIBIT 3.10

Types of Websites Visited by U.S. Internet Users

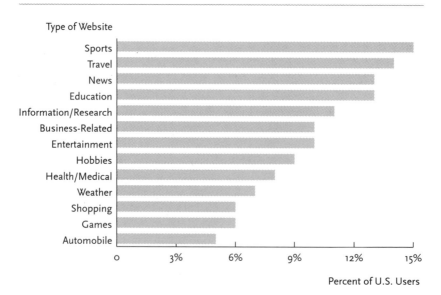

>> IntelliQuest, "Worldwide Internet/Online Tracking Service," Second Quarter 1999.

<<*Web Use and Opinion*>> In 1999 *Fast Company* conducted an online survey with Roper Starch Worldwide to determine what Web users did on the Net and what opinions they held about the Net. Like IntelliQuest's survey, the *Fast Company*/Roper Starch study found that people use the Internet for both business and pleasure but spend more time on the Internet for personal use. In addition, responses to the following statements show that Internet users have largely favorable attitudes toward the Internet, both as a medium and as a distribution channel:

Statement	*Percent Calling Statement True*
"The Internet makes it easier for people to communicate."	94%
"The Internet makes shopping easier and more enjoyable."	67%
"The Internet will fundamentally change the way we live."	85%

In addition, given pairs of options, three-quarters of respondents to the *Fast Company*/Roper Starch survey said they would rather have an hour to explore the Web than an hour to watch television. Almost half (48 percent) said they would rather have an hour to shop on the Internet than an hour to spend shopping in a mall.

Online Retail: Beyond E-Window-Shopping

The first Internet users to venture online were there primarily to browse, gather information, and maybe do a little e-window shopping. However, the share of Internet users who make online purchases has been growing. As shown in Exhibit 3.11, Internet buyers as a percentage of all Internet users has risen from just 19 percent in 1995 to 71 percent in 1999. In addition, an even larger share of Internet users go online to gather information for purchase decisions.

Like Internet users in general, Internet buyers tend to have higher incomes than the overall population. Also, the frequency of their purchases and amount spent per purchase is growing. Their online shopping appears to be a substitute for traveling to stores. According to a Greenfield Online study, 39 percent of U.S. Internet users spend less time shopping at offline stores and malls as their Internet use has increased.

The United States largely leads global online retail commerce, but other regions are growing quickly. According to International Data Corporation (IDC), the non-U.S. Internet population will generate almost 46 percent of global e-commerce spending by 2003, up from 26 percent in 1998.

For men and women alike, the primary motivation for buying online seems to be convenience. According to a survey by CDB Research & Consulting, the top reasons for shopping online are the ability to shop from home at any time and to find the best price. Exhibit 3.12 shows the percentage of men and women who gave various reasons for conducting their shopping online. Except for "Online shops offer best prices," the reasons emphasize the relative ease of shopping in the e-marketplace. (And even "best prices" reflects the ability of Internet tools to search for the lowest price from a global selection.)

EXHIBIT 3.11

Percent of Internet Users Who Made an Online Purchase

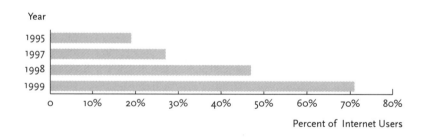

>> *Find/SVP; Greenfield Online.*

The most popular products purchased by online consumers include books, musical recording, computers, electronics, toys, clothing, travel, investments, and videos. In addition, online users are increasingly using the Internet for buying furniture, automobiles, health and beauty aids, pet supplies, homes, and appliances.

Generations Net

Each generation has distinct expectations of the Internet and motivations for using it, whether simply to surf or to buy online. Understanding these differences can help marketers anticipate market shifts, not only within each segment but overall. Today's young consumers are being exposed to sophisticated video games, computers, and the Inter-

EXHIBIT 3.12

Why Consumers Shop Online

>> CDB Research & Consulting.

net to a greater degree than other generations. As members of that generation exert their influence, marketers will see a different Web user who expects a Web experience that is not yet available.

Different expectations for computers and the Internet arise from each generation's unique life experiences. Yankelovich Partners, in its book *Rocking the Ages: The Yankelovich Report on Generational Marketing,* by J. Walker Smith and Ann S. Curlman, classified each U.S. generation as Matures, Baby Boomers, and Generation X. Don Tapscott, in *Growing Up Digital,* identified an additional U.S. generation, the Net Generation. The Net Generation has also been referred to as Generation Y.

>> *Matures*

People in the Matures generation were born between 1909 and 1945 and number more than sixty-eight million in the United States. A majority of Matures are married (64 percent) and own a home (65 percent). Only 36 percent of Matures are employed because a majority of them are retired, and their median annual household income is $24,000. Matures typically exhibit traditional brand loyalty.

Twenty percent of U.S. residents over the age of fifty are online, and 76 percent of them are online daily, according to CyberDialogue. Their main reasons for going online, according to a survey by the Third Age, are to try something new (67 percent), to keep in touch with family and loved ones by e-mail (53 percent), and encouragement to go online by children and grandchildren (20 percent). Matures use the Internet primarily for news, information, and shopping. In a 1999 study by the Consumer Electronics Manufacturers Association (CEMA), 28 percent of senior citizens said they visit a store to research a product and then buy it online. Even more, 45 percent, research a product online and then purchase it in the store. Top products bought online by this group include computer software, books, computer hardware, music, and clothing, according to Greenfield Online.

These characteristics suggest ways to tailor e-commerce to Matures. Members of this generation are likely to enjoy sites where they can keep in touch with friends and family, and they will gravitate to brand sites and Web ads for brands they know and trust.

>> Baby Boomers

The Baby Boomers are people born between 1946 and 1964, and they represent a U.S. population of over seventy-seven million. Like Matures, a majority of Boomers are married (72 percent) and own a home (63 percent). More than 83 percent of Boomers are employed, and they have a median household income of $43,000. Boomers are busy and under stress from balancing family and work.

Male Boomers were early adopters of the Internet and primarily used the Internet for work. Today about half of the Boomer population uses the Internet. Boomers' interests in the Internet include shopping, news, information, and family and educational activities. Websites with at least 50 percent of users coming from Boomers, according to Nielsen//NetRatings, include Intellicast.com, Travelscape.com, Expedia.com, Maps.com, Mapblast.com, City.net, Fidelity.com, Side walk.com, Southwest Airlines (iflyswa.com), News.com, and Quicken .com. According to the CEMA study, 36 percent of Boomers visit a store and then buy the product online, whereas 53 percent of Boomers research a product online and then buy it in a store. Boomers' busy lifestyles and demands for information are important in guiding e-commerce strategy. For brands that have Boomers as the major customer segment, the website and online ads may need to focus on convenience, time savings, information, and utility.

>> Generation X

The Generation X population was born between 1965 and 1976 and represents over forty-four million people. Only a third of Gen Xers are married, and one-fourth own a home. Seventy percent of Gen Xers are employed, and the group has a median household income of $31,000.

Eighty-two percent of Generation X users are online regularly. Generation Xers have been online since the early years of the Web, and they prefer to have fun and socialize on the Net. According to ZD Market Intelligence, Gen Xers use the Internet as a meeting place, with their e-mail use in excess of 90 percent, and they chat online 50 percent more than other Web users. They also shop and purchase online more than other age groups. Top sites for Generation X in a recent week were careerpath.com, babycenter.com, wellsfargo.com, monster.com, astronet.com, nfl.com, espn.go.com, realtor.com, ivillage.com, moviefone.com, imdb.com, berkeley.edu, priceline.com, bmgmusicservice.com, and usps.gov. According to CEMA, 41 percent of Gen Xers visit a store but purchase online, and 53 percent research a product online but purchase it in a store. For online marketers, key characteristics of Gen X are that this group goes online for social and fun activities and demonstrates high interest and ability in Web shopping. Therefore, sites that feature online buying capabilities and Web ads that allow an immediate transaction may appeal to this consumer segment.

>> Generation Y: The Net Generation

Generation Y, U.S. teens and kids, were born between 1977 and 1994. They represent a U.S. population of about sixty million. Members of Gen Y grew up with computer technology at home and at school. Gen Y prefers the Internet to other media. Gen Y likes to have fun on the Internet and use the Net for socializing—games, instant messaging, music downloading, and shopping. Members of Generation Y spend more time online than other generations, and most want higher-speed access.

According to a Jupiter/NFO survey of U.S. Internet use, 8.4 million teens and 8.6 million children were online in 1998. Forecasts for 2002 are 16.6 million teens and 12.9 million kids online. Top reasons teens go online, according to Nickelodeon/Yankelovich Youth Monitor 1999, include e-mail (67 percent), just surfing (63 percent), games (58 percent), homework or schoolwork (50 percent), chat rooms (48 percent), instant messaging (43 percent), and online encyclopedias (37 percent). A 1999 study by Cheskin Research and Cyberteens identified the favorite sites of teens: yahoo.com, hotmail.com, mtv.com, starwars.com, seventeen.com, wwf.com, gurl.com, angel fire.com, bolt.com, zone.com, teen.com, espn.com, nsync.com, teen mag.com, ebay.com, nba.com, backstreetboys.com, korn.com, excite .com, icq.com, geocities.com, delias.com, download.com, gap.com, bluemountain.com, altavista.com, cdnow.com, wbs.net, talkcity.com, and comedycentral.com.

For Generation Y, a brand may need to develop a community site where the Gen Y set can have fun. Possible features include the ability to create a personal website, get a free e-mail account, and spend time in online chat rooms. Brand marketers may need to use games or online promotions to get Gen Y's attention. For more ideas, see "Words from the Wise" on pages 78–79, reporting the views of Don Tapscott.

What the Customer Wants

Whatever their age, Web users are on a mission. When they go online, they have a purpose for spending the few precious hours available at work or home. Marketers' challenge is to get online customers to take notice of advertising messages. Online advertising is becoming more sophisticated, interactive, entertaining, and targeted to distract users from their primary motivations to go online: information, utility, entertainment, and community.

>> *Information*

In this Information Age, in spite of complaints about information overload, the primary reason people go online is to find information. The Internet tantalizes users with hundreds of millions of Web pages offering information on just about any subject. There were more than 800 million Web pages on the Internet as of early 1999, according to the NEC Research Institute. Many users' first stops on the Internet are visits to news sites. The Internet also has become popular as a resource for gathering information about many purchases—especially automobiles, homes, travel, computers, and electronics.

>> Don Tapscott on the Rise of the Ne(x)t Generation

Don Tapscott is the author of Growing Up Digital. *In that book, he identifies what he calls the Net Generation (N-Gen), those who in 1999 were between the ages of two and twenty-two years old. This group numbers eighty-eight million in the United States and Canada.*

The Net Generation is large and will be the "dominant voice in the 21st century." This generation is important because it is the first whose members grew up totally surrounded by digital media. In contrast to 1984, when only 29 percent of students in elementary and high schools used a computer, by 1997 almost three-quarters of students used a computer. Consequently, the Net Generation embraces Internet technology, while many members of older generations harbor some trepidation about using a computer.

The rise of the digital world is being influenced or even controlled by N-Gen. According to Tapscott, "Marketers have little comprehension on how this wave will shop and influence purchases of good and services." N-Gen-ers use digital media for learning, entertainment, communicating, and shopping. Online community is very popular among members of the N-Gen population, who participate in online chats with regularity.

As a consumer group, N-Gen consumers have wants that fit a few distinct themes. They want (1) options; (2) customization; (3) to change their minds; (4) to try before they buy; and (5) function and real value, not dazzle. These N-Gen themes pose a challenge for brand marketers. Options, customization, switching, research or experimentation, and desire for function can subvert the influence or strength of brand promises, messages, preferences, and loyalty. Still, Net Generation members are influenced by brands: "They want cool products, with cool names, used by cool friends and cool celebrities." Not only is the Internet changing the branding process in communications, but for marketers to the Net Generation, changes in the branding process will go deeper than messaging and media. Since this generation has grown up with technology, the messages and media will need to be technologically sophisticated and interactive. TV audio and visuals will take on a new level of pace and complexity. On the Web, the Net Generation will look for advertising and sites that have interactivity in the forms of games, chat, and streaming video/audio. Instead of presenting a product in a static, straightforward format, brand marketers will have to figure out how to translate the messages into an interactive format.

Of particular interest to marketers looking for trends in the Net Generation is the Internet's teen population, a very large group of future consumers. Teens prefer to surf the Web rather than watch television. As with any generation, the teenage years are marked by social development, and teens are highly involved in social activities. Thus, the most popular online activities for teens involve social interaction—exchanging e-mail with friends, sending instant messages, and hanging out in chat rooms. Teens would like to use the Internet as they use the telephone to communicate with friends. While online shopping is important to teens, it takes a backseat to socializing. Teens also are very aware of online advertising and are generally responsive to it. In particular, teens react positively to humorous and animated online ads.

The consumer behavior of the Net Generation is an important indicator of what e-commerce will look like. Writes Tapscott, "We should pay attention because the culture which flows from their experience in cyberspace foreshadows the culture they will create as the leaders of tomorrow in the workplace and society." >>

The availability of vast amounts of information influences buying habits. On the one hand, a person can do some comparison shopping across many sites faster than visiting many stores. On the other hand, the access to unprecedented and increasing amounts of information can lengthen the research and consideration part of the buying process. Consumers will take time to perform research online not necessarily because they want to, but because the information is there and because they can. In the traditional selling model, customers have to work harder to obtain information, so some customers forgo intense comparative shopping. On the Internet, where customers can easily zip around a few sites to gather comparative information, researched decisions are more common.

>> Utility

Although the Internet is interactive and entertaining, it is also very utilitarian. E-mail is a useful tool for communicating. Other Web-based applications allow people to perform other useful activities, such as calculate mortgages, find the local Barnes & Noble store, order groceries, keep track of stock investments, receive notices of events, book air travel and select a seat, obtain driving directions, check bank accounts, purchase gifts, manage calendars, send family photos or videos, trace family history, find a job, plan a meal, monitor children in day care, or research a health issue.

Web users' expectations for the utility of the Net continue to grow more sophisticated. Software developers are responding with another wave of applications: voice-enabled chat, Internet telephone, Web-based meetings, interactive TV, customized software applications, virtual trade shows, personal bots, digital publishing, online education, personal area networks, virtual neighborhoods, personal malls, wearable Internet, and election voting.

>> Entertainment

Over two-thirds of active Internet users go online for entertainment. The Cyber Dialogue study found that 70 percent of U.S. adults retrieved entertainment content, which led other content such as business (68 percent), local (67 percent), product (61 percent), and news (52 percent). Favorite entertainment content is sports, movies, television, music, and online games. Online entertainment activities include reading news about favorite stars, consulting TV schedules, playing online games, participating in celebrity chats, downloading music, gambling, and listening to the radio.

Marketers can attract users with brand-related entertainment. Web users are now interacting with very entertaining advertising, where the advertiser wants the user to spend some time with the brand. In-banner ad games or full-blown website games are becoming effective tools for motivating users to click.

>> *Community*

Human beings yearn to belong and to share, and the Internet is the perfect platform for community. Web users are active in using online chats, instant messaging, and e-mail to connect with other people who share the same interests. Online chat rooms, chat events, and discussion rooms also attract users. The Internet makes communication less intimidating because Web users can be anonymous, be another persona, or show their true selves from the comfort of their computer.

Early websites were dedicated to education, government, companies, and organizations. Now individuals can share interests with others. According to NPD Research, almost half of Internet users have their own websites in 2000. More than a third of these websites are about users' families. The new cyber neighborhood is a place for people to reach out and virtually touch others.

The "Super-Empowered" Customer

As discussed in the preceding chapter, online customers are super-empowered customers. Their empowerment comes from information, choice, control, trust, and speed. Besides the unprecedented amount of information, online shoppers have research tools such as shopping bots, comparison shopping sites, infomediaries, manufacturer sites, and retailer sites. Web users now have just about all the information they need, literally at their fingertips. In fact, they have almost too much, which sometimes results in a longer purchase process. One online auto dealer found that the average car-buying process increased from six to eight weeks.

With regard to marketing messages, super-empowered customers have the ultimate choice. While on the Net, customers don't passively receive commercials; instead, they actively point and click their way to a brand's website—or ignore the banner ad inviting them. Online customers' control makes it more challenging for the brand marketer to capture their attention. Similarly, when asked to provide personal information, Web users insist that they be given the choice of participating in the profiling process, and they want to know how their information is being used and how it will benefit them.

These super-empowered customers have little time to waste online. They have a mission and are willing to spend time with websites only as long as they provide value. Busy online consumers are looking for convenience. They want to find what they are looking for quickly and want it delivered to their home just as quickly. According to NetSmart, the top frustrations for Web users are difficult navigation (87 percent), slow downloading (84 percent), difficulty finding information (73 percent), too many clicks to find information (68 percent), confusing home page (61 percent), boring content (56 percent), no interactivity (38 percent), and need for plug-ins to use the site (37 percent). Speed and ease of use are therefore essential. If Web users can't get an idea of what a website is about within a few seconds of landing on a home page, then they are gone with a click of a mouse. In contrast, if users have a satisfactory experience with a website, they will spend a lot of time with the site and will continue to return time and again.

Privacy

Online customers have heightened awareness of security and privacy. Reports of hackers and concerns about secure shopping make it more difficult for marketers to establish a trusting relationship online. In a store, a customer can choose to be anonymous, but in cyberspace, the customer's anonymity is no longer. Companies identify website visitors by using cookies, user IDs, and passwords, and they can match this information with data on purchases and other information to build a customer profile. Similarly, broadcast and print advertisers know only aggregate data about consumers—for example, demographics of TV viewers associated with a programming time slot and channel. The situation for communicating with consumers in the opt-out online model more closely resembles direct and catalog marketing, where customers do not fully control the selling of their name, address, and telephone number to other companies, unless they go through the hassle of asking to be removed from phone or mailing lists.

Online customers are quite outspoken and vigilant when it comes to protecting the privacy of their personal information. They are adamant that information about themselves belongs to them, not to marketers or anyone else. They want to know what a company is going to do with the information. In a study by AT&T Labs titled "Beyond Concern," almost half of respondents said they would be more likely to provide personal information if a law prevented the site from using the information for any purpose other than processing their information request. Over one-fourth of respondents said they would be more likely to provide personal information if a privacy policy were displayed on the site. Over half said they would be more likely to provide personal information if a privacy policy and a privacy seal of approval (such as Better Business Bureau) were displayed on the website. A study by NFO Interactive echoed this concern. Almost 70 percent of respondents indicated that a key factor influencing whether they make a purchase is an assurance of privacy on the website.

To build trust in this context, online brands must visibly protect customer information. This consideration fosters a deeper, more loyal relationship with the customer. Protecting online privacy involves offering customers choice, control, and disclosure. The strategy for collecting customer data may be *opt-in* (Web users are asked to add themselves to the program) or *opt-out* (Web users are automatically added unless they select an option to take themselves out of the program). In general, online consumers prefer the obvious control of the opt-in strategy. Along with this, the website should include clear and visible communications explaining the use of customer information. These decisions are essential for success with the super-empowered customers of the e-marketplace. Marketers depend on customers to give them personal information because their future depends on how well they know their customers.

TOP–OF–MIND THOUGHTS

Like many other transforming technologies, the Internet will change
the product purchase cycle and other aspects of consumer behavior.
The coming generations—the customers of tomorrow—also will challenge the marketing models that brand marketers have become accus-
tomed to. Brand marketers involved with the Internet should become
investigators who intimately understand their online customers,
including their demographics, psychographics, and buying behavior.
The Internet helps marketers collect such data.

>> The U.S. Internet population is becoming more mainstream. While
the United States leads the adoption of the Net, other geographic
regions aren't far behind.

>> Web users are spending more time online, which takes them away
from other activities. Understanding online and offline habits will
help marketers develop the marketing mix, including messages.

>> The Internet is changing buyer behavior. Brand marketers will need
to watch and listen to customers in order to learn their needs and
motivations for the digital medium.

>> Anticipating the next generation of business buyers and consumers
is key to discovering new ways to leverage the Net marketplace. At
the same time, many brand marketers must achieve a return on
investment now, in the current state of the Net. They must understand the existing wants and needs of the customer, as well as the
possibilities that already exist for interacting with the brand via
the Web.

CHAPTER <4>

[# Brand Principles and Paradigm Shifts]

>> [ONLINE], THE BRAND IS EXPERIENCE, <u>NOT</u> THE NAME
OR SLOGAN. . . . BRAND IS A COMPLEX PHENOMENON. WE HAVE TO
CHANGE OUR IDEA THAT BRAND IS SIMPLY "AWARENESS."
CONSUMERS ARE AWARE OF MANY THINGS THAT DO NOTHING TO
CHANGE THEIR BEHAVIOR. ALL OTHER MEDIA IS ONE-WAY OR
BROADCAST. WITH THE INTERNET, THE POWER OF CHOICE IS
TOTALLY IN THE HANDS OF THE CONSUMER, AND FOR THAT REASON,
IT IS A REVOLUTION IN MARKETING. >>

-- REGIS MCKENNA, AUTHOR OF <u>REAL TIME</u> AND
<u>RELATIONSHIP MARKETING</u>

The new brand-marketing rules—like the Internet—are changing. The online medium is in the nascent stage, and so, too, are marketers' ideas about branding on the Web. Anyone conducting brand marketing online therefore should embrace experimentation.

As marketers substitute or supplement their activities in the physical marketplace with a presence on the Web, they need tactics suitable for an electronic marketspace that brings new communications models. Brand-marketing programs on the Web will incorporate marketing based on response, experience, speed, proximity, one-to-one relationships, real-time responsiveness, permission, viral/spiral communications, reach, community, and other Net models not yet invented. In sum, although the core brand marketing maxims will not change, the execution of these principles will change.

Brand-Marketing Principles

The practice of modern branding is about a hundred years old, and the core brand-marketing practices have been proved throughout the twentieth century. Although the basic maxims of brand marketing are very familiar, they are worth pondering in order to see how they apply in the e-marketplace.

>> Brand Association

Anything linked with the brand in the customer's mind is a brand association. Brand associations help a customer understand the brand, create a reason for the customer to purchase, and help the customer differentiate one brand from another. Associations can include lifestyle, personality, product attributes, customer benefits, price, product use, competitors, spokespersons, characters or icons, geography, and company employees. For example, when thinking of Volvo cars, many people associate the brand with safety—a product attribute and customer benefit.

How can marketers optimize brand associations within the Web medium? The website can tell the brand story in a way that allows the customer to experience the brand associations. The Volvo website (www.volvocars.com) communicates and reinforces the brand's concern for safety by making associations with lifestyle, people, and product attributes. For example, the "Volvo Saved My Life" Club, the Volvo Safety Center, and other safety-related areas on the site promote Volvo's reputation for and dedication to safety.

>> Brand Identity

A brand's identity is the collection of images, words, ideas, and brand associations that form the perception of the brand in the mind of the prospect or customer. A fundamental marketing principle is to keep the images, words, and so forth consistent, in order to maintain a clear brand identity. But should the brand identity also be consistent on the Web?

Many brands are approaching this fork in the road. For the *New York Times* website, the publisher decided to keep much of the identity of the print newspaper intact. When someone visits the website, he or she will see a layout that looks just like the print newspaper. With this strategy, the *New York Times* website leverages much of its offline brand image. At the same time, the website includes new features, such as up-to-the-minute news, that cannot be done in the print edition. These features help the newspaper reach an audience beyond its local geography, supporting the perception that its online presence is a worldwide source of news.

>> Brand Personality

When people are familiar with a brand, they tend to associate human characteristics with it. Taken together, the characteristics associated with a particular brand constitute its brand personality. For example, customers think of fatbrain.com as being smart and friendly. Marketers try to cultivate a brand personality that appeals to members of their target market. Just as people like to hang around with those who have pleasant personalities, marketers assume their customers will want to spend time with a brand whose personality they find attractive.

With many people saying the Web is impersonal and lacks emotion, how can online marketers make their brand personality shine through? Television has been a superior medium, because its sound and moving visuals help communicate the brand's personality. Audio and video are becoming more available to marketers for online advertising and Web marketing. Until these are widely used, the challenge for the Web is to exhibit brand personality using text, graphics, e-mail, chat, and other Web functionality.

>> Brand Positioning

For a brand, positioning is the way customers perceive the brand relative to its competition. Positioning is important because it helps customers identify a reason for choosing one brand over another or over a generic product. How can a brand's positioning come through loud and clear on the very cluttered, busy Web? In the e-marketplace, it is more critical than ever to communicate a brand's position precisely, because the Web surfer is impatient. Marketers must carefully test their online messages to ensure they can be understood quickly and accurately.

>> Brand Image

The elements of brand identity, including the brand's name, logo, color, and typeface, contribute to the brand image. That image is defined in terms of the brand's positioning, personality, and reputation. As the Internet opens up possibilities for new marketing strategies, should marketers change their brand image—and, if so, in an evolutionary way or in a radical way?

For Volvo cars, the Web helped the company evolve its brand to be hipper. Although the safety message is still at the core of Volvo's brand image, its Web effort (at www.volvocars.com) added hipness to the brand's personality. By appealing to the lifestyle of its core market, Volvo has enhanced its brand image. It has extended that strategy across all media, so the Web effort has broadened Volvo's appeal to its entire market.

>> Brand Quality

Perceived quality is a key element of branding. Customer satisfaction depends on the customer's perception of overall quality in terms of how well the product fulfills its intended use and how it compares to competitive offerings or alternatives. Thus, to satisfy customers, brands must not only deliver actual quality, but do so in a way that customers perceive that quality.

According to brand-marketing expert and author David Aaker, the quality dimensions that influence perceived quality for a tangible product include performance, features, conformance with specifications, reliability, durability, serviceability, and fit and finish. For services, the quality dimensions include tangibles, reliability, competence, responsiveness, and empathy. How does building perceived quality happen on the Internet? The Web requires online communications that form perceptions of quality. Web navigation, graphics and photography, functionality, copy and messaging, e-mail, Web customer care, and other Web elements should be implemented so that they contribute to perceived quality. Website features should operate as promised, be easy to understand, respond appropriately to user inputs, be aesthetically pleasing, and accurately communicate the brand's position regarding quality.

>> Brand Awareness

Marketers measure brand awareness in terms of a buyer's ability to recall or recognize the brand within a certain product category. Typical measures of brand awareness are top-of-mind recall, unaided recall, and aided recall. Marketing assumes that awareness is a necessary first step in the purchase process. For brand marketers, the more readily customers call a brand to mind, the better.

What is the secret to building brand awareness online? Which medium is the best for achieving desirable levels of brand awareness? Opinions vary. Some marketers say television is the premier medium for building brand awareness. Others say you can successfully build brand awareness online within the Web medium itself. Most say it takes an integrated cross-media plan.

>> Brand Promise

The brand promise is the promise that the brand will deliver the value proposition—the functional and emotional benefits of the brand—to the customer. Of course, the Web can help deliver on the brand promise, but the difficult question is, How? As with other media, online advertising and a website can communicate the promise. The product (good or service) itself, customer service, and other aspects of company performance all must deliver on the promises communicated in any medium. This and later chapters suggest ways to communicate and deliver on the promise, using the Internet.

>> Brand Loyalty

A successful brand strategy fosters a high degree of brand loyalty—the customer's level of commitment or attachment to the brand. A loyal customer base protects a brand from price competition and other competitive threats. The Internet challenges brand loyalty by offering easy ways for customers to shop around for the best price or to compare competitive brands. At the same time, the Web is a nearly perfect medium for encouraging and facilitating customer loyalty. In fact, many companies are using their websites as the catalyst for changes designed to build customer loyalty. The Internet offers tools for customer relationship management, including data mining to uncover customer needs and product ideas, as well as personalization of marketing messages and product offerings.

>> *Brand Equity*

Marketers position their brand, promote it, and cultivate brand loyalty because of the practical value of owning a well-known, well-loved brand. Customers perceive that a product backed by a valued brand is worth more than competing products. Such a brand therefore increases repeat purchases and perhaps the price customers are willing to pay. The quality of a brand that causes it to deliver these bottom-line benefits is called brand equity. In general, brand equity and its impact on profitability are the true measure of a branding strategy's success.

In the e-marketplace, the objectives are the same. Online marketers of dot-com and traditional brands want to build brand equity in order to build profits. This is an important measure by which to judge all of the branding tactics marketers are trying on the Web. Some companies have found that just being online seems to contribute to brand equity by signaling that the company is innovative and smart. As the Internet becomes more mainstream, that advantage will lose its meaning. Marketers will have to find other, more enduring ways to distinguish their brands and build brand equity.

The Web Impact

Marketers and their customers are only just beginning to experience the overall impact of the Web on branding. The nature of shopping and buying is changing. Customer expectations and behavior are changing. Let's look at the resulting paradigm shift in brand marketing.

>> *The Web Market*space

Traditionally, shopping involved a physical marketplace. That place could be an old-fashioned street market, an enormous steel-and-glass shopping mall, or even the buyer's own home. But in any case, the marketer had to consider the qualities of the place, from convenience to ambience. In addition, most traditional marketplace transactions involve some interchange between the buyer and seller.

On the Internet, place is largely irrelevant, or at least uncontrollable by the marketer. Especially as the devices used for accessing the Internet have grown smaller, online shoppers have been able to log on just about anywhere—office or home, cramped airplane seat or lounge chair on the beach. Furthermore, online shoppers rarely (so far) interact with a human seller.

Writing in the *Harvard Business Review* in 1994, when computerized transactions were becoming more common in the business arena, Jeffrey Rayport and John Sviokla proposed that the notion of physical location—marketplace—would be replaced by the virtual location of the computer screen. Rayport and Sviokla called this cyber-location "marketspace." Not only does the marketspace provide the means to learn about and carry out a transaction, it serves as a representation of the marketplace where people gather to buy and sell. Today Rayport and Sviokla's prediction is confirmed when online shoppers talk about "visiting" a website.

As the Web has made online marketing more commonplace than even Rayport and Sviokla might have imagined, marketspace becomes an essential element of the online marketing mix. To operate in marketspace, marketers must consider its limitations in demonstrating benefits that must be experienced firsthand, such as texture and taste. Another limitation is the difficulty in providing for human interaction. However, such limitations are more than offset by benefits, most notably the ability to be available to customers almost anytime, anywhere. Furthermore, marketers have ever more powerful tools for creating a marketspace in which shopping delivers convenience, fun, aesthetics, information, and whatever other benefits the marketer deems consistent with the brand's positioning. In effect, the Web requires any online marketer—not just store proprietors—to create a shopping environment.

>> Two-Way Communications

The Web also sets new standards for communicating about brands. Traditionally branding messages have been unidirectional, delivered to customers via radio, TV, magazines, and other media. In contrast, the Web allows two-way communications—a dialogue in which buyer and seller learn more about one another. Not only does it permit this, but Netizens *expect* to be listened to.

This interaction opens the door for a loyal brand relationship. Listening to customers enables the company to identify customers' expectations and meet those expectations more efficiently and satisfactorily. The challenge is to move fast enough. Companies can get instant feedback from customers via a website. Customers know the technology should enable the companies to respond just as quickly to their wants, needs, complaints, and suggestions. For companies that meet their customers' expectations, the dialogue is a valuable exchange that enriches the customers' experience over time—and enriches the company's customer database over time.

>> Web E-Motions

Some marketers believe that the Web's impact as a branding medium is limited by an inability to make an emotional connection. Many believe the Web is impersonal. They are correct in recognizing the difficulty of appealing to a person's emotions online. In contrast, television readily creates a bond with a brand because its sound and moving visual imagery can be used to evoke emotional reactions. Internet technologies still do not match the quality of audio and video experienced on TV.

This limitation is probably temporary. In a couple of years, significant advances in Web technologies and bandwidth (i.e., broadband access) will allow marketers to use sound and video for online brand-ing to tap into emotions. In the business-to-business market, compa-nies already have high-speed connections, so B2B brands can take advantage of audio and video in marketing programs. In the consumer market, Susan Bratton of Excite@Home predicts, "By 2003, one in five online consumers in the U.S. will have high-speed Internet access."

Until broadband access is common, should marketers wait to pro-mote their brands online? Of course not. No brand can afford to wait to make an impression with the online audience. Rather, there are many branding activities that marketers can conduct on the Net or within a website to appeal to the emotions. For instance, brand mar-keters can leverage the Web's interactive nature to create interactive applications, personalization, animation, e-mail, and community, all of which can stir warm feelings toward a brand. Also, personalization can save time and simplify someone's life or job—certainly generating a positive emotional response. Finally, many brand advertisers have found that using humor in online advertising or on their website has been an effective emotional tool.

>> Response and Tracking

Although media such as direct-response television and direct mail allow users to respond to marketing messages and allow marketers to track those responses, the Web provides an unprecedented level of response and tracking. HTML, hyperlinks, and cookies allow user response and tracking of people's online usage and behavior. With click-through tracking, marketers can assess the performance of online marketing programs and Web pages. Never before could you track performance down to the individual user.

The upside is that this allows marketers to measure return on investment (ROI) for online activities. However, a click-through meas-urement only tells marketers that the Web user responded to the online advertisement. It does not provide data about attitudes or brand awareness. For instance, if a Web user viewed an ad but didn't click on it, the user was exposed to the brand. This exposure might have had a positive impact on brand awareness, but click-through measurements would not have counted it.

To counter this disadvantage, marketing researchers are developing measures for online brand awareness. They are very similar to ad-tracking measurement for television, radio, print, and other media. Companies such as IntelliQuest, Harris Interactive, MB Interactive, and Nielsen//NetRatings can measure brand awareness and other brand performance measures for websites and interactive campaigns. An example is measuring whether an online brand has significant awareness by tracking the number of people who actually type in the Web address (URL), rather than find the site through other means. This measure presumes that the more people who type in the site URL, versus going through search engines or banner ads, the greater the top-of-mind brand awareness.

>> The Web Experience

Customers are used to experiencing brands in a few basic ways. Usually they receive advertising messages about brands, and they buy and use branded products. But as we have seen, using the Web encompasses much more than receiving messages or making purchases. Web users expect to find useful information, to have fun, and to interact with other people. Consequently, marketers face the challenge and potential benefits of incorporating these activities into the ways customers interact with their brands.

Online customers expect marketers to offer them not just a message, but a positive experience on their website. As shown in Exhibit 4.1, effective online marketing messages not only convey physical content about brand name, logo, and product characteristics or mental content about benefits, value, and brand personality. Rather, marketing messages in the Internet medium must allow customers to experience the exchange of information, useful applications, and personalized communications. In sum, the Web has erased the limits defining how customers can experience brands. Later in this chapter, we describe ways of providing a positive brand experience online.

>> *Relationships*

The Internet's fundamental purpose is the interconnection of computers, organizations, and people. This interconnection has encouraged the creation of relationships between organizations and people. To fully participate in this new environment, marketers need relationship-centered models like virtual communities, affiliate networks, and comarketing partnerships. Applying these models, marketers are using the Internet as an efficient way to communicate with a broader audience.

Marketers at United Parcel Service (www.ups.com) understand this concept. UPS has placed its online package-tracking application on thousands of websites so customers of those sites can track packages sent from those sites via UPS. "Every time a customer tracks a package that was sent using UPS from another website, United Parcel Service (UPS) has a branding opportunity," says Tom Daly, the company's online national brand manager. He adds, "It has extended our brand's reach across the Internet."

Another enterprise that has seized the advantages of networking is MSN Hotmail, a free e-mail service that signed up more than one

EXHIBIT 4.1

Moving to Brand Experience in the New Medium

Traditional Brand Communications		➞	Real-Time Brand Communications	
Physical	**Mental**		**Experiential**	
Name	Benefit		Information	
Logo	Values		Utility	
Color	Personality		Personalization	

>> *Copyright © 2000, Forrester Research, Inc.*

million e-mail subscribers within its first six months, spending only $50,000 for marketing. At the end of each e-mail message sent by a Hotmail user, Hotmail inserts a marketing message offering the recipient a free e-mail account. This caused Hotmail to spread like wildfire on the Net as people used it to communicate and keep in touch with others. A similar phenomenon spread the free instant-messaging software application, ICQ. For one Web user to send an instant message with ICQ, the Web user needed his or her friends, family members, and colleagues to have the software also. So if someone had ICQ, several others would download the software so they could receive and reply to messages.

With the attraction of network-wide reach, the Web has made it easier and quicker to forge marketing partnerships, from cobranding to exclusive sponsorships or alliances. However, extensive cobranding has the potential not only to create synergies, but to dilute the brand or generate negative perceptions. For every additional relationship, the brand takes on some of the characteristics of the brand it is associated with. For synergy, marketers must select the right brand relationship.

Other companies have leveraged an affiliate marketing model. For instance, Value America (www.valueamerica.com) has over 50,000 Web affiliates, which sell Value America merchandise. "Our affiliate program is an alternative sales channel. It would have taken us many years to build this kind of channel in the offline world," says Jennifer Lewis of Value America. The affiliate marketing model is attractive to marketers because they pay only when a sale is made. Instead of a heavy up-front advertising investment, marketers pay a commission to the affiliate. Even when sales volume is low, affiliate marketing yields brand exposure across many websites for little, if any, expense.

>> Net Speed

"Internet time" refers to the intense speed with which product cycles, deal making, and growth take place on the Internet. Not only has the Web sped up product development and introduction cycles, it has accelerated the buying cycle for many products, both goods and services. The Web shrinks marketing cycle times by enabling companies to test ideas, products, messages, and advertising quickly and cost-effectively. If a Web banner advertisement isn't performing well, it can be assessed and changed within days or even hours.

The increasing prevalence of the Internet puts all marketers on Internet time. Long-term marketing studies and carefully researched decisions are still important, but marketers cannot wait for their completion before acting. Brand marketers at traditional as well as dot-com businesses need the tools to act and react to minute-by-minute information. They will increasingly depend on those tools for marketing ventures with Internet-savvy colleagues like Tiffany Schlain, founder of the Webby Awards (www.webbyawards.com). Schlain declared, "Our main criteria for doing deals is speed. If potential partners aren't fast enough, we will not work with them."

>> Advertising Proximity and Integration

In meeting users' expectations for informational content and interactivity, Web marketers often have difficulty maintaining a clear distinction between advertising and editorial. Of course, the blurring between editorial and marketing messages didn't start with the Net. Television infomercials and advertising supplements that simulate editorial in magazines are two offline methods that blend information with selling. Still, TV and magazines provide disclaimers and labels clearly indicating content that is paid advertising. Website and e-mail content that includes advertising messages resembling editorial content has raised the suspicions of customers and governments. The *Wall Street Journal* (July 12, 1999) quotes Lee Peeler, associate director of the Division of Advertising Practices for the Federal Trade Commission (FTC), as saying, "We are very interested in consumers knowing the difference between objective presentation and presentation with financial interest." Many popular websites do make sure that users recognize advertisements, either by using recognizable formats such as Web banners or by labeling content "advertisement" or "sponsor."

Despite these risks, marketers for most of the brands and inter-active agencies participating in this book have said that Web spon-sorships are very effective at building brand awareness and preference. Consistent with those companies' experiences, a study by the Associ-ation of National Advertisers (ANA) found that 39 percent of respon-dents used online sponsorships in 1997, and 60 percent did so in 1999. Furthermore, cobranding and Web sponsorships are becoming more integrated, with the brand not just sponsoring a section of a web-site, but delivering a message integrated with content, distributed to many areas of a website, and included in e-mail marketing messages. Thus, the sponsorship is no longer a distinct, self-contained element. Instead, the sponsor's messages appear at the most appropriate, rele-vant, and targeted points of the user's website experience.

Net.Marketing.Com

This radically different environment requires new brand-marketing methods. Many marketing models and buzz phrases have been emerg-ing to help marketers leverage the Web for brand marketing. These range from solution branding to viral and spiral marketing.

>> Brand Marketing as Relationship Building

As Martha Rogers remarked in Chapter 2, the brand used to be a sub-stitute for a relationship. Mass marketers and even many business-to-business marketers couldn't know every customer personally, so they developed and promoted brands with "personalities" they thought would appeal to their customers. When people could relate to a brand, they tended to become more loyal customers, thereby continuing their pseudo-relationship. But as we have also seen, the Internet is making branding less acceptable as a substitute for customer relationships. Regis McKenna expressed a similar viewpoint in 1998 in *Business 2.0*: "For the past one hundred years, producers have been assuming that a well-known name is a shortcut to information. In a world where information is disposable and choice and price are higher values than brand, how we engage and retain our customers has to be reevaluated."

Successful marketers are reevaluating the role of brand and concluding that it can become the basis for creating true relationships between sellers and their customers. Technology, including widespread use of PCs, increased computer-processing power, and the ability to gather and sift through huge amounts of customer data, have made this new objective of brand marketing possible. Brand marketers not only can gather summary data about groups of customers, they can track the demographics and buying behavior of each customer, soliciting feedback along the way. With each new piece of information, brand marketers can tailor responses, as humans do when they are interacting. In addition, they can apply their customer data to other points of communication with their customer, such as store retailing, phone calls, and print catalogs. This style of brand marketing is organic. That is, it is flexible and responsive to individual customers, incorporating changes as the relationship develops over time. The result is a closer identification between customer and brand.

Using brand marketing to build relationships supports a strategy of *solution branding*. With this strategy, companies present brands as solutions to a customer's needs or problems, versus presenting brands simply as types of products. Solution branding is not a new concept, but the Web helps marketers offer individualized solutions. Whether on the Web or in a face-to-face selling environment, solution branding requires input from the customer. For example, Clinique cosmetics has a "computer" at its retail counters so the Clinique representative can work with each customer to find products suitable for the customer's skin type, eye color, hair color, and other criteria. Clinique also makes this solution tool available on its website (www.clinique.com). In the future, solution branding on the Internet will go beyond the interactive Web experience by offering the human touch. The human brain is a superior computer to the Web server. Marketers designing a solution-branding experience online should carefully consider the role of interactive tools, databases, and real human beings, using applications such as real-time chat, along the purchase cycle.

Experiential Marketing

As noted earlier in this chapter, online brand identity arises from customers' experiences with the brand. Experience with a brand has more impact than product features and benefits. The brand experience can produce a deeper meaning and be more memorable, which can yield greater customer loyalty. Thus, the goal for marketers is to provide a positive and unforgettable experience that establishes an unending relationship with a customer.

In *The Experience Economy*, Joseph Pine II and James Gilmore define experiences as one of the basic sources of economic value, along with commodities, goods, and services. Exhibit 4.2 details major differences in marketing each of these types of products. Commodities are typified by an agrarian economy, and the marketer's job is to extract, store, and offer them in trade to broadly defined markets. The type of product associated with an industrial economy is tangible goods, which traditionally are made according to standardized speci-

EXHIBIT 4.2

Economic Distinctions of Economic Offerings

	Commodities	Goods	Services	Experiences
Economy	Agrarian	Industrial	Service	Experience
Economic function	Extract	Make	Deliver	Stage
Nature of offering	Fungible	Tangible	Intangible	Memorable
Key attribute	Natural	Standardized	Customized	Personal
Method of supply	Stored in bulk	Inventoried after production	Delivered on demand	Revealed over a duration
Seller	Trader	Manufacturer	Provider	Stager
Buyer	Market	User	Client	Guest
Factors of demand	Characteristics	Features	Benefits	Sensations

>> *Reprinted by permission of Harvard Business School Press. From* The Experience Economy *by Joseph Pine II and James Gilmore. Boston, MA, 1999, p. 6.*

fications. Marketers offer them to users, stimulating demand based on their features. In a service economy, marketers deliver customized services to clients on demand, promoting the benefits. Experiences are not produced, but staged, and the buyer is the marketer's guest. Marketers build demand for experiences by connecting with customers on a personal level and offering desirable, memorable sensations.

Of course, each type of product is part of any economy. The entertainment industry, for example, has always marketed experiences. However, the marketing of experiences dominates in the e-marketplace. Online marketers therefore must master *experiential marketing*—the type of marketing defined in Exhibit 4.2 as the offering of experiences.

Experiential marketing has definite advantages for marketers who can demonstrate the memorability of their offerings. Desirable experiences can bring higher prices than commodities, goods, and services. Pine and Gilmore use the example of a cup of coffee. As a commodity, growers sell coffee for the equivalent of pennies a cup. Supermarkets sell it packaged as a good for the equivalent five to twenty-five cents per cup. In a diner a customer can buy a cup of coffee for as little as fifty cents per cup. At a five-star restaurant or trendy coffee bar, patrons are willing to pay two to five dollars for a cup of coffee in pleasant surroundings. Pine and Gilmore explain why: the coffee bar establishes "a distinctive experience that envelops the purchase of coffee, increasing its value (and therefore its price) by two orders of magnitude over the original commodity." In addition to the price benefit, experiential marketing can provide significant differentiation in a competitive market as well as enhance customer loyalty.

On a website a user needs to experience the brand in a dynamic and personal way. Something static does not create a real experience. Visiting a site needs to move beyond informational to experiential. Sarah Buxton, director of marketing at Virgin Entertainment Group, says Virgin Atlantic's website (www.virgin-atlantic.com) provides just such an experience: "When you are on the Virgin Atlantic website, you are wholly involved in creating the experience yourself." The website experience is consistent with the company's overall positioning.

Virgin Atlantic is known as an airline that makes flying a fun and rewarding experience rather than just a way to get from one place to another. Its flight experience includes massages, in-flight entertainment, limousines, and more. On its website, users are treated to a highly interactive experience that gives them a sense of the lively and entertaining Virgin Atlantic personality; features include a Shockwave-enabled presentation of the company's history, entertainment services, 360-degree views of cabins, and games. Exhibit 4.3 shows a brand experience on the Virgin Atlantic website.

To create a memorable brand experience, the Web provides chat, community, personalization, and interactive applications that are useful or fun. Online chat certainly taps into the expression of emotion,

EXHIBIT 4.3

The Brand Experience on the Virgin Atlantic Airways Website

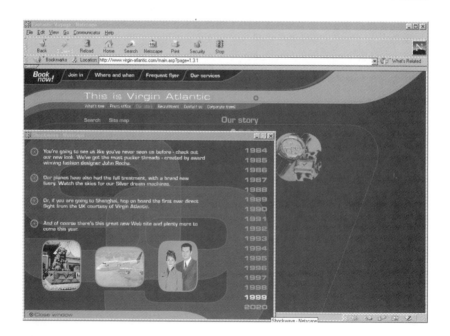

>> *Courtesy of Virgin Atlantic Airways.*

as people build a community based on like interests. With chat or community, people spend time bonding with other Web users or with a company representative. With Web-based personalization, the website makes a one-to-one connection with individual customers. The uniqueness of personalized communication and service can make a customer feel special and important, as anyone knows who has gone into a favorite store and been recognized by the staff. (See Chapter 8 for an in-depth discussion on interactivity and the Web experience.)

Volvo (volvocars.com) has used Web experiences to evolve its brand message from the singular idea of safety to the emotional benefits of safety. "In the car category over the past several years, the idea of safety no longer provided the huge differentiation Volvo used to enjoy," says Ron Berger, CEO of MVBMS, Volvo's ad agency. "So we had to evolve communications to add the emotional benefits by involving human aspects of saving lives." Volvo was one of the first automobile manufacturers on the Internet, where the relatively high-income and young demographics played to Volvo's strengths. Volvo used this medium to evolve its communications by providing more than information about the cars. Like other automobile manufacturers' websites, Volvo offers plenty of details, but its site puts as much emphasis on humanizing the brand with an extensive and engaging online experience.

Because experiential marketing requires a personalized approach, experiential marketing campaigns must be planned accordingly. Forrester Research suggests that in place of ad campaigns delivering a single message to millions, experiential campaigns should link exposure with the depth of Web offers. For example, clicking on a banner ad should take the user to a pitch page that features all of the benefits and features along with in-depth information about the promotion or special offer. The Web pages allow marketers to tell the whole interactive story, in a way that rewards the user for the time spent with the Web pages. This will ensure that the user will have a more positive impression about the brand, which can lead to a brand preference. Also, with *decision-point targeting* instead of demographic targeting, a marketer can find a more qualified audience. Decision-point targeting is a refined approach to targeting in which the online ad is presented based on time and place targeting. In other words, if a Web user's clickstream (collected through anonymous tracking and profile) indicates that he or she is shopping for a new set of golf clubs, then the golf retailer can have its ad displayed at the right time and at the right place—when the user is the most receptive to an ad for golf clubs or a site that sells golf clubs. Finally, whereas traditional advertising uses a push approach, with messages that interrupt what the audience is doing, Forrester advises creative approaches that "combine context, clarity and a come-on to lure customers."

>> Micro Marketing

The emphasis on marketing experiences is helping to propel a shift in target marketing to *micro marketing*. Marketers have traditionally identified segments within a product's market and tailored brand messages to selected segments, or target markets. Micro marketing takes targeting a step further by overlaying many segmentation criteria to carve up the market into many more, smaller market segments, or micro markets. For instance, a marketer might target women, ages thirty-five to forty-four, childless, high-income, with active lifestyles, own a Volvo, within particular zip codes, and own homes.

On the Web or within e-mail, segmentation can get even more precise, based on online behavior, registration profiles, and so on. Take the case of Art.com, the leading online art store, with the Web's largest selection of framed and unframed art and photography. Art.com has 300 to 400 different Web banner ads, which can be categorized by artist (for example, Monet), type of art movement (modern art), and other targeting criteria. This enables Art.com to target ads within search engines such as Yahoo. So when a user types in "Monet," for example, Art.com's Monet banner ad is displayed. Creating this many different advertisements for traditional media would be prohibitively expensive, but microtargeting can be done cost-effectively on the Web. It does, however, require that marketers understand their customers more intimately than they do when using traditional brand-marketing media.

>> *One-to-One Web Marketing*

Some marketers even go a step beyond micro marketing and target individuals. This strategy, which Don Peppers and Martha Rogers call *one-to-one marketing*, is possible when a message or product can be customized to meet an individual customer's need. The Web is a perfect medium for one-to-one marketing because it is individually addressable. In other words, a unique piece of data or request for information from a user can trigger a response to that user alone. We have already considered most of the Web applications that enable one-to-one marketing: interactivity, e-mail, personalization, community and chat, Web presentations and conferencing, advertising, tracking Web use, integration of Web data gathering with company databases, auctions, shopping bots, and real-time customer service and customer relationship management.

Thanks to these applications, each of the most popular sites on the Internet uses one or more one-to-one features. For example, CNN's website lets registered users create their own version of the website, called MyCNN, where they can personalize their weather, sports, business, and lifestyle news.

Building customer profiles based on declared information (customer data captured from site registration) and behavioral data (Web users' site usage and purchasing habits) can be powerful tools to maximize brand loyalty and financial value from each customer. Customer profiles enable marketers to create more brand value in the mind of the customer. This in turn builds a stronger connection with the brand and increases costs (real or perceived) of switching to a competitor.

>> *Riding the "Cluetrain"*

As marketers adopt an increasingly personalized approach, they are being challenged to consider the implications. In *The Cluetrain Manifesto* (at www.cluetrain.com), Christopher Locke, Rick Levine, Doc Searls, and David Weinberger present ninety-five theses that ask companies to rethink how they interact with and market to people in the e-marketplace. *The Cluetrain Manifesto* asks marketers to stop thinking about their customers as demographic sectors and think of them as human beings. According to the authors, "The Internet is enabling conversations among human beings that were simply not possible in the era of mass media." These conversations (i.e., marketing communications) need to sound human, since they are taking place with human beings.

Now that people have more information available to them on the Internet, they are more savvy. This development, along with the proliferation of advertising that is shouting at customers rather than conversing with them, has rendered customers immune to traditional advertising. Customers are in control of the conversations online, and they quickly make a getaway to a competitor if they feel that the website is merely using them as conduits to achieve their financial goals. According to Locke, "We need an alternative to traditional branding. People are looking for substance instead of sizzle. The message should be a meaningful narrative that makes sense in someone's life."

>> Permission Marketing

One way that marketers might meet the challenge of humanizing their communication is with what Seth Godin has called *permission marketing*. Godin advocates using this approach in place of traditional advertising, which he calls "interruption marketing." Interruption marketing uses advertising messages that interrupt what a person is doing. This no longer works because there is too much interruption, too much noise, too much clutter. Marketers respond to this clutter by interrupting more often or with stronger messages, which intensifies the problem and continues to erode the effectiveness of advertising.

In contrast, permission marketing invites a customer to volunteer to receive marketing. The use of permission marketing therefore ensures that the audience consists entirely of people who have volunteered to receive marketing messages. These volunteers are interested, so they will pay more attention to the messages. In Godin's words, permission marketing should be "anticipated, personal and relevant," meaning customers are expecting the marketing messages, the message is directed personally to each customer, and the marketing is relevant to each recipient. This attention to customers' wants results in a highly targeted (and therefore cost-effective) approach to marketing communications.

>> Real Time

In an environment operating on Internet time, marketers must meet new standards for speed. In his book *Real Time*, marketing guru Regis McKenna sets the standard as what he calls *real-time marketing*. This means marketing that provides immediate responses and instant decisions, connecting with customers before they can click over to a competitor's website. Warns McKenna, "The competitive environment will no longer tolerate slow response or delayed decision making."

What does real-time marketing look like? In terms of marketing channels, it involves getting a website online in a matter of weeks. And rather than spending months preparing and testing a print or broadcast advertisement, Internet marketers quickly produce banner ads and then gather data as users start clicking on the ads. If necessary, they replace a poor performer in the course of about a week. For customer service, marketers must provide immediate answers when someone e-mails a comment or complaint. Today's customer wants a response now!

>> Viral and Spiral Marketing

The networked communications inherent in cyberspace can help marketers with real-time marketing efforts. Two related marketing methods that optimize the Internet's inherent networking capability are called viral marketing and spiral branding. As its name describes, *viral marketing* is marketing that spreads like a virus—growing itself in an epidemic manner. It is word-of-mouth marketing facilitated by the product itself or the marketing activities. Viral marketing draws on customers' sense of affinity, where they want to belong or want others to belong with them.

With viral marketing, the company doesn't do the selling, its customers do. As discussed earlier, every Hotmail e-mail message contains a link advertising Hotmail's free e-mail service. According to Steve Jervetson, one of Hotmail's investors, viral marketing can succeed only if the product or service offers benefits or features that a customer would want to share with others. In Hotmail's case, customers are willing to share the message that their e-mail service is free.

Instead of spreading outward to new customers, *spiral* branding spreads inward, solidifying the customer relationship. According to Jesse Berst, editorial director of ZDNet AnchorDesk, *spiral branding* is a three-stage process:

1. The marketer uses TV, print, or radio advertising to generate interest and Web traffic.

2. The marketer uses interactivity and specialized content at the website to engage a customer. At this stage, the marketer collects the customer's e-mail address.

3. The marketer develops e-mail communications that remind and give customers incentives to return to the Web.

As described by its name, spiral branding thus moves around a fixed point, the customer, in a coil-like manner. This continuous spiral is a closed loop that encourages customers to be part of the process for the long term.

Spiral branding involves a feedback loop that enables companies to learn more about customers and offerings in an iterative manner. It also involves integration that benefits both the customer and the brand. Companies must tie together the media and databases to collect and track behavioral and declared information from the customer. The long-run benefits of a closed-loop marketing process far outweigh the headaches and costs of creating such a process.

>> E-Reach

The global reach of the Internet can create opportunities as well as challenges. When a company sets up a website, it has a global opportunity overnight, but there is more to globalization than translating websites into local languages of key markets. As global brands already know, they need to engage in localization, taking into account the business and/or consumer cultures in each region or country.

It is helpful to rank the priority of localization by the country's Internet penetration, as well as the likelihood that people in other countries will visit or buy from the company's website. Some companies will determine that they need a local physical presence in the country, in addition to a localized website. Also, marketers must determine how much their websites should vary from country to country—beyond translation to merchandising, style, tone, and so forth. For example, Amazon.com's book sites for the United States and United Kingdom have similar site architecture and appearance, but that is about as far as similarities go. Each site features different merchandise on the home page. In fact, Amazon.com.uk is a British subsidiary of Amazon.com. In this case, localization of a website requires staff made up of people from the local area.

The Net Brand Organization

Already marketing organizations are changing. Internet companies have come up with creative titles to describe new functions that were never on the marketing team before. Doug Rice, CEO of Interactive8 (now Luminant), advises against tacking online marketing onto the brand manager's already-full list of responsibilities:

> *An organization must realign itself to deliver the brand promise from the website. A company will need to dedicate key online people or teams within the organization. Like TV, print, and other advertising vehicles, you should have a specialist within each media. If you don't have them in-house, then outsourcing the responsibility to an interactive agency is a good short-term move.*

According to Ian Ryder, director of global branding at Hewlett-Packard, "A company must have someone in the brand-marketing organization [who] is well-skilled in visual communications, in addition to good written communications." Ryder adds that "designing the right kind of team for online initiatives requires the full support of the organization's executives; unless they buy in, the effort will fail."

To create online marketing programs for the Internet, the brand-marketing organization will require new skills, including relationship or one-to-one marketing, data warehousing and data mining, direct marketing, broad marketing communications with integrated media experience, retail marketing, and sales promotion. So in addition to Web designers, architects, and developers, the Web team should include key marketing resources to create the best customer experience in the online medium. The new marketing team for the Internet Age will need people who understand how people interact with the Web interface, including graphics, text, and hyperlinking. Usability and information-architecture experts should be on the team. If the Web projects involve sound, video, and moving visuals, another key person would be a producer, who can create the vision of the application or presentation as well as integrate the different visual and sound elements. Also, the team should be adept at integrating the Web with other branding activities. In general, a Web team is cross-functional, with team members involved in Web design, editorial, e-mail, marketing, public relations, order fulfillment, Web performance measurement and reporting, programming, site hosting, technical support, and project management.

At the Sharper Image (www.sharperimage.com), the Internet team is a separate division comprising media (online and offline), marketing (e-mail and promotions), website (administration, development, and hosting), auction (dedicated personnel, separate profit and loss), and creative services. The entire team reports to the director of the Internet division, who reports directly to the president.

At UPS, the marketing team works much more closely with the information technology (IT) group than it has in the past. "Our team is made up from experts in each function," says Tom Daly, online national brand manager for UPS. "The team is cross-functional, representing marketing, marketing communications, operations, IT, customer service, and other key functional areas of the company to ensure the site meets every area's requirements as they relate to the customer."

Since the Internet continues to change, so will the brand-marketing organization. We will continue to see new and interesting titles such as content producer, vice president of customer experience, relationship marketing manager, customer care champion, manager of interactive services, captain of community, director of Internet revenue, interactive brand manager, and more. Such new titles are a logical outgrowth of what Lynn Upshaw says about brand building in the following interview: that it is not only a marketing activity but requires transforming the entire organization.

>> **Lynn Upshaw on the Future of E-Brand Building**

The following interview is Lynn Upshaw's point of view on the future of branding on the Internet. Lynn Upshaw is an internationally known brand/e-brand marketing consultant, principal of Upshaw & Associates, and author of Building Brand Identity *(John Wiley & Sons, 1995) and author of* The Masterbrand Mandate *(Wiley, 2000). He can be reached at upshaw@brandbuilding.com.*

Deborah Kania: *How has the Internet affected the relationship between the customer and the brand?*

Lynn Upshaw: Online channels have created an environment in which brands can finally reach their full potential as relationship builders. Extended and pure-play online brands must deal with a new set of operating rules with their prospective customers. For example, trust has always been the hallmark of great brands, but online brands must ask prospects to trust *everything* associated with a purchase. Buyers must trust that the product or service will look and perform the way it does online, that their credit card number is safe on the Net, that their order will be filled promptly, and that their questions or complaints will be addressed by live human beings who really care, and on a 24/7 basis.

(continued)

Past offline brands were largely built by selling *at* the customer. More recently, brands have been built by assuming that the purchase was only the beginning of a customer relationship experience. In the future, brands will be built through a continuous, mutually beneficial interaction between seller and buyer, which, like the Star Wars "force," will run under, around, and through brand marketing. And, as always, it will be the customer who will be the ultimate judge of what is or is not beneficial.

D.K.: *How can a brand compete effectively in the online marketplace?*

L.U.: The e-commerce phenomenon has accelerated the speed at which relationships are built. Day traders at E*Trade and working moms visiting eToys and bank customers at WingSpan are all happily enjoying the benefits of disintermediation, interacting with brands that are committed to being the number one place for their patrons to shop, regardless of channel. They are evolving experiential brands that can build awareness and patronage at light speed compared to their offline competitors. They fight the overwhelming clutter and competition on the Web with a core set of features, including:

- A strong sense of community that moves one-dimensional customer relationships into multidimensional seller-buyer-buyer "brand triangles" (e.g., eBay, iVillage, ESPNet);
- Customization, followed by personalization of a brand, once sufficient databases are compiled and profiling is established (Amazon, Yahoo!);
- 24/7/365 service, ideally a combination of online and live, and with instantaneous response to customer inquiry (Charles Schwab);
- Alliances with relevant, brand-reinforcing partners (AOL, MSN);
- Reliable, scalable, server farm support (*New York Times* website);
- Simple-to-navigate site architecture (Drugstore.com);
- Strong branding components, i.e., name, graphic system, strategic selling line, etc. (Saturn.com);
- Substantial "stickiness" to encourage multiple usage and long-term loyalty, via attractive content and/or promotional incentives (CBS.Marketwatch, PCMall); and

- Creative customer relationship management (CRM): strategically sound and tactically fresh approaches to managing ongoing customer relationships (Harley-Davidson HOGs [Harley Owners Groups]).

D.K.: *What are the challenges in the future that brand marketers should prepare themselves for?*

L.U.: Even as everyone jumps into the e-commerce pool, marketers need to be coldly realistic about a few dark clouds that threaten to rain on the parade. The first hovers over the issue of brand loyalty. Modern marketing in developed economies has evolved through several eras, from the mass-market stage to segmented targeting to today's one-to-one relationship era. Customers are now elevated to the status of CEO of their own service acceptance companies. Whatever they wish to read, eat, drive, use, or play with, marketers are there to create the world they seek.

At first glance, such made-to-order service should trigger more loyalty. Yet, paradoxically, even as customers gain more control over what is sold to them, they seem less inclined to commit their loyalty. Why? Because the incentives to shop around exceed those that induce loyalty. There are more choices offered by more companies clamoring to provide ultrapersonalized goods and services. In such an environment, the customer is rewarded more for shopping around (made easy by the Web) than for sticking with tried-and-true favorites, which increasingly seem to be commoditized. (eBay, to name just one example, lost its uniqueness the minute Amazon and others joined the auction party.)

E-marketers may be more skilled at creating relationships with customers, but those relationships may at best create short-term habits, rather than build long-term loyalties, as in the past.

D.K.: *Many online brands are using aggressive promotional tactics to acquire customers—such as discounting and free products or services. What impact will this have on brand loyalty?*

L.U.: In terms of brand loyalty, anyone who has been in marketing for more than ten minutes knows that brands have traditionally been built on persuasive positioning and steady marketing support . . . and undermined by dis-

(continued)

counting and promotional incentives. For better or worse, it appears that most e-brands are being built by just such incentives. The question is, Can they hold onto a core base of users with carrots on a stick, or will they have to make their revenue hurdles by churning customers through the turnstiles indefinitely? At last count, there were a half dozen management consultant studies that have proven that the latter strategy is a sure formula for red ink. (Of course, if the new name of the game is to build capitalization and indefinitely postpone earnings, that approach might work out just fine.)

D.K.: *What is the Internet technology's impact on the brand?*

L.U.: Technological breakdown is not just a bothersome inconvenience, it is a strategic flaw. Technology is simply moving too fast to guarantee 100 percent or even 98 percent reliability. Priceline, eBay, E*Trade, and Schwab are but a few of the many online businesses that have been crippled by server crashes. These may be temporary glitches for those firms, but they are indicative of a broader industry problem that must be solved—namely, the temptation to expand faster than the hardware and software support can handle.

Trust—and therefore brands—may soon be measured by the number of crashes per quarter.

D.K.: *How has the Internet changed how we determine a brand's valuation?*

L.U.: In the past decade, much has been written about Moore's law (the speed of computing will double every eighteen months at a constant cost), and the market is now being influenced even more directly by Metcalf's law (the value of a network is based on the value of its users, squared). To these profound observations, "Upshaw's law" suggests that, in the near future, the value of a brand will be a function of the mutually beneficial interaction between that brand and its customers.

Brand valuation firms have created assessments of the financial equity in brands. Those assessments take into account such attributes as the quality of the brand's leadership (often defined as the brand's ability to influence its market), its stability of strength over time, its globalness, the impact of its marketing communications, and the security of its legal titles. But these approaches to evaluations may have to be updated to measure the living relationships that brands create.

In the future, brand marketers will need to come up with a quantitative measure for the potential of a brand to generate relationship-driven revenue with customers. While there is no specific formula in mind at this time, some key factors might focus on brands that [do certain things]:

- Are positioned in a way that is demonstrable as superior in an interactive environment—For example, Amazon demonstrates its personalization capabilities at every turn in its site.

- Carry a brand personality that is inviting in a highly repetitive relationship with customers—To some, Yahoo! may have a more accessible personality as a brand of portal than, say, the Go Network.

- Live up to customer assumptions about online brands—For instance, online buyers assume eToys and Outpost.com and Buy.com provide discounted goods and services versus offline competitors. When and if that is not the case, these brands are vulnerable to customer erosion.

- Are inherently relationship-driven—Information sites that visitors check daily (CBS Marketwatch), e-commerce sites that carry staples (Peapod), and community-based sites (eBay) are most likely to grab and hold audiences, because they are tapping into a fundamental trait of the Net.

D.K.: *How will the Internet affect the brand-building process?*

L.U.: The Internet—its progeny the Web, intranets, and extranets—has also spawned the creation of a new form of holistic, digitized marketing, in which the company, its employees and constituencies, its brand(s), and its customers can be commingled in a dance that benefits all. In short, for marketers to fully capitalize on the virtually unlimited possibilities of e-branding, they must

(continued)

first recognize that "branding" and "brand building" are two related but different disciplines.

Branding is the act of differentiating a product or service or corporation with a unique name, logo, positioning, selling theme, etc. Branding is essential to the establishment and sustaining of e-businesses, but it is only part of the brand-building process.

Brand building, on the other hand, includes branding but involves creating more than a well-branded product or service. It also requires transforming the entire selling organization into a brand-driven company which works collaboratively with its customers to establish the strongest possible brand-based relationships. In such cases, the brand *becomes* the company, and vice versa.

Down the road, the key to creating ongoing, mutually beneficial relationships between sellers and buyers lies as much in (1) how brand-oriented the company is [in the way it is] organized, and (2) how its people are motivated to build e-brands, as it does in their chosen style of marketing. Just as Charles Schwab, Saturn, Gap, Starbucks, and other leaders have organized their resources into brand-driven companies for the sake of their customers and stakeholders, so e-branders must establish similarly strong selling organizations, molded to fit the unique opportunities and challenges of online brand building. >>

"The brand is the brand," proclaims Tom Daly of UPS. "The Web doesn't change that fact." On the one hand, the Web is just another channel. On the other hand, the Web is an entirely different medium altogether. The Web medium differs from other media in significant ways. It is profoundly changing both buyers and sellers. The brand itself may not change fundamentally, but how it is presented to the online audience will be consistent but different.

For some companies, the Web will be a catalyst for completely changing the brand. They are recasting their entire positioning and brand communications because of the Internet. Other companies are gaining understanding about what the Web medium is strongly suited to do, instead of shoehorning past brand methods into the Web framework. In other words, when it comes to the Web, these companies get it. Of course, marketers still don't have all of the answers; the Internet continues to evolve.

A good practice for marketers who have much experience in traditional media is to look at building online programs from the ground up. This means erasing the legacy of traditional branding from one's mind. Some brand organizations have admitted that they have no idea how to proceed on the Internet, or that they cannot afford to wait for change within the organization. These companies have found smart interactive agencies and Web development firms to get them there faster and to educate them on the idiosyncrasies of the Web vehicle. One thing is for sure, every brand marketer must go forward with an open mind.

>> The core principles of brand marketing are not changing because of the Web.

>> How brand marketing is accomplished is a totally different experience on the Web. The brand is the experience, and the experience is the brand.

CHAPTER <5>

[Building the Online Brand]

>> PRODUCTS, LIKE PEOPLE, HAVE PERSONALITIES, AND
THEY CAN MAKE OR BREAK THEM IN THE MARKETPLACE. >>

-- DAVID OGILVY

Building a brand online requires an approach that is unique, like the Web medium itself. Though the fundamentals of building brand awareness, preference, and loyalty are still intact regardless of the Internet, the challenge of establishing a presence online requires a new approach based on integration and interactivity. Many companies have already found that building the online brand requires an integrated media plan. TV, radio, print magazines, and other traditional media have a place in establishing the online brand. Marketers have also discovered that a website is potentially a powerful medium for establishing brand preference and brand loyalty, if it keeps customers engaged and entices them back to the site often. To do this, marketers must build not only a website, but an online brand experience.

Taking It to the Web

The e-branding process starts with the company's objectives for going online. Some companies want to reach a new target market. Some companies want a cost-efficient way to sell to customers. Others see

[119]

that their competition is online and conclude that they too must be online. Still other companies go online to show that they are progressive. Most companies' objectives include serving a growing segment of customers who research purchases and prefer to buy online. Exhibit 5.1 shows the primary website objectives identified by respondents in a study by the Association of National Advertisers. The survey respondents, mostly marketers of traditional brands, were asked to rank their top five objectives for their website. Their ranking gave priority to brand awareness, brand image, and brand loyalty.

The brand's Web presence should be part of an overall branding strategy. Today's well-known dot-coms were the first movers on the

EXHIBIT 5.1

Why Go Online? Primary Objectives for Websites

>> Association of National Advertisers, Web Site Management & Internet Advertising Trends, 3rd ed.

Web, so they were largely unchallenged as they built awareness with the small but growing online audience. All they needed was some limited online advertising to make their presence known online. Now strong offline brands are forging onto the Net, and in this newly competitive environment, dot-com brands must spend many millions, or even hundreds of millions, of dollars to establish and maintain their brands. Many dot-coms have begun to play the same branding game as traditional offline brands by buying expensive TV ads during the Super Bowl or sponsoring race cars and sporting events. Monster.com even put its name on a blimp. An Interbrand study recently found that major dot-com brands such as AOL, Yahoo!, and Amazon.com are spending a significant percentage of revenue on marketing—16.9 percent, 35.9 percent, and 25.9 percent, respectively. These percentages top those of the leading brands: Coca-Cola, 20.5 percent; Microsoft, 16.7 percent; and IBM, 1.1 percent. (Interbrand determines leading brands based on a company's financial strength and the role that brand plays in influencing that strength.)

Brand marketing for e-commerce is at a critical stage. As we saw in Chapter 1, top-of-mind awareness for online brands has been established for only a very few product categories. In some categories it is relatively easy to name the number one brand online. Books? Amazon.com. Auctions? eBay. But, who offers insurance or fitness products on the Web? Most consumers don't know—yet.

How Important Is Brand?

Many marketers believe that the Internet is a direct-response medium and people who shop on the Net are only looking for the best price. Web technology certainly supports this application. Online customers can easily surf from site to site, comparing offerings from brands. With superpowered shopping bots, online customers can scour the Net for the best prices. In addition, marketing research indicates that getting a good price is important to most online shoppers. When researchers in a 1999 Ernst & Young study asked consumers about their reasons for buying online, three-quarters of respondents said they wanted to save money or get a lower price. (Other reasons cited included convenience, product variety, and fun.)

Still, the perception of the Internet as being a place to price-shop may not be the reality. Online customers are declaring that they go online to save money, but their actual shopping behavior does not necessarily show that they are spending a lot of time price-shopping. An Ernst & Young study of consumers' online behavior found that only 16 percent of U.S. online shoppers use a comparison-shopping engine or guide. Likewise, a study by Massachusetts Institute of Technology's Sloan School of Management found that Amazon.com, which has 80 percent of the online book market, did not necessarily have the lowest prices. In the study, Books.com's prices were, on average, $1.60 lower than Amazon.com's prices.

Even if consumers care about price, many situations allow for the influence of a brand. In some situations, Web users may obtain a listing of several companies offering the same price. Also, Internet searches have the potential to turn up thousands of alternatives meeting basic criteria. Brand theory predicts that in these situations, where choosing may be difficult, consumers are likely to pick brands they prefer or are at least familiar with.

The evidence so far is consistent with brand theory. For example, online users tend to return to the same websites again and again. According to Nielsen//NetRatings, Web users visit an average of just ten websites a month. They spend most of their time visiting their favorite few sites, not seeking out new ones. Similarly, Ernst & Young's study of online consumer behavior found that Web users mostly go to sites they know about already. Of the U.S. Web shoppers surveyed, 67 percent get to websites from their menu of favorite sites, 63 percent type in a Web address they already know, and just 33 percent get to sites via a search engine (suggesting that these are sites the users didn't think of on their own).

Studies that ask consumers about the reasons underlying their purchase decisions also support the principle that brand influences choices. For example, a PC Data study found that the top factor influencing visits to apparel websites was familiarity with the brand (15 percent). (Other influences were prior shopping experience, historically low price, recommendations from friends, and advertisements.) In the 1999 study by Ernst & Young, 82 percent of respondents said that knowing a product's brand name was important or very important in their decision to buy on the Web. Another 79 percent of the survey respondents said that familiarity with the online retailer was important or very important. The study's report quotes Fred Crawford, national director of retail and consumer products at Ernst & Young, as saying, "Consumers online reinforce what leading consumer goods companies have known for many years: there is a lot of equity in brands, whether it's the company or product brand."

A few other studies indicate that brand is not influential. For example, Forrester Research found that younger Internet consumers found activity and utility more important than brand when it comes to their online usage. This preference may be a result of younger consumers growing up in a digital environment. Marketers targeting the teen market may need to communicate their brand in a more interactive way with games and chat. For brands to exert an influence on teens, they need a suitable marketing approach.

Brand Awareness, Preference, and Loyalty Online

Building a relationship between a customer and a brand starts with creating awareness of the brand in its market. Marketers are using a combination of online and offline media to increase brand awareness.

As a rule, brands with high awareness shortcut the process of achieving brand preference and brand loyalty. For example, among clothing websites, IntelliQuest measured a strong correlation between top-of-mind awareness and conversion rates (percent of website visitors who make a purchase), as shown in Exhibit 5.2. The importance of brand awareness is also borne out by the fact that the very first website in a category or a dot-com brand that was first in the market does not necessarily have a guarantee of future success. Fashionmall.com was on the Net in 1994, before the Gap appeared online in 1997. However, the overall strength of the Gap brand has given it a significant advantage online.

Even at a respectable level, however, brand awareness does not necessarily translate to brand preference. In general marketing terms, the reasons for low conversion could be that the marketer's advertis-

EXHIBIT 5.2

Those Who Know, Buy: Top-of-Mind Recall and Conversion Rates

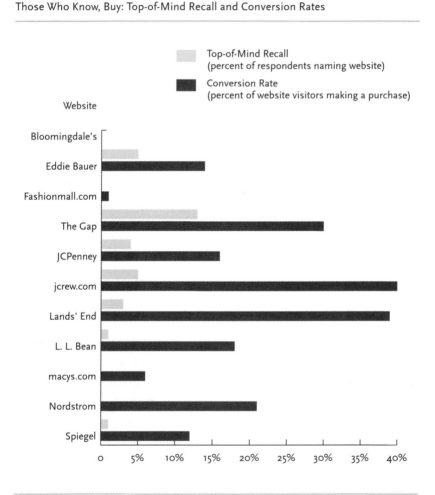

>> IntelliQuest Consumer eBranding Study, First Quarter, 1999.

ing messages and media buying are not attracting the type of people who are most likely to become customers of that particular brand. In the case of a website, some reasons for low conversion could include poor website navigation, slow Web page loading, too little brand trust, difficulty placing an order or making an inquiry, and lack of security or communication about security.

Conversely, some brands have low awareness but high preference, which means that the website did a better job at converting prospects to customers than the company did at building awareness of the site. A case in point is Nordstrom, whose website lacks top-of-mind or unaided awareness, according to the IntelliQuest study. Nordstrom's site has a good conversion rate—even higher than for Eddie Bauer, which has more brand awareness. Nordstrom has always exemplified best-in-class service in the retail industry, and it has brought that standard to the Web.

Despite these exceptions, marketers generally use advertising to build brand awareness and get prospective customers to a website where they attempt to influence brand preference. The combination of brand awareness and preference may encourage customers to make a purchase. To produce this result, converting the first-time browser into a first-time buyer, a website must exhibit excellence in key areas. These same characteristics should also enhance a brand's ability to achieve repeat visits and purchases, leading to brand loyalty. For example, as discussed in Chapter 1, Web users are most likely to buy from sites they trust. In their recent study of e-commerce trust, Cheskin Research and Sapient report, "In short, even if a company can combine a well-known brand, strong navigation and strong fulfillment, it can't ensure that its site will be perceived as trustworthy if its brand isn't considered trustworthy."

Consider how trust plays a role in some examples from the Cheskin/Sapient study. Of the two toy websites studied, eToys.com and Toys "R" Us, respondents were more familiar with the Toys "R" Us brand than the eToys.com brand. Both websites had about the same level of use by respondents. However, respondents indicated they would trust Toys "R" Us more than eToys.com. The correlation between familiarity and trust was consistent across many product categories, including books, computers, drugstores, flowers, investment, online malls, music, travel, and video. In the case of video retailers online, Blockbuster.com had the most familiarity and most trust, despite the fact that its website was being used less than Reel.com's. In sum, brand familiarity can enable a brand to move faster and further toward brand trust and loyalty, but the online customer's perceptions about the brand also depend on the site's functionality, look, and feel and communication about security and privacy. The company that leverages its customers' trust in the brand and creates a superior site will be successful with its online presence.

The Internet significantly influences customers' perception of a brand. A CyberDialogue study found that 36 percent of Internet users' opinions about one or more product brands changed as a result of using the Internet. For some brands, an online presence can have a positive influence on brand perceptions. People generally view companies with websites as progressive and leaders in their industry. However, if a well-known, trusted brand has a poorly designed website, that site can damage perceptions of the brand. The negative perception can diminish brand loyalty among existing customers. Consequently, the brand's website deserves the same investment and commitment to quality as other media receive.

Nothing but Net: The Dot-Com Phenoms

Interbrand's 1999 ranking of the world's top brands included three dot-com brands: AOL, Yahoo!, and Amazon.com. In just a few short years, these brands have become household names. AOL is ranked just below the Wrigley's chewing gum brand, introduced more than 100 years ago.

Yahoo!, introduced in 1994 as a directory and search engine site, now has more than sixty million registered users and has increased its functionality to include content and shopping. Its advertising campaign, "Do You Yahoo?" has successfully defined the brand by focusing on the brand's attributes rather than the product's technical aspects. If you use Yahoo!, your life is that much better. Those who visit www.yahoo.com find the common features of a Web portal: news, search engines, shopping, weather, chat, maps, auctions, and more. Yahoo! users also can download some content to a handheld device such as the Palm VII. Still, Yahoo! is the epitome of what a brand was traditionally—more sizzle than substance. In a similar way, Coca-Cola is essentially sugar-flavored and caffeine-laden water, but it means so much more in the mind of the consumer. Like Coke, Yahoo! has brand equity. According to Karen Edwards, director of branding at Yahoo!, "Technology can be leapfrogged. Brands cannot."

Thus, Yahoo! and other top dot-com brands seem to have successfully executed traditional brand-marketing practices on the Internet. They know that the path to the customer's heart is not feature and functions, but the brand and what it means to the customer. To that end, many dot-com brands and brand names are not communicating just the specific function or attribute of the associated product. Brand names like eBay, Beyond.com, More.com, Streamline.com, About.com, and Gloss.com don't restrict their expansion to other areas of business. However, these broad names will require significant brand education to build meaning in the minds of the customers. These dot-com brands will have a bit more of a challenge to translate and define their identities, in contrast to websites like WebMD, Plan etRx.com, Plastics.net, iPrint.com, Digitalwork.com, and Furniture .com, all of which have more clearly understood brand identities.

Amazon.com was created with the mission of being the Internet's largest bookstore. To communicate that scale of activity, Amazon's founders named the company after the Amazon River, one of the world's longest rivers. From July 1995 to mid-1998, the Amazon.com brand was synonymous with books. Since then, as proclaimed by the slogan "Books, music and more," Amazon.com has extended its offerings to electronics, toys, auctions, videos, games, women's apparel, garden and patio supplies, office supplies, pet products, and more. The site also offers zShops, a collection of independent retailers and sellers that has been described as an online flea market. All of the products offered on the Amazon.com site are available from other retailers, but Amazon.com's focus is on its main product attribute of selection. Thus, Amazon.com has evolved its brand away from books to a variety of products, using its brand positioning of having the largest selection of many of the product categories it offers.

In contrast to Amazon.com's emphasis on product attributes, gloss.com defines itself in the market in terms of brand attributes. The word *gloss*, in the context of a beauty site, can be associated with lip gloss, which is a beauty product—a type of lipstick that is very shiny. The word also suggests a glossy or slick presentation of beauty and fashion. Like Amazon.com, gloss.com offers products available from other retailers, but its brand meaning is based on brand attributes. The site's positioning emphasizes an emotional appeal and overall brand image with the slogan "beauty. inspiration. shopping."

Many Net industry professionals believe the future is going to be much more difficult for dot-com brands. Unless they are the number one or number two online brand, they will be acquired or required to merge with other companies. One possible reason is that the traditional brands have been coming online in droves, and they have the significant advantage of their offline brand equity. Also, building a brand can be very expensive. The dot-com brands dominated in the early Web years because they were there first. At this point, the top branding spots in popular e-commerce categories are evenly split among dot-com and traditional brands.

Wiring Traditional Brands

Marketers of traditional brands have had to revisit their branding strategies. A fundamental question is, Should our brand messages and marketing be different for the Web? The *New York Times,* for example, determined that the brand online would need to mean something different than its traditional newspaper. Volvo used the Internet to evolve its brand to encompass the emotional benefits of safety. For other traditional brands, branding online is all about consistency, because the Web is just another channel or medium. Ben Jones, senior creative director at Agency.com, says Texaco looked for consistency in establishing its Internet presence: "When we designed the Texaco site, we built it from the company's core brand attributes of nimble, responsible, passionate, no nonsense, forward thinking, and smart. This is what we call 'living the brand.'" Some traditional brands have ignored the Web completely, either out of fear of the unknown or concern over cannibalizing other channels. Finally, Egghead and other brands have totally abandoned their offline persona to become a completely wired dot-com brand. In some form, most of these strategies try to find a balance between maintaining the brand's core positioning, promises, and image, while using new practices to convey these attributes to the online audience.

>> Dual Personality

The online audience of many traditional companies is slightly or significantly different from their offline audience. The *New York Times*, for example, launched its website in January 1996. By 1999 only about 20 percent of the million-plus print subscribers used its online version (the site now has more than ten million registered users). Susan Hunt Stevens, director of marketing for the *New York Times* website, says the *Times* decided to differentiate this market segment: "When we created the website, we knew we wouldn't just put the newspaper online. We wanted to extend the brand, but we also knew that people had different reasons for reading a print newspaper versus looking for news on the Web." People tend to read a print newspaper passively, page by page. In some cases, readers will seek out specific areas of the newspaper and read it in a linear manner, from the first page to the last. Online, people tend to seek out particular stories in a nonlinear manner because of the hyperlink nature of a Web page. Also, whereas the newspaper was traditionally very geographic, the Web gives the *Times* national and international audiences.

To serve this new audience, the *New York Times* website has the same style, format, and color of the print newspaper, but the news is very dynamic—updating hourly and at any moment with round-the-clock continuous news. In contrast, the print newspaper has a twenty-four-hour cycle. Also reflecting the difference in the consumption of news offline versus online, the *New York Times* positions its online brand differently, as a news *source* instead of a news*paper*. A news source on the Web provides changing and up-to-the-moment coverage of a story as well as related and more in-depth analyses associated with feature stories. A newspaper is static, reporting what has happened in the past, whereas a news website can report on what is happening in the present. It is serving a whole different market with a different product and a different set of competitors.

Despite these differences, the online and offline brands are unified by the same key brand attribute: quality. To the print newspaper, this means a quality newspaper experience—how people browse and read the paper. On the Web, this brand attribute means a quality online experience—how people navigate the site. The website has the look and feel of the print edition, but it has features that people expect on the Web, including more color and up-to-the-minute news, stock information, weather, and the option to receive news via e-mail.

>> Brand Evolution

As we have already seen in the example of Volvo Corporation, some companies have leveraged the demographics of the online audience to evolve their brands. In the thirty-five years during which Volvo has sold cars in the United States, it has developed a strong brand image of safety. The challenge for Volvo is that other car companies have also promoted safety. Volvo had to update its image. First, the simple step of getting online ahead of the competition positioned the brand as contemporary. In addition, the website focuses on lifestyle, not product attributes. Ron Berger, CEO of Volvo's U.S. advertising agency, MVBMS, explains, "We evolved the communications to deepen the meaning of safety to include the emotional benefit of a safe car. Volvo was famous for its ad that showed its cars driving off the cliff. Now Volvo humanizes the core benefit of safety."

Humanizing that benefit means focusing on people. Visitors to Volvo's online showroom (see Exhibit 5.3) first encounter images of people, not automobiles. These images suggest the lifestyles and emotions of each car's owners. In this way, Volvo upgrades the brand image to focus on Volvo's role in people's lives.

>> Extending the Brand

For an already-strong brand, the e-marketplace is an opportunity to extend the brand. A case in point is the Gap, recently ranked by Interbrand among the top sixty brands in the world. The Gap's position as number twenty-nine puts the brand right below Nike and right above Kellogg's. So when the Gap launched www.gap.com in 1997, it gave the website a look and feel very consistent with its stores and its magazine, TV, and outdoor advertising. Gap's website uses the brand's crisp

---

EXHIBIT 5.3

Volvo's Web Showroom: Displaying the Human Side of a Commitment to Safety

---

>> *Courtesy of Volvo Corporation.*

white background with minimalist color palette and silhouetted models, matching the look and feel of the retailer's TV commercials. The website exhibits the Gap's brand personality of hip, young, and easy. Although some retailers consider the Web a threat to their retail revenue, the Gap has embraced the Web as another way for its customers to buy, as well as another way to build customers' relationship with the Gap brand.

Another company that extends its brand online is QVC, a full-time televised shopping service reaching seventy million U.S. cable and satellite television homes. QVC launched its interactive iQVC brand website (www.iqvc.com) in September 1996. "We believe the online world is an extension of the QVC brand," says Steve Hamlin, vice president of iQVC. The company's strategy is to integrate the Web seamlessly with the television programming. This strategy enables the company to broaden its appeal by meeting different needs of the TV and Web audience. According to Hamlin, "On the television our viewers are impulse buyers, because they are watching a show and don't know what product will be shown next. On the Web our customers are given all the products and more choice where they are making a more considered purchase." For instance, if QVC is featuring a particular product line such as glass craft kits from Carol Smith, the channel can show only a limited number of items during the program's time slot. On the website, however, a complete selection of Carol Smith craft kits are available. The website also features an "On the Air" button that customers can click on to see what products are currently featured on TV. Conversely, the QVC television programming includes ten minutes of advertising for the iQVC website every day. "The trust we have built for our TV brand has helped us establish a trust for our online brand," says Hamlin.

Activities for Building the Online Brand

Building the online brand and using the Web for brand marketing have been challenging from the start, but that challenge is becoming more difficult. Dot-com companies have been spending a major percentage of their revenues on marketing without much worry for profitability. Profitability keeps the reins tight on traditional brands, so it is difficult for them to rely on the online medium that has had a high cost per thousand (CPM) relative to some other media. Many companies instead are pouring dollars into advertising that uses more traditional media to promote the dot-com portion of their businesses. Not long ago, using ".com" in an advertisement brought great interest, but now that a website is no longer a huge differentiating factor and most customers expect companies to have websites, companies must again focus on their brand. To build a media plan that gets the message across and rises above the clutter, marketers can learn from what others are already doing. Consumers are learning about online brands through many advertising and promotional activities. The Association of National Advertisers has found that most companies take the simple step of including their Web address (URL) in advertisements

EXHIBIT 5.4

How Marketers Are Drawing Traffic to Their Websites

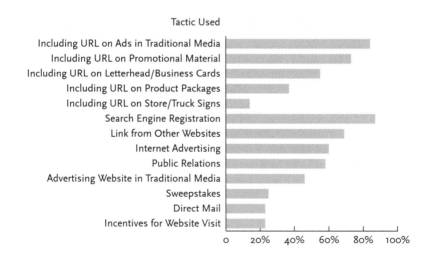

Tactic Used

>> Association of National Advertisers, "Web Site Management & Internet Advertising Trends," 3rd ed.

and promotional material. Most also have registered their site with search engines. In addition, many marketers are communicating their online brand with website links, Internet advertising, and public relations activities. Exhibit 5.4 details these and other methods identified in the ANA study.

Monster.com, a top job-recruiting website, has used several methods to build awareness of its brand. These include targeted promotions with relevant offers, targeted banner ads, TV Super Bowl advertising, and public relations—especially the company's bright orange blimp.

Television has become one of the most popular methods dot-coms use to establish brand awareness. Most believe that the TV is best suited for building brand awareness because of its audio and video elements, which can really make an emotional connection. Early on, most sites settled for just doing online advertising and placing their URLs on company literature to attract people to their websites. Now, as traditional marketers have long known, dot-com marketers appreciate that the most effective way to increase awareness of an online brand or website is to use an integrated media mix.

>> Acquiring a Customer

The most important goal of any marketer—brand or direct-response—is to acquire customers profitably. According to a Shop.org report in conjunction with the Boston Consulting Group, dot-com retailers spend an average of $42 per customer, whereas multichannel retailers spend an average of $22 to acquire a customer. Exhibit 5.5 compares typical goals of the online advertising budgets for the dot-com and multichannel retailer. As this comparison shows, dot-com marketers are devoting a greater share of their advertising budgets to acquiring customers and building brand awareness than their multichannel competitors are.

Multichannel retailers already have the benefits of an offline customer base and some brand awareness, so they can devote more of their advertising to customer retention. This gives the traditional retailers an advantage, in light of the oft-cited maxim that keeping a customer costs far less than obtaining a new customer. To stay competitive, the dot-coms need strategies as creative as that of Art.com (see page 136).

>> Online Advertising

As an advertising medium, the Internet still has a ways to go. Traditional brands have dedicated only a small percentage of their advertising budgets to online media. Dot-coms used to devote a majority of the marketing budget to online advertising, but over the past few years, they have increased the share of spending for traditional media. The lack of audience measurement standards and brand-marketing measurement methods is an important reason why marketers have not moved more dollars to online marketing. Over the next couple of years, online and offline brands will increase their online share of

EXHIBIT 5.5

Goals of Advertising for Dot-Com and Multichannel Retailers

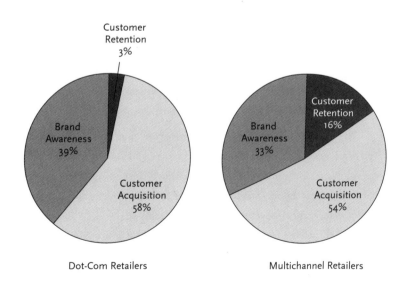

Dot-Com Retailers   Multichannel Retailers

>> *Shop.org and Boston Consulting Group.*

>> Online Brand Building Paints a Bright Future
for Art.com

A well-known maxim of advertising executive Leo Burnett is "You need to have share of mind before you can have share of market." This quote is exemplified by the core branding strategy for Art.com, an e-commerce site that carries the Web's largest collection of framed and unframed art. Art.com has created an online art store with many tools to make buying art a satisfying and comfortable experience—essentially a new business model for buying art and photography.

According to Michael Kahn, Art.com's vice president of marketing, the company's approach to acquiring customers is based on some solid principles:

- Art.com may be an online business and reached through a modem or T1 line, but at the end of the day, we are another retail brand selling through a new channel of distribution.

- Art.com needs to "own" a really right definition of who our target is, what our positioning is, and what our personality will become.

- Art.com needs to use the power of the Web as an incremental customer connection point to create an integrated campaign that combines and unifies brand building and direct response.

- Art.com must continuously ask how what we are doing is building the brand and what kind of response it is generating.

The Art.com brand is targeted to female consumers and other art buyers. The company's positioning is "to be the inviting and fun destination for discovering and buying art and art-related products the consumer has never had before . . . not in 2,000 years of civilization." The personality of Art.com is cool and sophisticated, yet simple and accessible.

The company's marketing objectives are to be a household brand name and one of the top 500 e-commerce sites. To do this, Art.com is combining offline and online marketing. With the online advertising efforts, the company is a master of "selling in context." For this advertising, the company has created hundreds of banner ads, including ads for works of different artists such as Edward Hopper and Rembrandt. These banners are placed on sites and on search engines with appropriate keywords that will serve the ad when someone indicates an interest in one of the artists. "What has worked for us," says Kahn, "is relentless optimization of creative messages and media buys. For an online retailer, being good at building the brand and at generating response is one and the same." He adds, "Your Web experience is your brand." >>

budget as the audience gets larger, more creative options become available, the online audience continues to accept online advertising, and the measurement tools for branding are made available. Internet marketing already began to stabilize a little in 1999, when there was enough history to determine some basic measures.

The primary advantage of using the Web for advertising is the ability to target ads based on Web surfers' online habits and personal interests. This level of detail in customer information has not been available with other media. Although the profiling capability is available to online advertisers, most online media buyers do not leverage user clickstream data (the data captured from Web users' Internet usage)—site visits, time spent online, online transactions, etc. Only one out of four media buyers make optimal use of user data, according to Jupiter Communications. So far, media planners are used to relying on demographics and pre- and post-ad-tracking studies. Online advertising that applies user profile targeting and tracking is new territory for the media buyer who previously did not have the depth of information and the tracking capabilities. Also, it requires more time and attention than traditional means of targeting. (For in-depth discussions about online advertising, see Chapters 6 and 7.)

>> *Website Marketing*

Marketing activities within the website are key to converting prospects into buyers and first-time visitors into loyal customers. According to eMarketer, the top five factors influencing buyer conversion include convenience, security, price, customer service, and variety. With the exception of security, this list looks very familiar to direct-response and catalog marketers. Most websites do pretty well with convenience, variety, and security. Web customer service and competitive pricing are the next issues for marketers to tackle. Web users have had difficulty getting service and finding a real, live human being to help them. Price is an interesting issue in that many believe that saving money is a huge reason people use the Web for purchases. In an NFO Interactive study, 29 percent of respondents said they would be more loyal to a website if they had the certainty of finding the lowest price. Although new pricing models have emerged—notably online auctions—it has not yet been proved that people pay less for the things they buy online than they would from a store or catalog.

Marketers have spent a lot of time, attention, and dollars on acquiring new customers, but keeping them requires a big shift in attention inward, to website activities. These website marketing techniques can keep customers interested while they are on a website. A website should be engaging and memorable enough that customers will want to return to it. Website marketing activities also must be meaningful because many require significant investment. ActivMedia has identified key Web marketing activities that work well for the top sites:

- E-mail newsletters and special promotional offers
- Links and partnerships to spread reach
- Memberships to deepen relationships and loyalty among core customers
- Gathering and building customer data
- Free services leading to subscriptions
- Building on friendship circles—that is, each customer's personal network

- Building a sense of community
- Leveraging offline-online synergy
- Multilingual marketing
- Being local (the Web's next frontier)
- Sticking to core competencies
- Value-added publishing
- Expressions of personality
- Personalization and customization
- Cyber-avatars that offer personal support
- Personal endorsements and customer imagery

When it comes to activities, information, and tools, websites have many ways to convert visitors into loyal visitors or buyers. E-mail marketing, in-depth content, community, profiling and personalization, and other activities are efficient marketing expenditures, because they pull customers back repeatedly toward the desired breakeven point and onward to the goal for customer lifetime value. Web marketing activities can include points of customer contact that create and enrich the customer profile. Over time, such interactions give the marketer more data points beyond transaction history, name, address, and telephone number. The marketer can fill out the profile by obtaining demographic, psychographic, and preference information.

Web profiling applications allow marketers to profile and identify the most profitable customers. The deeper the customer profile, the more easily marketers can identify, rank, and individualize customers. This information and the resulting insight will help marketers optimize creative and media selection to acquire the most profitable types of customers, knowing with a higher degree of assurance that they will be loyal enough for the brand to achieve the desired financial payback. These in-depth customer profiles can also enable marketers to maximize the value of each customer. By building profiles based on each and every Web transaction and interaction, a company can determine what its customers need and how to satisfy them. (For an in-depth discussion of the website marketing experience, see Chapter 8.)

Interactive Identity

Brand-building activities on the Web are distinctive largely because they create a distinctive kind of brand identity. Whereas most brand building involves the customer observing a brand, the online customer is more engaged in the process. The result is an *interactive identity*— that is, an identity that grows from the customer's active experience of the brand.

The marketer forging an interactive identity cannot simply devise an animated logo or audio/video applications to be played on a site. That approach provides a passive experience, whereas an interactive identity arises from an active—or interactive—experience. Unlike TV, radio, and other one-way broadcast media, which provide for no interactivity, the Web is a two-way medium, so marketers must think in terms of making their brand interactive. When a user clicks on a hyperlink, for example, the user is interacting with the website. Inputting information in order to receive a result involves interacting. Participating in a chat dialogue with other users or with the brand or company also is interacting. Lynn Upshaw, author of *Building Brand Identity*, sums up the significance of this interaction:

> Generally speaking, we don't like people who talk at us; we are more inclined toward those who talk with us. We feel an affinity with individuals who pull us into a conversation by letting us talk, too. The interactive communications evolution is, more than anything else, a recognition of what we are all most comfortable with, that is, information exchange instead of information dump.

The interactive identity can be accomplished in many ways. Interactive applications can be built as tools, such as the Kraft Foods Interactive Kitchen (www.kraft.com), which allows visitors to find recipes and build shopping lists. Some brands use games to build an interactive exchange between the brand and the user. The Lifesavers Candystand (www.candystand.com) features numerous games such as crossword puzzles, card games, and video poker that involve many brands such as Lifesavers candy, Bubble Yum gum, Carefree gum, and Snack-Well's cookies. Levi's ties in music with its online brand experience. The Levi's Music Channel (www.levismusic.com) lets users play music, see a concert calendar, participate in a petition, and enter a contest. The Ralston Purina website (www.purina.com) has other interactive applications. Its dog breed selector takes the user through an interactive question-and-answer session to determine which breed of dog is best suited to the user's preferences and lifestyle. The Purina site also features the iVillage.com Pet Namer and iVillage.com Vet Finder tools, Pet Talk chat, and an advice service where users can e-mail questions to Purina's Internet representatives. ABC Sports and ESPN websites (abcsports.go.com and espn.go.com) have a special feature from ABC called Enhanced TV, which allows TV viewers to go online while watching a football game. Enhanced TV gives users real-time statistics, lets users play games with other people online using Primetime Player, and offers the Live Push feature, which sends statistics, sports trivia, and other information while the game is on the TV. During the 2000 Super Bowl, 650,000 football fans logged onto supporting sites such as www.superbowl.com and www.espn.com, and spent an average of forty-two minutes apiece with Enhanced TV.

Depending upon a brand's identity and attributes, an interactive identity can be humorous, helpful, entertaining, serious, imaginative, or informational. It all depends on the brand's identity and attributes. The obvious benefit of an interactive identity is that users will spend more than a few moments on a website—quite a contrast with the brief time spent viewing a TV ad. The time spent by the website customer, along with the memorable user experience, can help a brand build preference and loyalty. The interactive identity creates an indelible experience, not just an indelible image, resulting in considerably more impact on a customer than marketers can achieve with traditional branding.

In the Web We Trust

Besides the already difficult job of moving from brand awareness to brand preference, marketers on the Web must establish brand trust. Unfortunately, the media have fueled controversies over protecting customers' privacy and security. Many people are therefore fearful about using the Internet. Studies have shown that a large number of online consumers are unlikely to trust a website even with a prominently displayed privacy policy.

Fortunately, as identified earlier, there are ways to increase trust among website users. As mentioned in Chapter 1, Jupiter Communications identified six favorable factors: a strong offline brand, word-of-mouth customer referrals, using branded products on the site, a good Web experience, a high-quality site, and high-quality information. Another study previously mentioned, Cheskin Research and Sapient's joint research project, titled "eCommerce Trust Study," determined six primary components that establish trust with Web users:

1. *Seals of approval*—security symbols like Visa and VeriSign, signifying that the site is secure
2. *Brand*—the brand promise to deliver specific attributes and the brand's reputation and credibility
3. *Navigation*—site design and tools that make it easy for customers to find what they are looking for
4. *Fulfillment*—dependable order processing, shipping, and customer service
5. *Presentation*—a high-quality, professional website design
6. *Technology*—state-of-the-art technology (i.e., speed, functionality) and its professional connotations

The study also identified additional factors that influence the use of websites by customers: convenience, ease of use, good prices, and wide product selection. Especially for a company or product with a lesser-known brand, strong site navigation and fulfillment are key to building trust. Of course, it is most advantageous to have a strong brand along with those other benefits.

If any website needs customer trust, an online bank does. Trust is crucial to any bank's success. Traditional bricks-and-mortar banks demonstrate security with cues such as a vault and the thick safety glass at the teller windows. A virtual bank like CompuBank (www.com pubank.com) has to convey these same feelings of security, virtually, which is much more difficult. Also, a traditional bank that goes online has the advantage of its legacy of offline trust to give its customers confidence in online banking. A dot-com virtual bank has a greater challenge in establishing brand trust. Therefore, CompuBank has found new ways to build brand trust, according to Jonathan Lack, the online bank's executive vice president of marketing and planning. Lack says, "In addition to the requirement of security and privacy, we have the benefit of third-party endorsements like our ranking by Smart-Money.com as the best brand in the category, which is extremely important to any financial company." Word-of-mouth referrals are a key component of CompuBank's success in acquiring new customers, and this signals the bank's ability to build trust. A customer must feel trust and loyalty toward a brand in order to refer friends and colleagues.

At CompuBank and other websites, brand trust is about the total customer experience. The customer's experience on a website doesn't stop at front end with the browser. Website growth and performance also depend on whether customers get quick responses and resolutions from the company. Back-end systems that integrate process and communication are therefore of equal importance. (For an in-depth discussion about the customer's Web experience, see Chapter 8.)

TOP-OF-MIND THOUGHTS

Building the online brand is a challenge for both dot-com and tradi-tional offline brands. Traditional brands have a wild card—a legacy that can be an asset or a liability in their execution of the brand online. In general, strong offline brands will be at a significant advantage on the Web. However, dot-com brands have the advantage of an interac-tive mind-set—no baggage, nothing to unlearn. Still the ".com" is all about the technology. Fundamentally, brand building methodology is the same in any medium. Familiarity and trust in the mind of the cus-tomer are key to branding success. On the Web, familiarity and trust have become more important than ever.

>> Brand is more important on the Web than in other media. The more choices a customer has, the more important the brand becomes. Customers are becoming empowered with information, and they can easily find competitive goods, services, and prices.

>> Establishing a brand, whether a dot-com brand or a traditional brand, requires the tried-and-true aims of brand marketing—aware-ness, preference, and loyalty. Traditional brands have some options on how they take their offline brand to the Internet, but choosing is not easy. The best avenue depends on the online audience and the brand legacy.

>> Evolution or revolution? Some brands have broken completely with their past, some have used the Web to evolve the brand, and others are taking their traditional brand legacy online.

>> In traditional brand marketing, establishing trust has been a key ele-ment of building brand loyalty. Reports of security and privacy prob-lems on the Internet have made people a bit skeptical and fearful of e-commerce, so brands must take even further steps to build trust online.

CHAPTER <6>

[The Web Medium]

>> THE INTERACTIVE WORLD IS WHERE CONSUMERS
ARE GOING, WHERE IT'S HAPPENING, AND WE NEED TO BE
THERE. >>

-- DENIS BEAUSEJOUR, VICE PRESIDENT OF
GLOBAL MARKETING, PROCTER & GAMBLE

Because Web users, unlike the audiences for TV, radio, and print advertising, visit a website only when they actively choose to do so, brand-marketing managers have a more difficult job to do online. Besides rising above the clutter, they must give users a compelling reason to visit websites and click on banner ads. This objective has become even harder since the novelty of the Web banner ad has worn off.

To meet the challenge of the Web medium, marketers apply the traditional questions. Where does online advertising fit into the overall media mix? How can online advertising contribute to the desired brand-building results? When, where, how, and how much should the brand appear online? Should the online advertising objective be direct response or branding?

Marketers have developed a variety of strategies for the Web. One popular approach is to use traditional media such as TV to drive the bulk of customers to the website rather than using a lot of online advertising. Other marketers use online advertising to reach mass audiences by placing brand banners or sponsorships on the most heavily trafficked websites, such as Yahoo! and Excite. Online advertising also can be used to reach a target audience across a network of sites. Or an advertiser can pick websites that reach the desired target market.

The Web medium is more flexible than other traditional media. It is the best direct-response medium ever created. It collapses the trial and purchase cycle. Some marketers have created banner ads that enable the Web user to complete a transaction right within the banner. Marketers also are figuring out how to use the online advertising to achieve brand-marketing objectives. New online advertising formats continue to emerge, increasing marketers' ability to convey brand messages in an interactive and memorable way.

The Next Generation Media Mix

Before the Web, marketers were already allocating media budgets among a host of media and events—TV, radio, magazines, outdoor, direct mail, newspapers, freestanding inserts, coupons, cobranding, telemarketing, toll-free telephone, direct-response TV, promotions, event sponsorships, public relations, packaging, trade shows, etc. The Internet has added a whole new channel, comprising websites, Web ads, and e-mail. Where should the Web fit in the already complex media mix? How much of the media budget should go to online advertising?

The answers depend on Web users' responses to Internet advertising. The influence of online advertising on buyer behavior is becoming apparent as marketers become more sophisticated in using this medium. Early on, users happily clicked on Web banner ads, but as the novelty wore off, response to these ads plummeted. The advertising industry reacted by creating new ad formats and technology to get response and recall back up to acceptable levels. According to a survey conducted by @d:Tech and Talk City, 21 percent of online users have made purchases online as a result of an e-mail advertisement, in contrast to 32 percent making purchases online as a result of word-of-mouth referrals and 36 percent buying because of a TV, radio, or print advertisement. Also, Web search engines prompted 36 percent of users to visit websites.

Determining how much of the online advertising should be allocated to direct response or branding also is an important task. Marketers have both branding and direct-response objectives, and the budget should support these objectives. Art.com, the leading online art and frame retailer, recently allocated 60 percent of its total advertising budget to branding and 40 percent to direct response. "Not only are we a brand, our offering is a whole new online category, which requires us to invest to build our presence to become a household name and to educate the market that there is a new way to buy art," says Michael Kahn, vice president of marketing for Art.com. At the same time, Art.com is an e-commerce site, so advertising must also produce responses that lead to sales.

If a marketer has a branding objective for the Web medium, then the media budget should cover online brand advertising, not just response advertising, no matter how enticing it may be to achieve a high click-through rate. Because the Web is the perfect response medium, reliance on direct response is hard to resist. Luckily, there are new online ad formats and measurements that enable marketers to create online brand ads such as integrated site sponsorships and interstitials and to measure their impact on branding objectives. Advances in both direct-response measurement and brand impact measurement will help marketers determine the viability of the online medium versus other media. Such comparisons are important for a company where limits on ad budgets require that new investments in online media be offset by cuts in other media, in order to fit online marketing into the overall media mix.

Marketers to the Next Generation must include online advertising as a part of the media mix. Still, marketers of top traditional and dot-com brands mostly agree that television is the superior medium for building brand awareness. Many dot-com brands also use radio to build brand awareness. For example, Monster.com uses media such as TV and radio to create broad awareness of the brand. The company considers traditional media to propel top-down brand activity and the

Web to stimulate a bottom-up brand activity. Thus, Monster.com was one of the first dot-com brands to advertise on TV during the 1999 Super Bowl game.

Marketers generally think of the Web as a great medium for increasing brand preference and loyalty. Monster.com uses online banner advertising and e-mail marketing to generate response. Online communities also have become popular vehicles for building brand affinity. Overall, many marketers are finding that an integrated approach to selecting and using media is the most effective way to build the online brand.

Internet Advertising Growth

The Internet's role in the media mix is growing. According to the Internet Advertising Bureau and PricewaterhouseCoopers, Internet advertising in the United States grew to nearly $2 billion in 1998 from $267 million in 1996, an annual growth rate of 111.8 percent. Jupiter Communications projects that online advertising will grow to $11.5 billion in 2003, when it will exceed cable TV advertising and reach approximately 75 percent of radio advertising. Similarly, eMarketer estimates that Internet advertising will represent 3.4 percent of total U.S. advertising by 2002 and 7.6 percent by 2005 (see Exhibit 6.1).

Even with this growth, the medium is still highly concentrated among a small percentage of websites that sell advertising. About three-quarters of online advertising revenue is received by the top ten websites. As marketers expand their online ad budgets, they will begin to spread the online ad dollars over more and more sites.

Compared to other media, the Internet had a much smaller household penetration in the United States in 1999, according to eMarketer. Among U.S. households, 25 percent had Internet access, compared to 67 percent with cable service and 98 percent with television. Marketers of some brands have waited for further penetration, believing that the online audience is not big enough to warrant online advertising.

Many advertisers are also waiting for better odds that their online ad dollars will be a good investment. In the previously cited study by the Association of National Advertisers, over two-thirds of respondents said a major reason they don't spend more for online advertising is that there is no proof of return on investment. A majority of respondents named a lack of reliable and accurate measurement information as a reason for not spending more, and 48 percent said the cost per thousand of online advertising is too high. In addition, one-third of respondents to the ANA survey said they were holding back because of a lack of experience with online advertising. Such experience is especially crucial for a medium that requires convincing Web users to stop whatever they went online to do, click on an ad, and interact with the brand.

Online advertising is still an experimental medium. Although most marketers agree that the Web will become a permanent part of the media mix, it is difficult to figure out how much effort should go

EXHIBIT 6.1

Projected U.S. Advertising 1998 and 2004 (in billions)

Medium	1998	% of Total in 1998	2004	% of Total in 2005
Newspapers	$44.3	20.7%	$46.9	16.9%
Broadcast TV	$39.9	18.7%	$49.3	17.8%
Direct Mail	$39.7	18.6%	$38.0	13.7%
Cable TV	$9.1	4.2%	$27.8	10.0%
Radio	$15.0	7.0%	$20.6	7.4%
Magazines	$10.4	4.9%	$15.0	5.4%
Yellow Pages	$12.1	5.7%	$11.6	4.2%
Outdoor	$1.6	0.7%	$5.0	1.8%
Other	$40.0	18.7%	$42.2	15.2%
Media Subtotal	$212.0	99.2%	$256.3	92.4%
Internet	$1.7	0.8%	$21.0	7.6%
Total Offline and Online	$213.7	100.0%	$277.3	100.0%

>> *Myers Group, 1999, eMarketer 2000.*

to online marketing and when it should become a bigger part of the total mix. "Traditional media is so well established, but there are so many issues to resolve for Internet marketing," says Bruce MacEvoy, Ph.D., director of advertising research at Yahoo! MacEvoy adds, "We really don't quite know what the Internet can do yet. It took thirty to forty years to optimize traditional media."

As online advertising becomes more acceptable to online consumers, the results from online advertising will become similar to those for other media. In the meantime, the companies that lead in purchases of Web ads are those marketing to an Internet-savvy clientele. EMarketer's ranking of Web ad buying by category recently found that 32 percent of Web ads were for search/new media content (e.g., Yahoo!), followed by computer-related and other technology (28 percent), consumer and retail (16 percent), financial services (12 percent), telecommunications (6 percent), and other (6 percent).

>> Marketers Motivated to Advertise Online

Online advertising offers many benefits that are motivating marketers to move some of their budget to online advertising. The Web allows companies and brands to reach new markets, segments, and countries more efficiently. The lower communication costs and higher targeting capabilities of Web advertising are fueling its adoption by marketers as a viable medium. For example, a company can create hundreds of banner ads at a fraction of the production cost for creating a variety of print ads or TV commercials. Also, the cost for sending an e-mail message is significantly less than producing and mailing a print direct mailer. An e-mail message can be produced and sent to a customer for a few cents, whereas a direct-mail piece can cost a dollar or two apiece to produce and mail.

In addition to offering potential savings in marketing costs, the online medium is adaptable to a variety of objectives. In a survey by the Myers Group, marketers said they used online advertising because it could deliver targeting (81 percent), brand building (77 percent), e-commerce (60 percent), audience reach (56 percent), and click rates to corporate sites (47 percent). Online advertising has the potential to return significant results for all marketing objectives because it provides cost-effective targeting, can minimize wasted ad exposures, and can be tracked better than most traditional media.

>> Cost per Thousand (CPM)

Online advertising reach and cost still concern most advertisers. EMarketer found that on a per capita basis, Web advertising spent on the Net population of 54 million was $27.80 in 1998. If the same Web advertising expenditures had been spread over the entire U.S. population of 270 million, the cost per person would have been only $5.60. In the early days of the Web, many marketers were excited because they felt that the online medium would be more cost-efficient than other marketing media. In terms of cost per thousand (CPM), however, the Internet has been in the middle of the media cost ranking—not the highest or lowest. Exhibit 6.2 compares advertising rates of major media. These numbers provide some general guidelines, but as with traditional media, the cost of online ad creative and media varies widely. The CPM for online advertising can vary from approximately $2 to $200.

EXHIBIT 6.2

Cost per Thousand of Selected Media

Medium	Vehicle	Cost	Reach	CPM
Television	30-sec. network prime time	$120,000	10 million households	$12
Online service	Banner on CompuServe	$10,000 per month	750,000 visitors	$13
Website	Banner on Infoseek	$10,000 per month	500,000 page views	$20
Consumer magazine	Full-page color ad	$86,155	2.5 million paid circulation	$35

>> Jupiter Communications.

Although the Web isn't necessarily the least expensive medium for advertising, it can be cost-efficient. Marketers can target online advertising to smaller segments based on content, demographics, and other criteria, thereby potentially minimizing wasted ad exposures and increasing the response and conversion rates. In general, marketers are willing to pay more to reach each audience member in order to obtain those benefits. Jupiter Communications has estimated that the CPM for mass marketing generally ranges from $13 to $20 to reach an audience of 10,000 to 1 million, the CPM for targeted marketing is $25 to $50 to reach an audience of 100 to 1,000, and the CPM for one-to-one marketing is $75 to $200 to reach an audience of 1.

>> Customer Acquisition Cost

For the Internet medium to play a larger role, it must provide an attractive return on investment (ROI). That return depends on the cost of acquiring each customer and the amount each customer spends. Customer acquisition costs vary by market, by industry, and by many marketing variables such as creative and media vehicle. Therefore, it is hard to establish benchmarks for the cost of acquiring a customer. Consider, for example, the wide range of 1998 customer acquisition costs for Art.com:

Medium	*Cost per Customer Aquired*
Broadcast advertising (TV)	$100
Print advertising	$80
Search engine advertising	$60
Keyword advertising	$40
Banner advertising	$30
Direct mail	$20
Public relations	$10
Affiliate marketing (Web)	$4

The variation is not surprising, considering the many factors that influence the effectiveness of an online marketing campaign, including creative execution, messages, choice of media, call to action, and promotional offers. An advantage of online advertising in this regard is that it can be changed and optimized quickly during a campaign— in a few short weeks.

With industry averages gathered from several sources, we can estimate the cost of converting a Web surfer into a lead, then into a customer. Exhibit 6.3 details the steps involved. First, we use the ad's reach and click-through rate to find the cost to get each Web user to click on the ad. If we also take into account the average conversion rate, we can find the number of customers acquired, and from that, the

EXHIBIT 6.3

Estimating Customer Acquisition Cost

Assumptions:

Average CPM for a Web banner ad	$34.23
Reach	100,000 Web users
Media budget	$3,423
Median click-through rate	1.5%
Average conversion rate	6%

Cost per Lead:

$$\frac{\text{Media Budget}}{\text{Click-Through} \times \text{Reach}} = \frac{\$3,423}{.015 \times 100,000} = \$2.28$$

Number of Customers Acquired:

Reach × Click-Through × Conversion Rate = 100,000 × .015 × .06 = 90

Acquisition Cost (Cost per Customer):

$$\frac{\text{Media Budget}}{\text{Customers Acquired}} = \frac{\$3,423}{90} = \$38.03$$

>> AdKnowledge, Q2 1999 [average banner ad CPM]; Association of National Advertisers, 1999 [click-through rate].

customer acquisition cost. Based on average experiences for Web banner ads, the acquisition cost is $38.03 for each new customer.

For the sake of simplicity, this example considers only the media cost. The time and expense of creating the banner ads and the fees associated with buying the media are not included. The cost of Web ad creation can vary from a few hundred dollars for producing a simple banner ad to a few thousand dollars for producing a highly interactive interstitial advertisement. (See Chapter 7 for an overview of online advertising formats.)

As demonstrated by the example in Exhibit 6.2, the cost to acquire a customer with online advertising isn't necessarily lower than for other media. Many variables can affect the success of a particular online advertising campaign—media cost, effectiveness of creative, effectiveness of media outlet (the website), and others. These may affect response (click-through) and conversion (of the people who click through, the percentage that actually place an order on the site).

>> Share of Budget

During 1999, dot-com brands shifted from online to offline spending, with a larger share of marketing budgets going to offline media such as radio, television, and outdoor. Traditional brands, in contrast, increased the share of budget devoted to online advertising, although that portion remained small. Some industries—among them computers, software, technology, and financial—are dedicating larger portions of their budgets than other industries. Exhibit 6.4 shows how the share of online advertising has changed at some companies that rely heavily on this medium.

The companies in Exhibit 6.4 are unusual in their heavy reliance on the Web as an advertising medium. Although many companies use the Web, online advertising's typical share of the ad budget is much lower. According to InterMedia Advertising Solutions, Internet advertising represented 1.3 percent of overall advertising budgets at the start of 1998. A 1999 survey by the American Advertising Federation (AAF) supports this estimate. In the AAF survey of senior executives in U.S. corporations, Internet advertising topped respondents' lists

(39 percent) as the marketing activity most likely to receive a 5 percent or greater increase in its budget, followed by direct mail (36 percent), sales promotion (34 percent), magazine ads (25 percent), and newspaper ads (24 percent).

As Internet advertising grows, overall marketing budgets will change. Forrester Research, in a survey of executives from traditional and dot-com companies, found that over half expect their online advertising budgets to grow without cutting into traditional media expenditures. The remaining respondents said they will pay for online advertising by shifting expenditures from traditional media to online media. On average, they plan to cut TV ad spending the most (about 5 percent), followed by magazines (2 percent). As marketers make these changes, online advertising will end up being a respectable share of most advertisers' budgets.

EXHIBIT 6.4

Big Spenders: Share of Advertising Budget Spent Online

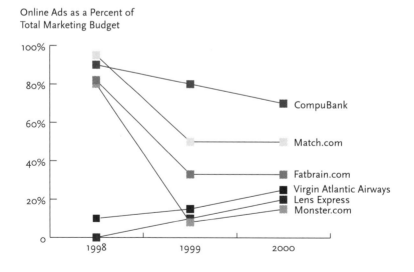

Online Ads as a Percent of
Total Marketing Budget

The online advertising budget itself must be allocated among various ad formats. The first form of online advertising, the ad banner, still has the lion's share of the online budget. Exhibit 6.5 shows trends in allocating Web advertising dollars among banners, sponsorships, interstitials, and other ad formats. Sponsorships typically include sponsorship of entire or partial website content as well as cobranding content. A relatively new ad format is e-mail. E-mail is becoming very popular as an ad medium, especially for direct-response marketers.

Besides advertising, online promotions such as contests, price promotions, and sweepstakes have become increasingly popular. In 1999 Forrester Research estimated that between 50 and 70 percent of Internet marketing budgets will be spent on promotional activities over the next five years. Marketers will offer coupons, sweepstakes, contests, price promotions, and memberships (loyalty/reward) on the Internet—the same tools they have used in traditional brand marketing but in a new electronic format. Web users have already shown

EXHIBIT 6.5

Formats Used for Internet Advertising

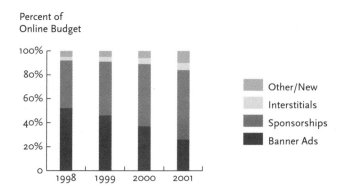

>> *eMarketer,* eAdvertising Report.

rapid acceptance of these promotional techniques in their online versions.

The New Creative Process

The Web has certainly influenced the creative process for branding. In some cases the advertising cycle has been shortened to a few days, instead of weeks and months. For example, a banner ad campaign can be created within a month's time. If one Web banner isn't performing, it can be replaced with an entirely new ad within a week.

Besides this ability to react quickly, the Web enables marketers to pinpoint their successes and failures. Companies can create hundreds of web banner ads. The Web ad server can track all of these banners appearing on each site to find out how they are performing. A marketer can identify which particular banner ad was performing well on a specific website. This ability is new. It is a powerful tool for making online marketing expenditures efficient.

Also unique to Web advertising is the ability to target audiences to an unprecedented degree. This alters the creative process. For online advertising, messages and creative elements such as text and visuals may be created to meet each market segment's characteristics. For its online ad campaign, Art.com created over 300 ad banners that were targeted by context. As detailed in the preceding chapter, if a Web user typed "van Gogh" in one of the search engines, up popped Art.com's van Gogh banner.

Internet users are information seekers, so marketers are adding more editorial options to online campaigns. For example, Procter & Gamble's Tide.com website includes many editorial features that educate the customer on Tide detergent products, as well as the chore of doing laundry. These features go beyond the benefit-focused TV commercials for Tide. Brands also have become content providers on sites that the brand sponsors or on which it advertises. For example, on iVillage.com, a leading women's content website, Charles Schwab sponsors the MoneyLife section. As part of the relationship, Schwab produces financial editorial content—articles such as "Interpreting

Stock Listings" and "Tracking Your Portfolio on the Web." According to iVillage.com, Charles Schwab has seen a significant growth in new accounts since it began doing advertising sponsorships and campaigns on iVillage.com.

In addition to its capabilities, the Web also influences the creative process because of its constraints. Currently, some marketers are waiting for improvement in such limitations as Internet access speed. One source of creative challenges is the Web banner ad format itself, which is small and very horizontal. However, advertisers can animate a banner with several frames that automatically change, so the banner can tell more of the brand story than a single static frame. Also, advertising formats now include more "real estate," with larger verticals; square, pop-up windows and browsers; and multi–Web page ads. Other formats will follow. In addition, marketers can supplement banner ads with content sponsorships and site cobranding. Even with these options, the Web is still limited in the use of sound and video—but only for the time being. Already one-inch by four-inch Web banners are incorporating animation (based on multiple banner frames), rich media, and sound. These allow brand marketers to flex their creative muscles.

Despite the limitations of Web advertising, talented advertisers can make it work. According to Maryanne Foley, senior vice president of IPSOS-ASI, about four in ten people notice Web banners—about the same rate achieved by TV ads. In addition, says Foley, consumers who see online advertising say they are more interested in purchasing the brands advertised. Foley names some features associated with successful online advertising:

- Bigger ads increase notability.
- Interactivity within a banner can greatly increase click-through rates.
- Broadband (high-speed access) appears to present significant upside potential because its higher speed allows advertisers to create more attention-getting and response-generating ads using rich-media technologies (e.g., sound, animation, interactivity).

• Increasing the file size of a banner results in increased notice-ability up to a point.

In sum, effective creative plus growing technological capabilities can add up to effective Web advertising.

At the same time, Web advertising requires not just creativity, but also diplomacy. Advertisers have to come up with innovative ad formats, but they must present them without being intrusive or interrupting to the customer. Online ad interaction is unique relative to other media. If TV viewing were like Web surfing, people would typically change channels to find a specific television show, stopping along the way to view a commercial advertisement. In reality, TV viewers are in a passive mode. On the Web, people are active. They are "on a mission" to find some information, so getting them to stop and view or click on an advertisement is a challenge.

Nevertheless, Web users are becoming more accepting of online advertising. Over time, Web users will accept online advertising as the norm and begin to think of it as an everyday occurrence.

Brand vs. Direct Response Advertising

Brand advertising makes people aware of the brand and communicates the brand's identity, image, positioning, value proposition, promotion, essence, personality, and associations. The goal of branding is to increase awareness and preference, strengthening the customer's relationship with the brand. Brand advertising educates the customer on how the brand differs from the competitive brands. It communicates the emotional and functional benefits of the brand, product, or service. Building the brand is a long-term process, and brand advertising is a long-term tool.

In contrast, direct-response advertising is usually retail focused in order to stimulate immediate action. It often involves sales or price promotions, and it is a short-term proposition that usually doesn't spend much time or space on communicating many of the brand's attributes or characteristics. Exhibit 6.6 shows an example: a special short-term promotion on Garden.com. Since the banner ad is action oriented, it focuses on specific brand attributes and a promotion or price communication to get desired action. The Garden.com banner ad doesn't convey much brand marketing other than the brand identity elements of typeface, picture, and colors associated with the Garden.com brand.

>> The Web: The Ultimate Response Vehicle

The Web is the perfect response-marketing tool. Users can click on banner ads or hyperlinks and be whisked off to a website or Web page to take action—buy, inquire, or provide data about themselves. The usual measurement of the online campaign is the click-through rate (CTR), the percentage of people who clicked on a banner ad to be taken to a website or Web page. Another key performance criterion is the rate of conversion to sale or inquiry.

If it weren't for the hyperlink and other Internet technologies such as e-mail and animation, marketers wouldn't be half as excited as they are about the Web medium. The click is music to any marketer's ears. Serve up a Web banner ad, and people can respond at that very moment. But as we have seen, today's click-through rates are not what they once were. The overall CTR has plummeted to less than 1 percent. From May 1998 to November 1998, Nielsen//NetRatings tracked CTR as it decreased from 1.4 percent to 0.5 percent.

Still, marketers are hopeful that the Web's targeting capability can increase CTR and conversion to sale. The more targeted the message,

EXHIBIT 6.6

Direct Response Advertisement for Garden.com.

>> *Courtesy of Garden.com*

the more likely the user will click, and the more likely the user will buy, participate, or inquire. Because of the increased value of a targeted online ad, advertisers pay a higher CPM. Even if your click-through on a target ad is in the 1 percent range, targeting is a way to minimize wasted impressions because the ad is only reaching the highly targeted audience.

Online ads can be targeted in a variety of ways including by content or context, keyword, key phrase, demographics, geography, and time of day or day of week. Also, a type of targeting unique to the Web is based on user profiles. User profiles typically contain data on Web usage and user-declared information. Data on users' Web behavior (also known as clickstream) includes what users clicked on and which Web pages they repeatedly visited. In addition, users may provide demographic and psychographic information to be used anonymously (meaning the advertiser doesn't know who is being served an ad). Using these two types of data, the advertiser displays the most relevant advertisement to each member of the target audience. Targeting not only helps response-ad campaigns, it allows brand marketers to find market segments for targeted messages. Marketers can identify clusters of customers based on their characteristics, find out where they hang out on the Web, and target them with razor-sharp precision.

>> The Web: A Branding Medium, Too

Since the Web's technological characteristics make it so response oriented, many marketers have rebuffed the notion that the Web can be effective at branding. However, many other advertisers and analysts have found that the Web can be an effective branding medium. It gives marketers the best of both worlds. This resembles the way in which television has become an excellent direct-response medium with the addition of toll-free telephone numbers (direct-response TV), television shopping networks, and infomercials. Likewise, business reply cards and toll-free phone numbers have made print advertising a direct-response medium. However, no other medium makes response as easy as the Web does. The Web's unmatched ability to permit fast response can improve brand response and impact. Brand campaigns can include response activities such as inquiries, samples, coupons, and sweepstakes right from the site.

The challenge is to measure online advertising's impact on branding. Since on average 99 percent of banner ads don't get clicked on, is there any evidence of brand impact? In 1997 the IAB and Millward Brown Interactive (MB Interactive) did a study to determine whether advertising and brand awareness could be achieved by ad impressions, rather than click-through. First, the study determined that acceptance of online advertising was on par with traditional media such as television and print. Second, it showed that online advertising dramatically increased advertisement awareness after a single additional exposure of a banner ad. Finally, the study found that online ads were associated with greater brand awareness and more positive brand perceptions. An IPSOS-ASI study in early 1999 showed that Web banner ad recall (at 40 percent) was similar to the recall for a thirty-second television commercial (41 percent).

Considering that the primary objective of brand advertising is to make a permanent connection that transcends short-term promotions—and not to stimulate immediate action—click-through and conversion rates are not necessarily the right performance measures for a brand-advertising campaign. To help companies with brand marketing objectives, marketing researchers have been developing more appropriate measures. For example, MB Interactive uses online surveys of Web users to gauge the performance of an online ad in terms of brand awareness, recall, and other performance criteria.

In a brand campaign, click-through rate is important only if the objective of the brand-marketing campaign is to drive trial, sampling, mail response, or short-term sales promotion. If the objective of the online campaign is brand awareness, then CTR is not the best measure. A fervent advocate of this viewpoint is advertising executive Rex Briggs, who wrote the essay on pages 163–166.

Not only measurement tools but also online creative approaches, advertising formats, and advertising technologies differ when the campaign's objective is related to branding. As online advertising opportunities have expanded beyond the 468- by 60-pixel Web banner,

>> Abolish Click-Through Now!
by Rex Briggs

Rex Briggs, executive vice president of Millward Brown Interactive (www.mbinter active.com), sits in a unique position to address the question of branding versus direct marketing. As the winner of the Atticus Award for direct marketing and the Tenagra Award for quantifying online branding, Millward Brown Interactive knows how the Web can be used for brand building and how it can be used for direct marketing. Mr. Briggs's articles and research tackle online marketing measurement and strategy.

Let me begin by clearly stating my bias. Do you know the metric we call click-through (the percentage of people who transfer from an advertisement to the advertiser's Web page)? Well, I loathe it. Not just a little bit either. As a researcher by training, I typically love data, but never have I seen a metric responsible for more confusion and poor marketing choices. Click-through is a treacherous metric that ought to be abolished.

Before I argue for the abolition of click-through, though, let me first give a brief history of why it exists, both from a direct marketer's and a brand advertiser's perspective. In the early days, the Web publishers needed a hook. They wanted the billions of dollars spent on direct marketing and advertising. To get it, they needed something to demonstrate that online banners were doing something for marketers. Focused on the needs of direct marketers, website engineers cooked up click-through (using a redirect page on the Web server to allow the Web publisher to count the people leaving the site through an ad banner). Click-through was born.

Click-through, it was thought, would be similar to measuring the number of people who open up a direct-mail envelope. Problem is that direct marketers don't really care about how many people open the "envelope." They care about how many people "buy" the offer. The same thing holds true for direct-response banners. It doesn't matter how many click. What matters is how many buy.

Direct-response marketers used click-through while they waited for their website engineers to develop systems to track sales rather than clicks. Once

(continued)

these systems were built, direct-response advertisers rejected click-through like the bad habit it is. Savvy direct marketers will tell you, "Never mistake direct response for any possible type of activity that occurs after you have laid down hard cash. Direct response is marketing communication that prompts an *immediate* and *specific* action. Anything less isn't success." Click-through, in other words, is meaningless to direct-response advertisers, and most have abandoned the metric.

But while direct marketers have ditched click-through, many brand-oriented advertisers still use it. Why? Let's first draw a distinction between brand and direct-response advertising. Emily Soell, a well-respected direct marketer put it best:

> The primary purpose of communication in direct marketing is to pro-
> voke a discrete, concrete action—to get a prospect to buy, try, join,
> donate, subscribe, request additional information—respond to the mes-
> sage (hence "direct-response"). . . . Like a retail environment, direct-
> response must elicit an instant, impulsive purchase, inquiry or
> demonstration of interest from the consumer before they leave "the
> store." . . . Direct-response creative, therefore, needs the stopping power
> of a bad accident and the magnetism of a solar eclipse. . . . Conversely,
> general advertising assumes (and in fact benefits from) the built-in time
> lapse between receipt of the message and the actual purchase. The mis-
> sion of general advertising creative is to implant and replant a reason to
> purchase that prospects carry with them—often at a subconscious level.
> Then, when a need or buying opportunity presents itself, customers will
> reach for the advertised product, for reasons they may not even be
> aware of at the time.

(Emphasis added.)

Ultimately, direct response and branding have the same goal—to sell. Simply put, direct response and branding go about achieving the same goal in a different manner. Direct response focuses on getting someone to buy the product now. Brand advertising focuses on getting consumers to buy the product the *next time* they have an opportunity to buy.

So why do brand advertisers use click-through? The use of click-through is symptomatic of brand advertisers losing sight of the nature of the product they are marketing. The art of the brand advertiser works by building and enhancing key perceptions and relationships with the consumer such that the next time the consumer reaches out to buy the product, he or she is more likely to consider the brand. The fact is that many products must focus on "branding" precisely because there is no compelling reason why a consumer must really "act now." Why anyone believed that a successful branding ad would garner clicks is beyond me. Looking for clicks on a general brand advertisement represents a fundamental misunderstanding of how brand advertising works.

This argument that click-through runs counter to successful brand advertising isn't just supposition on my part. We came to the conclusion based on empirical research. We documented the fact that clicking on the ad banner has *nothing* to do with effective online brand advertising in 1997 when Millward Brown Interactive conducted the Online Advertising Effectiveness Study. We observed nearly 17,000 Web users as they surfed twelve websites. We tracked their exposure to online ads and click-throughs, and then intercepted them online to measure their responses to the twelve advertisements running on the twelve websites. The single most important finding was that click-through is not a valid metric to measure the effectiveness of online advertising. In fact, 97 percent of the increase in sales came from exposure to the ad (not click-through).

For the online direct marketer, the measurement of an impulsive purchase is relatively straightforward, since the transaction takes place immediately upon seeing the direct-response ad online. But for the brand-oriented marketer, which is anyone selling a product or service that is not purely purchased on impulse and relies on longer-term associations to fuel sales, the means of measuring effectiveness has not always been within their grasp. Many brand-oriented advertisers aren't even aware that they can measure the effectiveness of their brand-oriented campaigns.

When I ask the brand marketers that use click-through why they use it, most say, "I can't measure branding. I can measure click-through." Never

(continued)

mistake general advertising (or "branding") for an unobservable and magic phenomenon that you must accept by faith alone. Branding can be directly observed. It is measurable and can be directly linked to sales. We have measured hundreds of online ads with our "brandimpact" measurement approach. Other research companies quantify branding for traditional media all the time. The traditional arm of Millward Brown, for example, measures the effectiveness of television advertising for over one-third of the top 100 advertisers. Like traditional media advertisers, online marketers can and should measure the effectiveness of their online campaigns.

How do you ensure you are getting a positive return on investment from branding? Talk to the consumers and measure their responses. It takes fifteen minutes to set up a "brandimpact study," involves talking to the consumer for less than ten minutes, provides quantifiable results within one day, and costs a fraction of most media buys. I can't fault advertisers for not measuring branding results earlier—it hasn't always been this easy and cost-effective to measure branding effectiveness. But now that it is easy and cost-effective, there is really no excuse for relying on click-through to measure online ad effectiveness.

So why am I so dead set against click-through? Why do I think it should be abolished? Click-through doesn't measure success. It doesn't work for direct marketers, and it certainly doesn't work for general brand advertising. In fact, it undermines the success of both! Direct marketers understand their goal is to trigger a direct and immediate response (be it a sale, a trial, a subscription, etc.), and they have quickly migrated away from click-through to the appropriate metrics of their success. Some brand-oriented advertisers seem stuck using click-through. Perhaps that is because alternatives to measuring online advertising effectiveness have not been affordable and easy to use. Research companies like Millward Brown Interactive have struggled to build systems to cut the cycle time for branding results down from weeks to hours to keep pace with the online marketers' need for instant information. And now that these solutions exist, it is time to shed the inaccurate click-through metric for true "brandimpact results." >>

marketers have more appropriate formats for conducting brand marketing on the Web. Although the banner will maintain a significant share of online ads placed, marketers will increase their use of other ad formats for brand marketing. Not only are some of the other online ad formats, such as interstitials and rich media, great for brand recall, some of them are achieving higher click-through rates as well. Some marketers believe that these newer online advertising formats are excellent awareness vehicles—on par with TV advertising.

The online medium may be best suited for parts of the branding process other than just brand awareness. Many marketers think traditional media such as broadcast media are best suited for brand awareness and the Web is best suited for other goals of brand marketing such as brand preference, which may best be accomplished via the website. (See Chapter 8 for an in-depth discussion of website brand marketing.)

Susan Bratton, vice president of development at Excite@Home, has her own term for this: "In addition to transactions, online marketing can facilitate 'brandactions' where the online audience can respond to online ads for requesting information, coupons, or samples." Bratton adds, "Television and print advertising are simple in message delivery. The Web provides a good balance of information and brand personality. The Net enables a value exchange." Some of the banner campaigns that created brandactions on the Excite@Home website have included an ad allowing users to request an Oldsmobile Bravada automobile brochure, and Cooking.com banners that allowed users to print a recipe directly from a banner, along with a coupon for free shipping. "Marketers should start thinking 'click-within' in addition to click-through for online advertising," says Bratton. Rand Ragusa, vice president at Freestyle Interactive, is another advocate of brand advertising on the Web. He says, "There really is no debate. Web banner ads can brand. For branding, banners need to be created according to brand objectives instead of pure response objectives. If Web users are participating with a banner ad that contains a game or a form, then they are interacting with the brand for a few minutes or more. You cannot get this level of brand awareness interaction in traditional media."

>> The Web: Response Versus Branding?

When it comes to response or branding, the Web isn't an either/or proposition. The online medium has methods and technologies that are suitable for both objectives. As shown in Exhibit 6.7, after an initial surge in direct marketing, companies are expected to devote an increasingly large portion of Internet advertising expenditures to brand advertising.

The shrinking ratio of direct response to branding over the next few years is greatly influenced by advances in technologies such as sound and video. These make the Web a better branding vehicle, so brand advertising is growing faster than direct response.

For brand marketing on the Internet, the best measures of brand awareness are ad recall and brand recall. Exhibit 6.8 samples average brand impact and response result of various online advertising types.

EXHIBIT 6.7

How Companies Allocate Internet Advertising Dollars

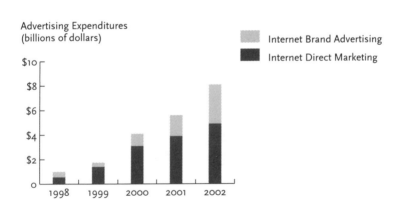

>> Forrester Research, 1998.

EXHIBIT 6.8

Branding Performance and Response Rates for Online Ad Types

Online Ad Type	Brand Impact	Average Response
Web banner (standard 468- × 60-pixel static banner)	40% brand recall (AOL; IPSOS-ASI) 9% irritation factor (Grey; ASI)	0.5% overall click-through (CTR)
Broadband (ads served on high-speed consumer Internet access connections such as cable modem)	34% greater brand recall than for narrow-band ad banners (AtHome-Intel; IPSOS-ASI)	Potential doubling of CTR (IPSOS-ASI)
Rich media (Interactive multimedia ads using advancedad technologies—sound, motion, interaction, and transaction)	61% brand-linked recall for rich media versus 30%for GIF ads (Wired Digital; MB Interactive Rich Media Study)	4%–15% CTR on rich media vs. 1.5% CTR on basic banner ads (Aberdeen Group)
Interstitial (ad launched as a pop-up browser window that uses animation, sound, video, interactivity, etc.)	64% increase in brand recall after 1 exposure (Berzerk.com) 64%–76% increase in ad recall (MarketAdvisor) 15% irritation factor (Grey; ASI)	44% higher CTR than for banners (Grey; ASI) 5% average CTR (MarketAdvisor)
Sound	24% greater brand awareness within the online context when using RealAudio streaming audio (MB Interactive; 800.com)	[N/A]

>> *AOL; IPSOS-ASI; Grey; ASI; AtHome-Intel; Wired Digital; MB Interactive Rich Media Study; Aberdeen Group;*
Berzerk.com; MarketAdvisor; 800.com.

One of the interesting phenomena with online advertising is the "three-banner rule." Many online marketers stop running a particular banner after three exposures because the CTR drops off dramatically. This is counter to the standard practice of using repetition for brand marketing, aiming for several ad exposures on television or in magazines. Experience with online ad campaigns has shown that this rule is more of a myth. The ability of online advertising to give immediate feedback on ad performance sometimes leads marketers to pull a banner that was actually effective, even though it didn't produce click-through. In fact, a Web banner might require more exposures to be noticed than other media, considering that an estimated two out of three online ads go unnoticed.

Ultimately, Web marketers are trying to figure out which online ad techniques, technologies, and formats will get the online user's attention. One who is far along that learning curve is Frank Camacho, staff vice president of marketing for Hertz Corporation. Camacho says, "Our goal with the Hertz website was to increase rental car reservation transactions, so our online advertising is focused entirely on response." Hertz's online banner ads are consistent with the company's offline retail advertising. The banners always include discounts, car upgrades, or other promotions. Camacho adds, "We continually optimize response at the 2 percent click-through rate. Above 2 percent, we are satisfied with the results. Between 1 and 2 percent, we work to optimize the banner creative and media placement. Below 1 percent, we analyze these nonperforming banners and media outlets to determine if we should stop this advertising."

TOP-OF-MIND THOUGHTS

The Web is a promising channel. It has already proved itself as a viable channel to move a small percentage of advertising budgets to online advertising. However, there is some hesitation. Any marketer conducting online advertising is experimenting. The Web channel is too young for stasis or optimization, which may be many years away. But with Internet time, online marketing cycle times are short. The promise of the Web is that marketers will learn and optimize much faster, since they have tracking technologies that give instant feedback for online campaigns. Other media don't have this benefit of timeliness.

>> Web advertising started with the simple banner ad in 1994. Now there are many different online marketing formats that fit well with brand-marketing objectives. More ad formats are to come, and marketers can now reach highly targeted segments, all the way down to an individual, with highly relevant advertisements. This was never before cost-effective with other media.

>> Click-through is a great measure for response-marketing campaigns, but not necessarily the right measure for brand-marketing campaigns. Marketers will be able to get beyond the CTR measure with the introduction of other online campaign performance measures like in-banner tracking and online intercept brand impact surveys. New performance measures allow marketers to get beyond measuring ad recall and brand recall and begin measuring brand comprehension, brand preference, and brand loyalty.

>> Experimentation is the order of the Internet, and results may vary, as results vary with other media. Performance depends on creative ideas, media outlets, media cost, offers, and other variables that must be tested and optimized. Luckily, marketers can test, track, improve, and optimize online advertising campaigns in days or weeks instead of months.

CHAPTER 7

[Online Advertising and Promotion]

>> THE MEDIUM IS THE MESSAGE.>>

-- MARSHALL MCLUHAN

In a very short period, online advertising has made its permanent place in everyday life. Although online advertising represents a small portion of marketer's budgets, it is a mainstay of those budgets.

In the few years the Web has been available for marketing and sales, online advertising has already changed considerably. It has extended beyond the small, static Web banner to totally interactive full-screen ads. Brand marketers now have more online advertising choices that help build brand awareness, comprehension, preference, and loyalty. Some traditional brand-marketing techniques, including sweepstakes and sponsorships, have made their way onto the Web. Brand marketers are beginning to take further advantage of the medium for branding as audio and video can be used to a greater degree. As we saw in the preceding chapter, the increased availability of performance tracking for brand awareness and other brand objectives is helping to increase the use of the Web for brand advertising. The increased usage, in turn, is moving Internet marketers like the *New York Times* website along the learning curve (see next page).

As new ad formats expand beyond the borders of the banner and high-speed connections become widespread, online advertising will

>> The <u>New York Times</u> on the Web Has Seen What Works

The *New York Times* on the Web has over eight million registered website users with less than 20 percent duplication of the print edition's subscribers. The *New York Times* on the Web is both a brand trying to establish itself on the Internet and a Web publisher selling online advertising. Along with its advertisers, the publisher has learned some key lessons when it comes to the success and failure of online advertising.

"One of the key issues with online advertising is that many times the creative execution is a mismatch with marketing objectives," says Christine Cook, director of sales for the *New York Times* on the Web. Cook adds,

Branding and direct response should have different creative and different media buying associated with each of these distinct objectives, respectively. Also, there is an issue with advertising networks that target ads based on demographics, because your advertisement may land on a website that meets the demographic criteria, but it may be the totally wrong content or context.

Susan Hunt Stevens, director of marketing for the *New York Times* on the Web, recommends that marketers aim for both brand marketing and direct response: "The Web is an interesting medium in that it can do both branding and response marketing. Advertisers should consider some combination of creative, ad formats, and media placements for both branding and response." To that end, Stevens and Cook advise brand marketers to consider including some call to action. Even if they do not sell online, they can use brochure request, sweepstakes, coupons, and sampling, because responses to these help marketers determine whether the audience is a qualified one. >>

begin to behave more like TV—particularly interactive TV, which is television that gives viewers the ability to respond to advertisements and offers. *Broadband advertising* is online advertising served to users on high-speed connections to the Internet, such as cable modem and

ADSL. Currently, the majority of Web advertising is *narrowband advertising*, typically understood to be ads capable of being viewed acceptably by users who connect to the Internet with dial-up analog modems. According to Forrester Research, high-speed access will be in sixteen million U.S. households in 2002. Because of broadband's promise of dynamic audio, video, and interactive capabilities, online advertising will become more interactive and behave more like TV advertising.

From Rags to Rich Media

The Web has moved from static clickable banners to interactive multimedia advertising. The impetus for this change happened when the novelty of the static banner wore off. Advertisers needed ways to capture the attention and interest of the fast-moving Web surfer. The next movement in online advertising was an animated version of the standard GIF banner, created by using several frames in succession to show a moving image to capture attention. Now higher-speed access lets advertisers create multimedia and transaction online ads that not only catch attention but move the user swiftly through the process of awareness, interest, desire, and action.

The use of the newer capabilities depends on the access speeds users have. An industry group called the Future of Advertising Stakeholders (FAST, www.fastinfo.org) has set guidelines to help advertisers increase Net users' acceptance of advertising. An Interactive Standard Advertising Unit (ISAU) should download in no more than five to six seconds. This means a 28.8 kilobytes per second connection will allow a 10- to 12-kilobyte banner, a 56 kilobytes per second connection should allow a 20- to 24 kilobyte banner, and an ADSL modem can handle up to a 288 kilobyte banner.

The "rich" in *rich media* means rich in interactivity, visuals, and bandwidth consumption. Such ads are also rich in expense relative to static or animated GIF banner ads. Rich-media ads usually involve HTML, sound, video, 3-D, animation, entry forms, games, pop-ups, and interstitials. These advertisements hold the promise of higher click-through rate (CTR), brand recall, and conversion rate. Rich-media ads are beginning to move marketers closer to the audio and video strengths of TV, but they also allow immediate interaction, action, and transaction that TV does not enable. "In contrast to traditional advertising, which is about branding, this [rich media] is really about giving the consumer an experience of the brand that's only second to using the product itself," states Jim Nail, senior analyst at Forrester Research.

Acceptance of rich media by websites that sell advertising is still small but growing. The GIF and JPEG Web ad formats are still accepted by an overwhelming majority of websites, according to AdKnowledge. The AdKnowledge report indicates that about a quarter of the websites accept rich-media ad formats. HTML, Java, Shockwave, and pop-up Javascript windows lead the list of formats used for the rich-media ads. According to Dr. Bill Pence, director of development with IBM's Internet Media group, there are hurdles to the adoption of rich media at this time:

> Currently, there are two challenges for rich media. First, rich-media ads require more bandwidth than most Web users have, so it will take some more time before rich media will become a greater part of the advertising mix. Second, Web users are skeptical of ad banners because they don't want to be taken away from the Web page they are on. The user doesn't know that with a rich-media banner, they can click on it and interact with it directly in the banner without being taken to another website. Therefore, the user may not interact with the enhanced rich-media ads.

>> Rich Media Pluses and Minuses

The major downside of rich media is greater cost. Creative production of rich media, with its many applications, simply costs more than for a static banner. According to Jupiter Communications, rich media can cost two to three times more to create than standard ad banners. Therefore, one of the biggest questions about rich media is its degree of acceptance by Web users—in particular, whether it is more effective and thus worth the incremental cost.

The evidence so far is that marketers get better results with rich media. One measure of rich media's success is greater click-through rates. IBM's Bill Pence says, "What we have seen so far is that rich-media banners get a four to five times better click-through than the regular banner ads." Almost as impressive, in a study conducted by MB Interactive for *Wired Digital*, the CTR for rich media was 1.72 percent, or 84 percent greater than the 0.93 percent for regular banner ads.

A possible reason for greater click-through is that rich-media ads are more engaging and allow the online audience to interact directly with the banner or other ad format without leaving a Web page. Instead of a user clicking on a banner ad that takes him or her to a website, the user can enter information or play a game right within the banner. Because users on a directed mission may not click on an ad banner that will take them to another site, interacting within a rich-media banner or pop-up ad, without leaving the Web page, can be more favorable. According to IBM's Pence, "Today, static banners require a binary decision from the user, which is to not click and stay, or to click and go to another site. Rich media is more interesting and packs more activity in a small amount of space."

Another advance in rich media that increases the likelihood of a response is *dynamic ad assembly*. This means the ad is built on the fly, based on criteria such as the user's Internet connection speed, demographic information, consumer interaction, etc. For example, a Web user with a dial-up connection such as 28.8 kilobytes per second is "detected" by the ad server and served an ad with animation, limited audio, interactivity, and/or low-resolution graphics, whereas a Web user with broadband access is served an ad with video, 3-D graphics, and/or high-quality audio. Also, if the user doesn't interact with the online ad, the subsequent incremental downloads are not displayed to the users. So instead of serving the entire ad, the ad server serves and assembles the appropriate individual ad components as the Web user criteria require.

With the in-banner activity of the rich-media ads, CTR becomes just one of the performance measures. Advertisers can now measure interaction rates, such as the time someone spent with the advertisement. This opens up an advertiser's ability to measure branding impact.

The branding impact of rich media also has been positive. The MB Interactive study for *Wired Digital* found that rich-media banners had a 31 percent higher brand-linked recall over regular banner ads. And in a study by Intel and Excite@Home, the brand recall for broadband ads was 38 percent, with a range of 15 to 54 percent, as compared to 36 to 38 percent for narrowband ads. The study looked at three ad models:

1. *Click-to-site ads*—typical banner ads that took users who clicked on them to a website

2. *Click-to-microsite ad*—ad that took users who clicked on the ad to a specially designed website for the product or service being advertised

3. *Click-within ad*—ad that allowed users to interact with the ad without being taken to another site, and that offered more features and functionality than the typical banner ad

Although brand recall for the three models studied was similar, the click-to-microsite and click-within models had an enhanced effect: in-depth comprehension of the brand. Brand comprehension has been a missing element in online advertising until now. The interactivity of the microsite and the click-within ad engaged users, which translated into more time spent with the ad or microsite and a more memorable brand experience.

>> Using Rich Media

A Java-based platform for developing rich-media advertising is HotMedia, a creation of the IBM Internet Media Group. HotMedia doesn't require a plug-in to be downloaded by the user. It allows advertisers to develop interactive banners that include 360-degree panoramas and panning, animated GIFs, scrolling images, audio and video clips, multitrack animation, and zoomable images. The HotMedia banner brings "infinite real estate" to the banner. For example, users can scroll through a list of products—a mini catalog where they can even place an order for a product. HotMedia ads allow secure transactions and printing right from the banner. Most importantly for advertisers, Hot-Media ads allow in-banner tracking using a tracking method that enables marketers to track different banner events such as clicking on a graphic within the banner or the amount of time the user spent with the banner—whatever interactions the Web marketer would like to measure. IBM's Pence advises that about five to seven events be the maximum number of activities tracked within a rich-media banner.

Further guidance comes from the Intel/Excite@Home study of brand recall and comprehension. The study's report advises that marketers focus on the following tactics when they are creating rich-media advertising:

- *Get "behind the click."* Greater interactivity gives users a deeper experience and, thus, better comprehension of marketing messages.

- *Give users information.* Consumers are motivated to interact with advertisements for an exchange of value, which requires useful information, not just clever and attention-getting ads.

- *Influence the take-away.* A user's experience behind the click influences what he or she takes away from the advertisement in terms of brand comprehension.

- *Find a creative balance.* Delivering on the brand value promise is just as important as the creative enticement for the users to interact with the ad. The ads (like websites) need to be intuitive, so people who interact with an ad will quickly receive the brand value exchange instead of becoming frustrated.

Besides making ads interactive and fun, marketers should take advantage of dynamic ad assembly to tailor the message to the audience. For this, the ad server needs to refer to user profiles. Typically, an ad server stores millions of anonymous user profiles (no personally identifiable data), built using cookie technology. If a user already has a profile in the system, the system will detect the user's profile and serve the appropriate ad. These user profiles are typically based on cookies that track and store the users' *clickstream*, or history of clicking on items. For example, if a user's profile shows he or she has visited several golf websites or clicked on other golf-related online ads, then the ad server would serve a golf-related ad that is associated with this profile. The system also uses demographic information, if available, that is typically captured during a website registration. Excite@Home introduced the first dynamically created online ad in 1999 using its Enliven and TrueMatch technologies. Demographics in the Excite@Home TrueMatch service can include age (for users over eighteen years old), sex, marital status, presence of children, income, education, geographic location, time of day, connection speed, and Web browser version.

Online advertising is beginning to behave much like a website in that marketers are primarily interested in the branding impact of the user's experience with the ad. Karim Sanjabi, CEO and founder of Freestyle Interactive, explains how this can work:

> The use of audio in online advertising is on a small scale today, but it
> will be a significant element to make Web advertising a serious
> branding platform. However, there are many tools for advertisers to
> create interactive experiences today that can be very effective at
> brand marketing. Emotions like humor, surprise, joy, excitement,
> and others can be effectively implemented with online advertising
> without the use of audio and video. These interactive experiences are
> unmatched in other media.

Fundamentally, success in brand advertising requires good creative placed intelligently in the most effective media. On the Web, this means that proven techniques and best practices for technologies— like fast downloading—succeed only with the magic of all the advertising elements working together. Successful e-branding is not just about using a particular ad format like rich media. It is about maximizing each format selected for the media mix. It is about creative that meets the campaign's objective. In the words of Excite@Home's

Susan Bratton, "Brand recall is the same for good creative, whether it is rich media or not."

Beyond the Banner

The Internet Advertising Bureau's "IAB Internet Advertising Revenue Report" shows that banners so far remain the predominant format of online advertising, at 58 percent of online ad revenue. However, many other advertising formats can be effective at branding (and response). And even though the online media mix is already giving marketers many options, much is still left to the imagination. As soon as marketers have figured out how to optimize a particular online ad format, more formats emerge. These range from interstitials and microsites to sponsorships and e-mail. In addition, marketers are incorporating promotional activities like games, contests, coupons, and public relations into their online advertising.

With so many options to choose from, Web marketers are becoming more creative and moving beyond the banner ad. In a recent study, Quicken.com's marketing partners reported they were considering the use of e-mail, new media technology, microsites, and real digital video.

In choosing a format, an obvious consideration is cost. The production costs of online advertising types vary considerably. In a 1999 Association of National Advertisers study, respondents paid the following average production costs:

Type of Ad Format	Average Production Costs
Animated banner/button	$7,494
Still banner/button	$4,142
Interstitial pages	$5,229
Jump pages	$4,368
Microsites	$25,000
Push ad	$9,800
Rich-media ad	$33,675
Sponsorship	$90,964

Marketers therefore need to consider whether the incremental results of using particular ad types will exceed the incremental costs.

>> *Interstitials*

An *interstitial* is a pop-up ad that incorporates such rich-media elements as audio, video, 3-D VRML (virtual reality modeling language), Java, HTML (HyperText Markup Language), and Shockwave. Interstitials can behave much like television advertising, with moving graphics and sound. According to MarketAdvisor, features that make an interstitial user-friendly are *daughter windows* (pop-up browser windows), ad size of 250 by 250 pixels, ability of users to open or close the ad, and a file size of fifteen to twenty kilobytes. As shown in Exhibit 7.1, interstitials dramatically outperform banner ads in terms of ad recall, brand awareness, ad noticeability, and click-through rate.

Interstitials created by Unicast Superstitials consist of files of up to 100 kilobytes. A file is loaded into cache memory in the background on the user's computer without disrupting the user. Once loaded, the Superstitial ad is displayed to the user. A Unicast Superstitial campaign for New Line Cinema's movie *Austin Powers: The Spy Who Shagged Me* generated an average click-through rate of over 15 percent, versus the average CTR of 0.5 percent for a banner ad. According to an MB Interactive study of Unicast Superstitials, the ad awareness was 66 percent, versus 32 percent for a banner ad.

EXHIBIT 7.1

Better Results with Interstitials

Performance Measure	Interstitials	Banner Ads
Ad recall	64%–76%	30%–51%
Increase in brand awareness	107%–200%	100%
Noticeability	36%	9%
Click-through rate	5%	1%

>> *MarketAdvisor.*

>> *Site and Content Sponsorships*

Many marketers have determined that sponsorships of websites and online content are good brand-marketing vehicles. Advertisers can create useful content or interactive applications on subjects related to the companies' products, then provide it free to willing websites. These arrangements are known as *syndicated sponsorships.*

Offline, syndicated sponsorships are not a new brand-advertising model. They go back to radio and TV soap operas that were sponsored by major brands. The first hour-long radio show was sponsored by Goodrich tires and was broadcast over a network of nine radio stations in 1924. Online, there has been a frenzy for website-wide and content sponsorships by brands.

Sponsorships and content cobranding are more of a branding activity than a direct-response activity—unless the sponsorship has a specific call to action or e-commerce component. For example, on the Preview Travel website, a section called Destination Guides features content by Fodor's, a leading publisher of travel guides. Although Fodor's has its own website with travel information and book ordering, it doesn't promote its books in the Destination Guides. In fact, there isn't even a link to the Fodor's website, so this is a branding activity for Fodor's.

The benefit to the advertisers is the credibility associated with the content, the brand name label on the content (i.e., "sponsored by"), and the ability to leverage the network and syndicate the content across hundreds or thousands of websites. For the website publisher, syndicated content is generally free, high-quality content the site can provide to its audience, thereby increasing the value of the site. For Preview Travel, the Fodor's content adds to its credibility as a travel site brand, because the Fodor's brand is well known and trusted. According to Bill Harvey, CEO of Next Century Media and a member of the Advertising Research Foundation, "Sponsorships work to create a bonding effect, an attitude shift, and a higher degree of relationship between the consumer and the brand."

Most of the marketers interviewed for this book have increased the share of budget allocated to Web sponsorships for their brands.

Christine Cook, director of sales at the *New York Times* on the Web, says the reason is that sponsorship works: "Content sponsorships and cobranded microsites have been successful for our advertisers." Cook adds, "Our advertisers have found that the credibility of our brand plus the credibility of their brand is very powerful with online sponsorships. We have also found sponsoring and supplying content such as late-breaking news to other sites has been very effective at increasing our website's brand awareness."

A company that has benefited from syndicated content sponsorship is American Honda, which created automobile-related sponsorship content in the form of a website for car enthusiasts. Titled Driving Today (www.drivingtoday.com), the site has been syndicated by other sites, including AutoGuide.net (www.autoguide.net, www.drivingtoday.com/autoguide). Studio One Networks (www.studioone.net), the company that produces the Driving Today content, determined that the sponsorship influenced 40 percent of car buyers who visited the site to buy a Honda.

With the Internet's interactive nature, brands are also creating interactive tools, including calculators, product finders, and quizzes. A low-key display of the brand name and logo on the content signals that the brand creates and sponsors the content, thus building brand awareness without putting too much emphasis on selling or direct response. iVillage.com, the number one women's website, sponsors content and interactive tools on other sites to increase brand visibility and to position iVillage.com as the expert on a variety of topics. The content distribution also drives traffic to its website. Examples of iVillage's interactive tools are the iVillage Pet Namer and the iVillage Vet Finder, which appear on the Purina website (www.purina.com).

Creating sponsorship content or interactive tools can be very cost-effective because the content is distributed through a network free to the website. Also, the advertiser typically doesn't have to pay an advertising fee to place the content on a syndicated website. Alternatively, the website publisher typically does not have to pay for the contact or tools. Since there are creative, production, and management costs, it is important for the advertiser to evaluate the potential syndicate affiliate. Studio One Networks advocates matching the content with the syndication partner in terms of quality and fit of audience at the affiliated website, as well as the amount of traffic on the website. According to Studio One Networks, success depends more on quality of audience than on size of audience. As with any type of content sponsorship, it is advantageous to be on a site that customers view as credible and useful. The resulting association with the brand can be very powerful and lasting.

>> Microsites and Jump Pages

Another approach to online advertising is to create stand-alone microsites for product lines, brands, contests, and campaigns. *Microsites* are small websites (in number of pages) focused on a particular advertising or promotional campaign. They typically serve as a way to focus the online audience's attention on the campaign, rather than sending them to a website's home page. Microsites may be permanent websites or used only for the duration of the ad campaign. Not only do microsites provide dedicated promotional messages, they can be used to track response to specific promotions, because marketers can track and analyze the traffic that is specific to the microsite. Microsites can be cobranded as well.

Sometimes advertisers use *jump pages*. These are single pages on the company's site to which the ad banner is linked. With jump pages, the user is sent to a specific page within a company's or brand's website, instead of to the home page. Jump pages usually focus on the advertising or promotional message. Once users view the jump page, they can click on hyperlinks to respond to the promotion or click on links to go to the rest of the website.

>> Online Advertorials and Ad Supplements

Advertorials—editorial advertisements—are a popular ad format for print magazines. The advertorial has also become a popular tool of online advertisers. Advertorials are somewhat similar to content sponsorships in that they are presented by an advertiser. However, advertorials usually have a more specific purpose, subject, or timing than content sponsorships. In other words, whereas content sponsorships typically are permanent sections of a website, advertorials can appear one month and not the next.

Online advertorials have caused some controversy because of their proximity to actual content online. Typically, print advertising makes a distinct separation by page. (This issue extends beyond the website to e-mail, where e-mail messages contain interlaced editorial and advertisement content.) Like magazine advertorials, online advertorials are marked with the word *advertisement* to ensure that Web users know the editorial is really an advertisement intended to influence a transaction. In contrast, content sponsorship doesn't have the direct relationship between editorial and sales. (See Chapter 4 for a brief discussion on advertising.)

>> Games, Quizzes, and Other "Intertainment"

The Internet is a great vehicle for interactive entertainment such as games and quizzes. A brand can take advantage of the experience by using single-player and multiplayer games. Again, these activities increase brand awareness through the interactive experience. The interactivity can produce several minutes of user involvement— something that most other media cannot achieve. Imagine the brand impact of a Web user spending ten minutes or more with the brand while playing a game. Games and other entertainment advertising can include games or quizzes inside banners or full-blown websites that are interactive games centering on the brand being advertised. The sole purpose of these games is to advertise the product in a fun and engaging way, and the user understands that these games are advertisements.

>> E-Mail

One of the fastest-growing areas for online advertising is e-mail. Brands can create their own e-mail newsletters or can advertise in opt-in e-mail lists or within the e-mail newsletters produced by other websites. *Opt-in e-mail* lists include only people who have signed up to receive the e-mail. Thus, opt-in differs from *spam*, or unsolicited e-mail. Opt-in e-mail lists can be quite targeted, and they produce a better-than-average click-through because the customer has elected to receive the messages. According to IMT Strategies, over 80 percent of e-mail users have granted marketers permission to send occasional e-mails, and 70 percent of customers have responded to at least one of these opt-in e-mail offers (versus 30 percent for spam). The Life-Minders.com e-mail service has achieved as much as a 45 percent response with an opt-in list that is highly customized.

In general, using e-mail that is targeted by subject or other user criteria can produce better-than-average CTR. For example, in April 1999 Charles Schwab (www.schwab.com) launched an e-mail campaign offering iVillage.com members the ability to open a tax-deferred IRA before filing their income taxes. The e-mail promotion was sent to iVillage.com members who had already indicated an interest in receiving financial information, advice, and special offers. The response was significant because the promotion was relevant and timely.

E-mail messages are typically text-based. However, the number of e-mail recipients able to accept HTML-enabled e-mail is growing. HTML e-mail can contain visual elements—just like having the Web page delivered via e-mail—so it is quite effective.

The relative simplicity of e-mail advertising plus high response rates combine to form a cost-effective medium for marketing communications. Exhibit 7.2 uses conservative assumptions about click-through and conversion rates to arrive at estimates of conversion cost per customer. According to these estimates, the conversion cost of e-mail is just $5, compared to $40 for direct mail and $100 for a Web banner ad.

Besides sending their own e-mail messages, advertisers can place brand messages in other companies' communications. Not only do e-mail newsletters within a website keep customers coming back to that website, but advertisers can promote themselves within the e-mail newsletter of another website. The iVillage.com website offers subscriptions to specialized e-newsletters on subjects such as health, beauty, and personal finance. Within each newsletter are a few opportunities for advertisers to feature their brand and special offers.

>> *Online Incentive and Loyalty Programs*

Rewards programs have been very popular among brands in traditional branding efforts, and now they are increasingly popular among Web marketers. On the Web, the user can sign up as a member who is willing to view ads, fill out surveys, buy products, or engage in other activities to earn bonus points that can be redeemed for products or discounts. Brand marketers can implement these programs on their own websites to facilitate brand loyalty. Alternatively, brands can join in other programs such as MyPoints.com, ClickRewards, CyberGold, or FreeRide. These rewards programs are managed by a third-party company and typically feature other brands as part of the total pro-

EXHIBIT 7.2

Estimated Conversion Costs of Marketing Media

Medium	Assumptions	Conversion Cost
Web banner	1% CTR	$100
	1% conversion rate	
	$10 CPM	
Direct mail (paper)	1% response	$40
	$0.40 per envelope	
Permission e-mail (opt-in)	10% CTR	$5
	10% conversion rate	$0.05 per e-mail message

>> *IMT Strategies.*

gram. In the case of MyPoints.com, which goes to members via e-mail, the response rates are as much as 50 percent.

Incentive and loyalty programs can be incredibly cost-efficient if they are conducted by e-mail. CBS Sportsline (www.sportsline.com), a leading sports website, launched the Sportsline Rewards program. Its members earn points, get discounts, enter contests, and enjoy other membership benefits. According to a study by Greenfield Online and MyPoints.com, 46 percent of MyPoints members shop online at least two to three times per month, whereas 26 percent of nonmembers participating in this study do so. Thus, reward programs give participants a significant incentive to stick with a particular brand or program.

>> Sweepstakes and Contests

Two more hugely popular offline branding activities are sweepstakes and contests. The Internet also is full of contests where brands capture names, addresses, and other demographic and psychographic information by giving users a chance to win prizes. The online sweepstakes and contests can increase awareness of and traffic to a website. Brand awareness and preference can be improved if the sweepstakes or contests are engaging, not simply an invitation to fill out an enter-and-win postcard. Another offline sweepstakes activity has gone online: RealTime Media produces electronic scratch-and-win promotions that act like the offline counterpart (without the messy shavings) to engage users in contests.

Brand marketers can create their own sweepstakes or use companies such as Webstakes and Yoyodyne (now part of Yahoo!).

>> Coupons and Samples

The Internet has taken the longtime brand promotion practice of couponing to the Interactive Age. Web users are downloading coupons from sites such as Coolsavings.com and H.O.T! Coupons, which can target coupons by geography and other demographics. Online coupons are offered for groceries, local retail stores, websites, and more. Three couponing methods involve the Web:

1. Online coupons may be printed and redeemed offline.

2. Offline coupons may be printed with unique numbers, and customers redeem them online by typing in the number on the coupon.

3. Online coupons may be redeemed online.

In an NPD Online Research study, roughly half of Internet users were aware of online coupons, and almost one-third said they obtain coupons online. The study also showed that among Internet users, the largest share (23 percent) discovered online coupons from online advertising. Another 10 percent said online coupons were recommended by friends, 7 percent were from in-store or point-of-purchase displays, and 4 percent were from newspapers.

Of all the sources of paper and electronic coupons, newspapers still lead with 48 percent of coupons; 3 percent come from the Internet. Perhaps that share will grow as Web marketers learn the value of couponing. According to Forrester Research, banner ads that offer coupons have an average CTR of 20 percent, much higher than the industry average of 0.5 percent.

In addition to couponing, the longtime brand practice of sampling can be conducted online to drive trial behavior. For example, Noxzema has created a new facial care line, Noxzema Skin Fitness, which is featured on a special website (www.fitskin.com), where visitors can request a sample of the new Noxzema products.

>> Desktop Branding

One of the newer online advertising models is desktop branding. With desktop branding, users have a branded task bar on their computer screen or receive episodic interactive e-mails. For instance, togglethis (www.togglethis.com) produces desktop-branding campaigns by creating special browsers that users will download instead of Netscape Navigator or Microsoft Internet Explorer. For the movie *Austin Powers: The Spy Who Shagged Me* togglethis created a twelve-episode promotion in which users could interact with movie characters in each episode. The campaign generated a 12 percent click-through rate. NeoPlanet created a custom desktop Web browser branded with the Austin

Powers character in which users could download the browser from the movie's website during the promotion.

The potential to create a special branded browser that can include chat, instant messaging, news, advertising, and other elements is significant. If customers download and use their favorite brand's browser every day, then brands have an opportunity to build solid relationships with their customers. But like sponsorships, e-mail, and other communications, desktop branding must be implemented in a way that is useful, entertains, or gives customers special treatment so that Web users will use the desktop-branding vehicle regularly.

>> Webmercials and Webcasts

Many brand marketers are eager to leverage the Internet much as they use television, creating webmercials and webcasts. *Webmercials* will be the next generation of interstitials with full-motion audio and video. *Webcasts* are audio and video broadcasts over the Web by companies such as Broadcast.com, InterVu, and RealNetworks. Webcasting is becoming a popular educational and entertainment tool, but it can also be a promotional tool. A well-known example was the introduction of the Victoria's Secret catalog website, which was broadcast on Broad cast.com. The obvious application of webcasts is to play TV commercials. Today, many U.S. news websites broadcast the TV news online, along with the commercials, using streaming media technology. Also, many companies sponsor events of all types as a branding activity.

Currently, online advertising that includes audio and video is less effective than television advertising. It depends on the level of Web traffic, so the broadcasts sometimes have pauses in them. These can be very distracting to users, resulting in a negative brand impression. With the growing use of high-speed Internet access from the home, webcasting will improve, giving marketers more flexibility in using audio and video in online advertising and events.

>> Branded Cursor

The Comet Cursor (www.cometcursor.com) is in its own online advertising category. It is a program that changes a user's cursor to a company logo, brand logo, graphic, or character (for example, the Energizer Bunny or the Dilbert cartoon character). Once a user down-loads the Comet Cursor, any site that he or she visits that supports the Comet Cursor will change the user's cursor to a graphic. The cursor can change in association with the website or in association with a par-ticular banner on a website. In a study by Comet Systems and MB In-teractive, the Comet Cursor–enabled banner ad increased brand recall by 39 percent on average, compared to 17 percent for the banner alone. The CTR on the Comet Cursor–enabled banner ad increased 97 per-cent over the banner alone.

>> Net Public Relations

Like other marketing activities, public relations activities are moving to the Internet. A company's website has made public relations more interactive and in-depth. A person can potentially get all of the infor-mation he or she needs about a company right from the company's site. Anyone can have a media outlet on the Internet. Specialized news and information websites are popping up everywhere. Newsgroups and online communities may act as media outlets that can reach many people quickly and inexpensively. On the Internet, brand marketers can create publicity events that reach many more constituencies than ever before. Companies can conduct online PR announcements that invite hundreds of thousands of people.

These developments put public relations departments on Internet time. The time compression of the Net has made it easier for mem-bers of the media industry to slip up on follow-through and fact check-ing. The network is a double-edged sword for PR departments, because news can spread across many media outlets instantly, but the expanded network is difficult to manage and monitor. Word-of-mouth spreads much more quickly on the Web than in the offline world, so companies have a harder time managing communications and even damage control. Also, brand marketers have to monitor and manage potentially thousands of sites, versus hundreds of key media in the offline world. E-mail, newsgroups, websites, and chat are therefore areas of both opportunity and challenge. The PR and media relations function must adjust the company's relationship with its various communities—financial and customer—to embrace communication that is more interactive and more immediate.

>> Portable Branding

Just as quickly as the Internet's appeal spread among consumers and businesses, the new wave of wireless communications is becoming another key brand communications vehicle. According to Dataquest, 3.9 million handheld computers were shipped in 1998 and 5.7 million in 1999 in the United States. Many websites are now sending content, advertising, and services to handheld devices such as the Palm VII. Just as the small 468- by 60-pixel banner ad challenged advertisers, the wireless devices will be as challenging with their small screens and, on most models black-and-white displays. (See Chapter 9 for an in-depth look at the future of branding on wireless devices.)

>> Sound Branding

Every marketer knows that sound is capable of making someone sing, cry, smile, laugh, hum, and most importantly, recognize, recall, and remember the brand. A catchy jingle is memorable and hard for people to resist. And whenever people hear the music on TV or radio, they are prompted to recall the brand. Using sound in online advertising and within websites is starting to become more popular among marketers. AudioBase, a company that provides streaming audio services for online marketers, has found that banner ad click-through increases significantly with the inclusion of audio (music and voice). In an e-mail campaign in the MyPoints.com rewards program, audio increased the CTR for online ads by 500 percent.

However, there are technological hurdles. In particular, the narrowband consumer connection can really hinder the use of sound. Currently, streaming audio (and video) from RealNetworks can optimize the delivery of sound over the dial-up Internet connection. Over the next few years, there will be increasing adoption of high-speed broadband access and online advertising served to businesses that already have high-speed access to the Internet. Then sound will be a regular occurrence in online advertising, on websites, and within e-mail.

Measuring Brand Impact Online

Advertisers who have branding objectives for their online advertising efforts need ways to track and measure brand awareness and other brand performance criteria. To overcome the limitations of click-through rate, the online ad industry has begun to create measurement models and methods to track brand awareness and the other brand dimensions that marketers expect to measure when they use off-line media. Many organizations, including Harris Interactive and IntelliQuest, are tracking overall brand awareness across the Internet audience.

Rich-media formats allow in-banner tracking to find out whether the user interacted with the ad and for how long. With interaction rate tracking, marketers can measure how online users are interacting with banner ads, regardless of click-through. MB Interactive's brandimpact service measures the impact of a particular online campaign relative to branding objectives. The brandimpact service determines whether the banner ads reached the target audience, enhanced brand perceptions, and increased the likelihood of purchase. Using brandimpact involves five steps:

1. The advertiser creates a customized online study on the brandimpact website by using a setup program, which asks for the brand, the website the ads will appear on, and the specific online ad to measure.

2. Test ads and control ads are served on the Web pages on which the study is running.

3. Website visitors are randomly intercepted and assigned to a test or control group.

4. A pop-up questionnaire asks a sample of test and control visitors about the test brand.

5. Once the questionnaire process is complete, the test and control data are analyzed.

The whole brandimpact study process can take just a few hours. It measures the advertisement's impact on brand awareness, image, customer-brand emotional relationship, and sales. This type of brand awareness study identifies the value of the ad, regardless of whether a Web user clicks on it. These studies help brand marketers understand whether the ad exposure itself had value in terms of awareness, perception, and other measures.

>> Ad Measurement

A sticking point for brand marketers is accurate ad tracking and audience measurement. According to an ANA study, the number two reason marketers aren't buying or spending more on online advertising is the "lack of reliable and accurate measurement information." Online ads have been served and counted as "impressions," but there has been no standard measurement—say, ads served, ads viewed, or ads requested. Advertising professionals addressed this problem by forming the FAST organization to find "a standard, practical methodology for counting Internet banner ad impressions and clicks."

FAST advocates tagging every ad to ensure accurate counting with less than a 5 percent variance. The base measure for online advertising campaigns has been click-throughs. With tagging, marketers also can measure conversion rate, cost per action, cost per sale, and ad interaction rates.

>> Response ROI

Although click-through rate measures a type of response, it probably isn't the best indicator of the success of an online direct-response campaign. According to AdKnowledge eAnalytics, the highest CTRs don't necessarily translate to the highest conversion rates—only 14.3 percent of high CTRs in its study were associated with high conversion rates. The AdKnowledge study also discovered that CTR optimization improved return on investment (ROI) only half of the time.

>> **Luminant Worldwide Sheds Light on Web Advertising**

Doug Rice, chief creative officer of Luminant Worldwide Corporation (formerly Interactive8), details the paradigm shift the Web has brought about for brand marketing: "The Web creates the opportunity for companies to have their finger on the pulse of the customer. Brands have traditionally spent a lot of money in expensive brand-tracking studies. With the Web, companies have real-time feedback with customers. . . . Customers desperately want to reach out to companies, and now the Web has set customers' expectation of being able to do so."

The bad news, Rice adds, is that companies must play catch-up with customers, and many of them are unprepared. He says, "Companies can't conceive how they are going to align themselves to the new model of being closer to the customer."

Fortunately, as Rice and Luminant have learned, advertisers can adapt to the online world. One way of doing this in the marketing arena is to recognize that measurement of advertising ROI requires the right tools: "Companies can use both quantitative and qualitative measures, just like traditional brand managers have done in the past. On the Web, the quantitative measures are click-through, site traffic, time spent on a website, pages viewed, etc. The qualitative measures are inbound customer e-mail analysis, opinion surveys, satisfaction surveys, and any other mechanism that opens up a dialogue between the customer and the brand/company."

One successful online advertising technique that Luminant has used for brand building is to think of the brand "within" the website, versus "on" the website. Thus, marketers don't simply dream up a banner ad or site/content sponsorship. The brand becomes an integrated part of the content, not just a label or a "brought to you by" moniker. The content can be created by the brand marketer as sponsored content, or the brand can be integrated within the content or context of the website. For example, to promote M&M's candy, Luminant featured one of the M&M's characters, Yellow, in an ad campaign on the Mr. Showbiz website (www.mrshowbiz.com). The ad campaign mimicked the biography format the site uses for entertainment celebrities it features. >>

Therefore, marketers are using newer measurement tools to track from click to sale—and beyond. Everything is trackable on the Internet. For instance, the AdKnowledge eAnalytics study found that within thirty to ninety days of an online ad campaign, 48.6 percent of the sales or leads associated with the campaign came from repeat visits. Advertisers can already track many ad types and associate ad messages with certain user characteristics. Over the next couple of years, tracking online advertising will become even more sophisticated and meaningful.

The tracking can help optimize messages and offers. For example, if an advertiser creates five ads and each has a distinct offer, the advertiser will know which combination of message and offer works best with each customer segment. This information about ad performance can also help marketers predict what type of ads will work in the future.

It is very easy to become caught up in the enormous tracking capabilities of online advertising. The key is to measure the most important performance indicators; everything else is a distraction.

>> Brand ROI

One simple measure of whether a website or online brand has top-of-mind awareness is to monitor the increase of people typing in the Web address (URL) or bookmarking the site, as well as the percentage of site visitors that went directly to the website. This is a good indicator of overall brand awareness or loyalty. On Web server logs, the top referring URL should be the website address to determine whether the brand has reached a high level of awareness and preference. For dotcom brands especially, other good measurement tools are traditional offline awareness techniques such as pre- and postcampaign surveys of prospects and customers. These surveys for tracking brand awareness and other brand dimensions may be conducted in person, on the telephone, on the Web, or via e-mail.

Other yardsticks measure brand preference and brand loyalty. Good indicators of brand preference are the number of site members or subscribers to the brand's e-mail newsletter. Changes in those numbers would signal customer growth or defection. Brand loyalty can be measured in terms of sales transactions, repurchase rates, or memberships (free or paid). Without sales data, the marketer can measure brand loyalty in terms of repeat site visits. Another brand loyalty activity is a referral program, which can be easily managed and tracked using Web technologies. Brand-loyal customers will enthusiastically refer brands to their friends, family, and colleagues.

In this time of great change, creativity in measuring advertising effectiveness is as important as creativity in producing ads. The example of Luminant Worldwide on page 196 describes a company that is leading the way.

Cross-Media Integration

The marketing potential of the Web is even more powerful when used in combination with other media. In the words of Rick Boyce, an early Web expert who joined *Wired Digital* as ad director in 1994 and is now its senior vice president of advertising sales and commerce, "All media and advertising work in a compounding fashion. It would be a mistake to evaluate the Web medium alone." Cross-media integration is not just putting a URL in a broadcast television ad.

Marketers are only scratching the surface of their ability to integrate the Web into the media mix. For the early Web years, the website was separated from the rest of the organization in many ways. Websites were created by distinct departments and were not integrated with companies' information systems. Moving into the future, the mind-set should be to put the customer at the center of the communications and find out how they want to communicate, whether it be online, by telephone, by mail, by a visit to a store, and so on. To support this customer-centric model, all marketing, communications, and databases need to be integrated. For example, direct marketing, word of mouth, and television, radio, print, and Web advertisements will drive people to websites. At a minimum, the brand messages should be communicated consistently across all media. That is easier said than done. For example, if a customer receives a direct-mail piece, its customer and promotional source codes should be supported on the website, just as they are via the telephone, store, and mail. If consumers see a discount offer on a retailer's website, they should be able to redeem this offer in the store. Cross-media integration is as simple and as complex as that. To see how this works, consider the following example.

LESSONS FROM THE WEB FRONT

>> Monster.com Takes a Giant Step with Cross-Media Campaign

Monster.com, a leading online career and job website, was formed when the Monster Board (launched in 1994) and the Online Career Center (launched in 1993) combined forces in January 1999. Monster.com is one of the Internet's leading brands. In addition to having its own airship (blimp), it has presence in all types of traditional and online media.

In July 1999, Monster.com launched a feature it called the Monster Talent Market (talentmarket.monster.com), which operates as an online auction where independent professionals—consultants, freelancers, contractors, etc.—can market their skills and services directly to employers. To promote the launch of this service, the company put together a $4.5 million marketing campaign that included television, radio, national and trade print, public relations, direct mail, online advertising, direct e-mail, and promotions. The primary objectives of the campaign were to increase website traffic, site registration, brand awareness, online offer response, and online sales. Monster.com's secondary objectives were to enhance the company's position as market leader and to maintain the brand's position as an innovator in the online career space.

The campaign for the Monster Talent Market (MTM) service ran from July 4, 1999, to December 31, 1999, with these activities:

(continued)

- Public relations activities aimed at national newspapers and national business print kicked off immediately before MTM's July 4 launch day. The public relations campaign used statistics gathered from multiple sources, as well as polling data garnered from the Monster.com site, to draw attention to the growing number of freelance professionals as a percentage of the workforce. The campaign positioned Monster.com as an industry leader that was best suited to provide a new kind of marketplace in which these types of people can connect with potential employers. As soon as MTM launched, Monster.com began offering reporters access to freelancers and employers who had successfully used Monster Talent Market to find jobs and to hire, respectively. The campaign itself received media coverage.

- A second PR outreach campaign centered around Labor Day took place in August and September. It used a satellite media tour featuring Monster.com's CEO, Jeff Taylor, and concentrated on consumer print and television outlets.

- Before the July 4 launch, an extensive direct e-mail campaign was conducted. E-mail messages went to the millions of freelance and permanent job seekers in Monster.com's database. The e-mail offered free trials to increase website membership registrations. A similar mailing went to Monster.com's existing database of employers.

- Offline, Monster.com spent $300,000 to send direct mail to its list of existing employers plus tactical list buys of employers in the four target categories. The mailing went out several weeks after launch to maintain registration momentum.

- Monster.com used a syndicated radio talk-show-related promotion in seventy-five markets nationwide for nine weeks over three months to further drive MTM awareness. The total radio budget was $2.6 million.

- Monster.com supplemented the radio promotion with three-week flights in July and October of a saturation promotion to CBS TV stations in eight key markets chosen for the number of wired citizens and number of freelance professionals resident in those markets. This was a prize-based promotion in which participants were required to register at a special CBS site online. Monster.com plans to continue offering promotion registrants e-mail updates related to MTM and other Monster.com activities.

- Monster.com combined brand-building activity in the third and fourth quarters of 1999 with a Monster Talent Market promotion on TV. It used its existing "When I Grow Up" TV spot, supplemented with a voice-over tag line referring specifically to the Monster Talent Market.

- A $400,000 online media budget targeted at online freelance professionals consisted of four Web ad banners rotated across two separate flights, first in July, then in October and November.

Monster.com rated the campaign successful. Within the first eight weeks of the campaign, more than 67,000 freelance professionals and employers registered to participate in the service.

Monster.com also learned from the experience. The company's marketing team indicated that if it could do the campaign again in the future, it would make the following changes:

- Increase the amount of spot radio, which performed better than syndicated radio on a single property (e.g., *Imus in the Morning*)

- Target the online advertising budget more specifically to opt-in e-mail and vertical business trade sites and information technology sites, relying less on business and news sites

- Concentrate print activity in vertical business trade publications, rather than general business print. In a product-specific campaign like this one, the relevance is much more direct in the trade publications.

As shown by Monster.com, online advertising—and any advertising, as a matter of fact—is a test-and-optimize process. The aim is media synchronization and message consistency across multiple media. Determining share of budget for each online or offline medium also is a test-and-optimize process.

(continued)

Marketers need to plan but also must be prepared to reallocate dollars to the medium that is working best for the objective.

As the Web matures as a medium and marketplace, more integration is beginning to occur. Amazon.com has sent out print coupons with unique user rebate IDs for $10 off an online purchase of toys. Nike has created TV commercials that begin on TV and end on its website (www.nike.com).

According to Forrester Research, the most successful optimization of media is "linking traditional advertising's branding strength with the Web's power to tailor messages based on a consumer's media consumption and purchase behavior." Forrester Research calls this practice *synchronized advertising*. It is the mixing and matching of online and offline media in order to shorten the buying cycle and to increase the connection between awareness and purchase. >>

TOP-OF-MIND THOUGHTS

Online advertising has expanded beyond the one- by four-inch horizontal banner ad that Web users were quite fond of in 1994. Now brand marketers have many more online ad formats to choose from in order to accomplish brand-marketing objectives. Interactive ads, audio, and sponsorships are becoming the most popular online branding activities. Online advertising is also expanding beyond the Web browser itself, as advertisers send messages to handheld computers and cell phones. Measuring brand impact is a new practice that is emerging for online advertising. Going beyond the CTR measure to other analysis of brand advertising will help marketers determine whether online advertising will produce the desired brand ROI. Cross-media integration is the future of online advertising. Being able to create a synchronized ad campaign that uses each offline and online medium to its strength is a potentially powerful approach for brand marketers.

>> Rich media will help the Web move from a static and silent medium to an interactive medium full of moving pictures and sound. Many brand marketers are eager for the growth in high-speed home Internet access in order to incorporate sound into online ads, since advertising with sound produces better recall and response. Until then, marketers have opportunities to use online advertising to increase brand awareness through the use of animated and rich-media banner ads, sponsorships, interstitial ads, online game ads, sweepstakes and sponsorships, and e-mail marketing. Marketers don't have to wait for Web audio and video technology enhancements when there already are online ad techniques that help brands establish a presence in the online marketplace.

>> Cross-media integration will be one of the next frontiers for online advertisers. In addition to ensuring consistency of messages in offline and online media, marketers can conduct cross-media promotion, sending users offline promotions to be redeemed online, and vice versa.

CHAPTER <8>

[The Website:
as Brand Experience]

>> THE NEW DIGITAL MEDIA FUNDAMENTALLY CHANGE THE
OLD BROADCAST MODEL FOR COMMUNICATION BETWEEN
INSTITUTIONS AND SOCIETY TO ONE OF ACCESS. IN BUSINESS,
SUCCEEDING WITH THESE MEDIA CALLS FOR BOTH IMAGINATION
AND VISION--THE FORMER TO DISCOVER AND EXPLORE UNCHARTED
SPACE, THE LATTER TO LEAD IN NEW, REAL TIME WAYS OF
ENGAGING CONSUMERS. ENGAGEMENT IS DIALOGUE: THE NEW
DIGITAL MEDIA WILL DELIVER INFORMATION WRAPPED IN FORMS
OF INTERACTIVE ENTERTAINMENT. >>

-- REGIS MCKENNA, IN REAL TIME

Every company wants new customers, and no one wants
them more than dot-com companies, which are spending millions
of dollars to acquire customers for top-line growth. And over the long
haul, profitability is as important as increasing revenue and acquiring customers. Marketers can achieve both revenue and profit by
building brand loyalty. A marketer doesn't have to spend money reac-
quiring a customer each time he or she repurchases a brand's product or places an additional order with a company. Thus, the more a
loyal customer buys from a company, the more profitable each subsequent sales transaction can be.

A website can facilitate the repeat purchase process. If it provides
a great user experience from the very first visit, the website can estab-

lish and sustain the user's brand preference. With features such as personalization, community, and e-mail, the website can pull customers back to place regular orders every time they think of the brand.

Television, Web, and other forms of advertising can drive users to websites, but the website is where window-shoppers are converted into buyers. In the words of Peter Sealey, Ph.D., adjunct professor of marketing at the University of California–Berkeley, "This [The Internet] is a powerful medium. It combines the persuasive power of TV with the shelf impact of a well-stocked Wal-Mart and the immediate gratification of a McDonald's." A website also allows marketers to get deeper into the minds of their customers. Sites can collect valuable customer information that gives marketers better insight and helps them make better marketing decisions, enabling them to serve the customer in a more personal way.

Currently, there is much controversy over building online user profiles. On a website, customers can choose how they want to interact with marketing messages. Customers also want control over marketing, especially with regard to providing personal information. If a marketer gives customers that control, they will be more willing to participate in the interaction and dialogue with the brand.

Brand Loyalty and the Web

Loyalty is the omnipotent profit builder. Companies spend a lot of time trying to identify loyal customers in order to find more customers like them. Companies also spend lots of time trying to turn customers into persistent buyers and recommenders of the brand. Marketers can apply the basic principles of brand loyalty to e-branding.

>> The Loyal Customer

The stages of branding are brand awareness, brand preference, and brand loyalty. Marketers move customers through these stages when they develop a positive brand identity, brand promise, value proposition, brand associations, brand positioning, and perceived quality. When this branding effort succeeds, marketers have loyal customers.

Their repeat purchases drive down marketing costs, increasing profit because the marketer doesn't have to reacquire the customer for every transaction or interaction.

Loyal customers also are strong advocates for a brand. This translates to the ultimate form of marketing communications: word-of-mouth advertising. Customers who are loyal will risk their personal reputation to recommend a brand to their friends, family, or colleagues. These new referral prospects tend to be better qualified (providing a higher conversion rate) and more likely to become loyal customers themselves.

Furthermore, a loyal customer base helps a brand fend off competition and protect prices. Brands with a loyal following have time to respond to competitive threats. Brand loyalty comes from the brand's value in the mind of the customer. Thus, customers who are delighted with their experience of a brand may be willing to pay more for the brand in order to obtain that experience.

In *The Loyalty Effect*, Frederick Reichheld explains how keeping customers is more profitable than simply acquiring new customers. Reichheld conducted extensive research to uncover the effect of increasing customer loyalty in various industries. One of his studies determined that a particular company that raised retention rates by 5 percent also increased the value of an average customer by 25 to 100 percent. According to Reichheld, customer loyalty has two important effects on a company:

1. *Customer volume effect*—If marketers reduce customer defection, their volume of existing customer revenue grows faster than if they tried to make up lost volume from customer attrition by acquiring new customers. These new customers cost five to six times more in marketing costs.

2. *Profit-per-customer effect*—In many industries, companies actually lose money when they acquire new customers. It takes several transactions for them to obtain a return of the investment associated with acquiring these new customers or to see a profit finally materialize from these customers. If a company loses

customers, it has actually lost the ability to recoup its investment in customer acquisition, thereby breaking even or receiving a profit from that customer. Also, a loyal customer's spending tends to accelerate over time. The more a customer orders over time, the more profit a company receives, because each interaction generally requires less investment by the company than initial transactions.

Based on these principles, the goal of brand marketing is to use loyalty-building efforts that increase repeat purchases in order to increase customer profitability. Of course, this process can be difficult. In terms of e-marketing, however, a variety of actionable Web features and functions can facilitate and enhance brand loyalty.

>> The Web Magnet

The website can be the key element that moves a customer's mind-set from brand awareness to preference, and ultimately to loyalty. The primary challenge of the Web is that a brand's site is out in cyberspace somewhere, with no constant reminder to the customer to come back. The brand marketer must figure out how to move the website from its far-flung location in cyberspace to a permanent location in the customer's mind. According to Nielsen//NetRatings, the average Internet user visited only eleven websites during September 1999. This suggests that Internet users limit their Web usage. Brands are therefore competing not only to get Web users to bookmark the brand's website, but also to achieve top-of-mind brand awareness, preference, and loyalty among users.

Web success goes beyond *stickiness*, a word used frequently to describe a site that customers visit frequently and for long periods of time. Rather, the website should be a *magnet* that continues to pull customers back at the moment a brand's category enters their minds. According to a Forrester Research poll of 8,600 online households in the United States, the key factors that drive repeat visits to websites include high-quality content, ease of use, quick downloading, and frequent updates. In addition, as detailed in the previous chapter, a website can build relationships with visitors through e-mail reminders, contests, games, personalization, membership programs, frequent-buyer programs, refer-a-friend reward programs, chat, community, and other electronic versions of traditional branding techniques.

Alone, however, these features are just that—features. They have value to customers only if the customers return to the website to take advantage of the associated benefits. For example, among online book retailers, the three top websites are Amazon.com, Barnesandnoble.com and Borders.com. As shown in Exhibit 8.1, each of these online bookstores has features and functionality that pull people back to the sites for purchase.

So what differentiates these retailers in the mind of the customer? Some of the Web features influence direct response, but brand awareness, preference, and loyalty operate at an even higher level in the customer's mind. As shown in Exhibit 8.2, unaided awareness is related to preference for online booksellers. Thus, the brand is important, and technology's role is to facilitate the movement of the customer from brand preference to loyalty on the website.

Creating a website's magnetic pull requires that the brand achieve preference in the customer's mind. This happens when the customer, responding to brand awareness techniques, comes to the website for the first time and has a good first experience. A good website experience is an event, built using technology to make using the site intu-

EXHIBIT 8.1

Website Features of Leading Online Booksellers

Amazon.com	Barnesandnoble.com	Borders.com
E-mail recommendations	E-mail announcements	E-mail newsletter
Wish lists	Author chats	NetCafe
Personal recommendations	ClickRewards	Author e-mails
Purchase circles	Membership	

itive and personal. To develop brand loyalty, the marketer then makes each return visit another positive brand experience. At each event, the marketer uses his or her knowledge of the customer—such as prior interactive or purchase history, user registration information, and user preferences—to present another satisfying experience. Also, Internet technology such as e-mail can be used to pull the customers back to the website. Technology obviously plays an important role in the experience, but it is the experience itself that makes the indelible impression in the customer's mind. In summary, the brand and the experience of the brand work in concert on a website to build lasting relationships with customers.

>> Measuring Loyalty

One of the Web's strengths is that it permits marketers to measure website behavior to determine whether customers are loyal. Measuring the differences between customers who stay with a brand and customers who leave a brand gives insights into how to close the gap. A

EXHIBIT 8.2

Unaided Awareness of and Preference for Online Book Retailers

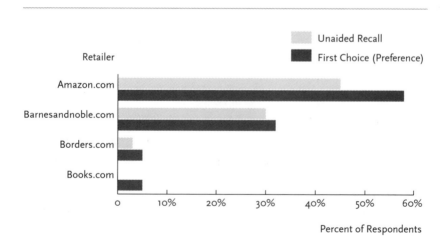

>> IntelliQuest Consumer eBranding Study, First Quarter 1999.

few key measures enable marketers to measure brand awareness, preference, and loyalty:

- *Website conversion rate*—Find the percentage of unique Web visitors who actually purchase a product or submit an inquiry on the website. Web server logs should offer this information. The conversion rate measures awareness and, potentially, preference. Similar measures are the percentage of site visitors who register personal data to subscribe to a newsletter or receive other membership benefits.

- *Buying habits*—The number of times a customer continues to buy from the site over a particular period of time can signal loyalty. Using company databases, marketers can measure customers' repurchase rates to determine whether buying the brand has become a habit with customers. In addition, they can identify whether a majority of the purchases in a particular product category are going to a specific brand. Comparing the average time spent on the website by browsers and buyers also can shed light on preference and loyalty.

- *Customer satisfaction*—Use exit surveys or e-mail to ask customers whether they are satisfied or dissatisfied with the brand and website. The satisfaction of Web visitors or Web buyers indicates preference and, possibly, loyalty.

- *Switching costs*—Measure the actual or perceived switching costs from the customer's perspective.

- *Commitment to the brand*—Ask customers if they will recommend the brand to others. Other indicators of commitment are the percentage of site users who redeem membership benefits and the percent who cancel e-mail newsletter subscriptions or other services.

By using these and similar measures, marketers can estimate the number of loyal customers that visit their website. In addition, the share of total website visitors who are loyal customers defines whether a website has a loyal customer base.

The Online Brand: Not a Thing, but an Experience

Four out of five Web users never revisit the average website, according to a study by U.K.-based Engage Technologies and NVision. A great website with a little-known or negative brand succeeds no better than a great brand with a poor website. The most successful websites exhibit great Web design and functionality coupled with great branding. Together, these create an experience, as introduced in Chapter 4 with the ideals from Joseph Pine and James Gilmore. That experience, in turn, builds relationships, as described by David Ropes, director of corporate advertising and integrated marketing at Ford Motor Company (quoted in *The Advertiser*, October/November 1999):

> *At Ford Motor Company we're more interested in the "what and why": the brand as a promise to the customer, fulfilled over time. And what the Internet is helping us do is rediscover what we've known all along. A company can't build successful brands for its customers all on its own. It has to build its brands with its customers, day after day, purchase after purchase, customer after customer. The Internet doesn't change this mission. It helps us accomplish it through a process of building interactive and highly personal relationships.*

A Web brand experience is a close proxy for the real-world buying experience. And just as customers want quality and convenience offline, they become loyal to sites that provide an online experience with those characteristics. According to a study by Cognitiative, 55 percent of Web buyers are already loyal to their favorite websites. The study identified the following factors that either unleash or destroy brand loyalty:

Keys to Web Brand Loyalty	*Killers of Web Brand Loyalty*
Ease of use and navigation	Outdated information
Fast response time	Slow response time
Familiarity	Slow download time
Relevant and accurate information	Poor customer service

A growing number of companies have succeeded in translating the real-world buying experience into a positive online experience. One such company is Avon Products.

>> Avon Gives Users a Beautiful Experience

Avon Products, the world's largest direct seller of beauty and related products, was founded in 1886. Avon products were and still are typically sold by an Avon representative, the famous Avon Lady, who visits women's living rooms in a personal interactive selling forum known as the Avon party. At an Avon party, the Avon representative demonstrates the products, and women share their experiences with the products. These shared experiences of the products solidify the women's relationship with the Avon organization and its products.

Today, however, Avon parties are rare. With more women working outside of the home in single-parent or dual-career households, people's free time is at a premium. The Avon representative still sells products, but much of the selling involves a catalog instead of an Avon party. In addition, with the growing use of the Internet, catalog sales are moving online. Avon now sells its products from its website (www.avon.com).

The challenge for the Avon website is to provide the same marketing and selling experience that made the company so successful. To do this, Avon's website includes features that give users a holistic experience rather than a standard e-commerce ordering process:

- Beauty tips
- Frequently asked questions (FAQs)
- Avon Beauty Bulletin Board, where visitors can post messages to share ideas about beauty techniques and products
- Virtual Beauty Advisor, which gives site visitors personalized recommendations
- Tip of the week, feature articles, and how-to advice

Together, these features give customers the "Avon experience." >>

With the obvious limitations of the Web, it is a challenge to re-create the real-world experience on a website. For many goods and services, physical attributes are key to the buying process. For other goods and services, people and personal selling are key to the buying process. Breaking through the customers' barriers to purchasing that have to do with product attributes is a major challenge for all marketers.

Certain Web applications, such as smart product finders and virtual retailing, can remove some of the barriers. The use of virtual applications is still in an early stage on the Web, however, because these applications typically require high-speed access to be effective.

To make the brand connection without the need for high-speed access, marketers can use databases to make the Web brand experience personal. With the personalization approach, the Web interface looks and behaves according to the preferences of each individual customer. In this way, one-to-one Web marketing builds brand relationships with each customer. Personalized Web branding presents a challenge, however. The practice of making each customer's experience unique may dilute the important brand messages that ensure that the brand "owns" a single word, phrase, or concept in the customer's mind. Owning the single brand concept has been the longtime practice for brand managers. Thus, it will be a balancing act for marketers to present concise messages about the brand yet deliver a personal experience for each customer. (Later, this chapter discusses website personalization in more depth.)

Brand Attributes in the Interactive Medium

Brand attributes are the physical or perceived features representing a brand. Some attributes are tangible, or associated with the senses—look, taste, feel, smell, and sound. Some attributes are intangible, representing an experience, a human characteristic, a benefit, or a feeling—speed, convenience, smart, leader, and so on. Brand attributes contribute to the representation of the brand's personality in the mind of the customer. Thus, to reinforce a brand attribute of speed, the obvious website feature would be fast downloading. To exhibit low-price leadership, a website could present prices on a Web page with a comparison against alternatives and competition.

Brand marketers should carefully examine brand attributes when they design or redesign their websites. The brand, not the technology, should take the lead in the Web development process. Building a brand experience based on the brand's attributes, rather than using technology for technology's sake, is the surest way for a website to accurately and interactively exhibit the essence of the brand.

>> Brand Attributes of Autobytel.com

Autobytel.com's primary brand attributes are empowerment and choice. Empowerment features on the Autobytel.com site include the site's wealth of information about automobile specifications, pricing, financing, and insurance. Autobytel.com's Your Garage feature empowers customers with a convenient service that creates an automated maintenance schedule and conveniently sends car service requests to a local car dealership. Autobytel.com acquired Chilton, a publisher of automobile repair guides, so that it could further empower customers by letting them use its labor and cost guide to find out how much a repair should cost and what parts are required. Autobytel.com's website focuses on empowering customers by giving them control over their auto purchases and repair needs.

>> Brand Attributes of Hertz Corporation

When the Hertz Corporation, the leading U.S. car rental company, redesigned its website in 1999, it went through a complex but worthwhile process of matching every key website function with the Hertz brand attributes. The primary Hertz brand attributes are quality, speed of service, and consistency. For the Hertz website, the quality brand attribute means that the website is up and running, meeting high standards for functionality and quality of Web graphics. For speed of service, the Hertz website ensures the fewest possible clicks, quick page loading, quick access to answers, and database integration that recognizes customers. Speedy service also involves quick access to help from people, because "there is no such thing as 100 percent self-service on the Web," according to Peter Budd, director of electronic distribution for Hertz. And to enable consistency, Hertz ensures that communications are consistent across all media channels.

The new Hertz home-page design is more consistent with the company's brand identity used in other media. But as with many site redesigns, much of the improvements companies focus on today are navigation and personalization. Another key attribute is represented by the Hertz marketing team's mantra, "Hertz knows and meets your needs." Hertz built its site to recognize the different needs of differ-

EXHIBIT 8.3

Hertz Corporation Home Page Before Makeover

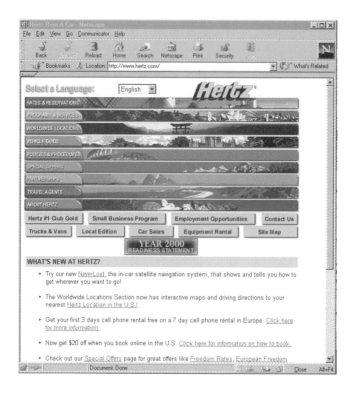

ent types of customers. For example, leisure travelers typically need local information on their destination (for instance, driving laws of a particular geographic location), and corporate travelers want quick and convenient service. The Hertz Club Gold service is a personal membership program that stores preferences and account information for each customer. It is designed to make renting a car fast and easy for Hertz Club Gold members. Against this need to save time, the website must balance the goal of providing personal service. The customer databases make this balance possible.

The result, says Peter Budd, is a website that is much easier to use:

With the previous Hertz site, leisure travel customers had to go to many different areas of the site to complete a rental transaction. With the new Hertz site, we store the customer's preferences as they browse through the site to make various selections, so when they get to the point of completing their transaction, they don't have to reenter this information. For our Hertz Club Gold members, we added sev-

EXHIBIT 8.4

Hertz Corporation Home Page After Makeover

eral features that allowed customers to store additional information
such as prior-trip booking data so they can quickly rebook the same
trip without having to reenter their information.

>> Brand Attributes of the Sharper Image

In the 1980s and 1990s, the Sharper Image was known as the store
to visit to buy something for the person who has everything. Sharper
Image stores are legendary as places for more than window-shopping
or a quick in-and-out shopping trip; rather, they are a whole shopping
experience. The stores draw people in and engage them in experiencing the unique products offered. In sum, the store experience *is* the
brand.

The Sharper Image was an early Web retailer, having launched its
online store in June 1995. "The biggest challenge for the company in
going online was to re-create the retail store experience on our website," says Meredith Medland, director of the Internet division at the
Sharper Image. She adds, "Our retail experience was entertaining,
where people would spend a lot of time touching and experiencing
the products and the atmosphere." On the website, the Sharper Image
has introduced three-dimensional product views, using Shockwave to
create a simulation of the in-store shopping experience.

With the Web as a catalyst, the Sharper Image has evolved the
company's primary brand attribute to be "The Sharper Image for
everyone." The goal is to change the market perception that Sharper
Image products are priced out of the reach of the average consumer.
According to Medland, "We added an auction site to appeal to the
e-generation and reach new users based on lifestyle, not demographics. The e-generation is totally wired, e-commerce savvy." The auction
site features Sharper Image products, and winning bids are handled
like traditional transactions between the customer and the company.

>> Brand Attributes of 1-800-Flowers.com

Jim McCann opened up his first flower shop over twenty years ago
and then purchased the faltering 1-800-Flowers. Since then, 1-800-
Flowers has been a category innovator in the floral and gift industry.

The company first went online in 1992 and introduced its own website in 1995. Four years later, when the company changed its name to 1-800-Flowers.com in order to convey its online presence in addition to its toll-free number business, it introduced the sixth version of its website.

The primary brand attributes of 1-800-Flowers.com are convenience and quality. The Web is a perfect fit for a company with a brand attribute of convenience. "Convenience on our website means that we flatten the shopping experience to make it fast and easy," states Donna Iucolano, the company's vice president of interactive services. The site's navigation is very simple, and it gives customers expert guidance in finding the best flowers and gifts for a specific occasion. Convenience also takes the form of personalization on the website, with features such as My Assistant, which allows customers to set up shopping preferences and gift reminders, perform account management, and create and maintain an address book to send gifts easily.

Historically, 1-800-Flowers.com has had a reputation for quality products and service. The website reflects the quality attribute with crisp photographs, attractive site design and graphics, and easy access to customer service representatives via the website.

The Information Connection

The primary reason people use the Internet is to gather information. This online activity is second only to e-mail, according to a study by Odyssey, L.P. The Odyssey report shows that while shopping is a reason for going online, information seeking and gathering are more important to the Web user. Also, many shoppers do their research about products on the Internet and then buy them in a store or by telephone.

The Information Age brought about a fundamental change in how people buy. Technology, especially the Internet, has increased the amount of information available to the average person. Customers have more choices and more information available to evaluate the choices. By providing that information, the Internet turns the mass-marketing buying model upside down. Traditional brands relied on advertising to push out singular messages to drive choice and decision. With the accessibility of information on the Internet, messages are pulled down by the customer. The customer is in control of the messaging.

If online research generates a set of competitive alternatives, consumers need a basis for making a choice. Is it the information, the brand, or a combination of both? On a website, the information represents the brand, and in some cases the information *is* the brand. Therefore, the availability of information doesn't necessarily decrease the need for branding. If anything, it increases the importance of branding.

The Web user's desire for information presents an opportunity and a challenge. The powerful opportunity is that the brand can provide useful and engaging information on a website to increase brand comprehension. Information seekers appreciate data from respectable sources such as a brand's own website. The challenge is that the online customer can shop around the many competitors online. The bottom line is that information should play an important role on a company or brand site because that is primarily why an online customer is going to a website. The demand for information is a demand that must be satisfied.

The problem is that customers are being overwhelmed by information and choice. In the early Web years, all of the information that was available was an exciting novelty. It still is, but Internet users now want guidance in applying the information. That requires something more helpful than search engines that present thousands of results that aren't very relevant. People want decision guides, product finders, personalized recommendations—tools that give them a selection to choose from. Choice doesn't necessarily mean more alternatives; it means that the customer wants the power of choice.

>> The Need for Content

Web users are information hunters and gatherers. They seek to find. If they don't find what they seek—and quickly—they may be onto another site that satisfies these needs. Information seekers are focused on their goal: hard data and solutions. In fact, they will spend a lot more time using the Internet to find information than in any other situation, such as in a store. The Internet has given them the power of information, making them the super-empowered customers described in Chapter 3.

Serving the super-empowered customer is a challenge and an opportunity. The challenge is that super-empowered customers will spend time evaluating alternatives. The brand must satisfy their need for information and make sure that the brand means something before the Web user exits the site to check out the nearest competitor's site a few clicks away. The opportunity is that these customers have an information-gathering mind-set, so they will take the time to research and inquire about a brand. This activity is key to creating brand preference. The information design in itself is key to forming the right impression about a brand.

A brand marketer must figure out what customers' information needs are. The role information plays in their buying process determines how to present information. Are products and applications of the products at the center of the process, or are customers at the center of the process? Many websites provide a few broad ways for people to seek information—typically product categories, applications, uses, search engines, and/or access to customer service representatives. In contrast, there is SciQuest.com, one of the dot-com intermediaries/infomediaries that have sprung up on the Net. In the marketplace for scientific and laboratory products, SciQuest.com serves as an intermediary by becoming an expert aggregator of information, products, and services. Besides smart search engines and a plethora of product information, SciQuest.com features an extensive resource center and Ask Joe, which connects users to a real person answering customer questions. In addition to the original Joe, an entire staff of scientists help customers in this form of one-to-one marketing. Thus, site visitors have many ways to find information.

The goal of content is to create the magnetic pull that draws customers regularly to the website and into the brand. As stated earlier, a Forrester Research poll indicated that high-quality content is the top factor driving repeat visits to a website. According to *Web Site Management & Internet Advertising Trends* (3rd ed.), a study by the Association of National Advertisers (ANA), respondents cited length of visit as the top measure for site performance (77 percent). Therefore, the information on a website should be valuable enough to site visitors that they spend a lot of time on the site. The content should make the site a "source" that is indispensable. This value can move people from using the site merely for practical information gathering to spending extra time learning more about the brand or company. The customer's time is limited and precious, so he or she is very discriminating when it comes to where he or she will spend time on the Net. But when customers are loyal, even if they are normally hurried in their expectations of a site, they will spend hours online with a website.

>> *Examples of Useful Content*

The best approach to becoming a useful source is to combine information and content features such as interactive tools. To determine information and content strategies, marketers should start by looking at a brand's attributes. For more ideas, consider the following websites, all of which have useful content:

- *Reynolds Wrap*—Reynolds Wrap products include aluminum foil and plastic wrap. The Reynolds Wrap website (www.reynoldswrap.com) has extensive content that helps customers optimize the use of the products and experience the brand. The site features Betty and Pat, the well-known home economists and company spokespersons, who work in the Reynolds Kitchens. The product and use information teaches customers many applications of the Reynolds Wrap products for successful cooking and food storage. This information is presented in features titled "Good Food Ideas," "Quick & Easy Packet Cooking," "Recipe Index," and "QuickTips." The value of the site's information and the interactive features engage the user in the brand experience.

- *Art.com*—Art.com, which sells fine art, photography, and frames, allows anyone to select art (including the frame and glass) online and have the finished piece shipped to home or office. In addition to a wide selection of product information, the site features advice and art education. For example, when a customer selects a mat for a picture, the customer can click on a link to a pop-up window that displays a short article written by an expert teaching about mat board and how to choose the right color. Other content on the Art.com site includes mini instructional guides to educate buyers about art, an online art dictionary, 1,000 art biographies, digital art cards that Web visitors can send via e-mail, artist signatures, and decor gallery recommendations. The online experience mimics the art gallery setting, where the buyer can learn about the artist who created the work.

- *American Express*—The American Express website (www .americanexpress.com) is divided up according to primary customer segments—personal, corporation, and small-business. Within the small-business section, American Express offers product and service information associated with credit cards, financing, and other relevant topics. In addition, there is the Small Business Exchange, which contains helpful content and resources related to small-business needs without promoting the American Express products. There are articles about marketing a business, a business book list, and a resident expert to whom customers can submit questions. Interactive business tools include help in creating a business plan and a financial fitness calculator.

- *Gloss.com*—Dot-com beauty retailer Gloss.com was created to bring trendy beauty products found in Los Angeles or New York City to anyone living anywhere. In fact, founders and beauty industry veterans Sarah Kugelman and Deanna Kangas created the concept while in Columbus, Ohio—far away from the fashion hot spots. They created a combination online store and beauty magazine to give merchandising information for product selection and provide beauty news and content that takes customers behind the scenes of the beauty industry.

- *REI*—Recreational Equipment Incorporated (REI) is a bricks-and-mortar retailer of outdoor clothes and gear that also has an e-commerce website. The REI website has an extensive content area, Learn and Share, related to outdoor activities and equipment. Learn and Share is a comprehensive and helpful online source with subtle cues for selling REI.com equipment. It offers information about camping, climbing, cycling, paddling, snow sports, and fitness. The content area even includes online clinics and community. (REI.com's community is covered later in this chapter.)

A key to success with content is to understand that content is really a service that a brand is providing to help the customer. Credible and trustworthy content enhances the brand's image and builds a customer relationship. However, if the customer senses that the content is used only to sell, he or she will lose interest in the content, and the investment in producing the content will be wasted. Content that achieves the desired results (stickiness, pull, or return on investment) is therefore based on customer's interests and needs, not on direct-selling objectives.

Fast 'n' Easy: The Intuitive Web Interface

An effective brand experience on the Web must be both engaging and satisfying. Therefore, in addition to the many factors involved with online branding, the website must deliver on two fundamentals: fast downloading and easy navigation. Web users don't get (and don't want) a user manual when they visit a website. Rather, a website has to be very intuitive, or customers will get frustrated. Some users who have a bad first experience will call the company, which defeats the purpose of the website, but most simply won't come back, and they will share their negative experience with others.

Early on the Web, many companies made the mistake of putting all the exciting bells and whistles on their websites. As a result, the pace of downloading was excruciatingly slow, and some of the features were hard to use. Poor site performance frustrated site visitors. According to a study by Georgia Institute of Technology, 50 percent of users abandon a site if it takes too long to download. Users are also frustrated by difficult navigation, information that is hard to find, and too many clicks to get to what they want. According to a recent report by Creative Good, an Internet strategy consulting firm specializing in user experience, over one-third of online shoppers in user tests did not buy because the websites were too difficult, and over half of search attempts failed in user tests. If the search attempts were successful, then half of them resulted in a purchase. Most companies have thus realized that when it comes to their websites, less is more, and simpler is better.

Of course, Web users are asking for everything—speed, personalization, attractive pictures, interactivity, information. The challenge is that some of these characteristics are antithetical. In particular, speed in navigation and downloading works against other features such as personalization and quality graphics. Pictures and database access present a big challenge to speedy downloads. However, a well-designed site architecture and flow can ensure that users don't become quickly frustrated with a website.

In the Cheskin/Sapient study cited earlier, one of the key elements for building Web user trust in the online medium and in the website is effective navigation. The study defined navigation as "the ease of finding what the visitor seeks." The study also found that a lesser-known brand must have an easy-to-navigate site in order to compete with well-known brands. The Creative Good study also found evidence that ease of use pays off. Providing a good customer experience can generate more incremental revenue than spending the money to generate website traffic. The study determined that $1 of advertising yielded less that $5 in incremental revenue, whereas $1 spent to create a good user experience yielded over $60 in incremental revenue.

As shown in these studies, website usability matters, whether or not the brand is well known. To achieve usability, there are many ways to design the site architecture and user interface. The site navigation should be designed in conjunction with an intimate knowledge of the customer, the buying process, and the brand. The design also should be based on the way people read on the Web. They don't read word by word, as they typically do with print media. People scan Web pages, so headings and subheadings must be clear and meaningful. Other useful devices are bulleted lists, short paragraphs, and an economy of words on a Web page. According to Web usability guru Jared Spool (www.uie.com), excellent examples of companies whose sites are usable include CNN (www.cnn.com), eBay (www.ebay.com), Fidelity (www.fidelity.com), and REI (www.rei.com).

Interactive Branding

We say that a website is an interactive medium because a user clicks on a hyperlink and an action results. Today website interactivity is becoming quite sophisticated, offering personalized communications, virtual-reality-type Web applications, games, tools, 3-D interactive product experiences, sound, and more. The hurdles for interactive technologies have been bandwidth limitations and the need for users to download plug-ins. The growth in high-speed access is already beginning to carry marketers over the first hurdle and toward interactive branding using more advanced Web technologies such as Java and VRML.

Interactive branding supports Volvo's slogan, "Volvo for life." Volvo's website (www.volvocars.com) emphasizes the way people can interact with its cars. The site shows the cars in a way that encourages Web users to interact with the Volvo brand and eventually leave the site with the brand's positioning well in mind. The online brand experience encompasses interactive menus, rollovers, animation, games, and 3-D virtual views of each model's exterior and interior. Visitors to Volvo's online showroom can choose a model and select colors and options (see Exhibit 8.5 for an example). Based on the model and options selected, the site displays the purchase price and offers a chance to order a brochure or make a purchase.

Although specifications and other information can help consumers select a car, building brand loyalty requires that Volvo also differentiate itself in terms of brand attributes. To that end, the Volvo website is more than a collection of models and product specifications. The site uses images as metaphors for the emotional and lifestyle benefits of driving one of the safest cars in the world. For example, in Exhibit 8.6, images and words depict the intersection of form and function: a charming pet alongside a Volvo convertible with the caption "Ahh, . . . the sun, the moon, the side impact protection." Surely, many would-be car owners long to grab the shaggy dog, hop into the gleaming convertible—and click to learn more.

EXHIBIT 8.5

Volvo's Interactive Auto Specifications

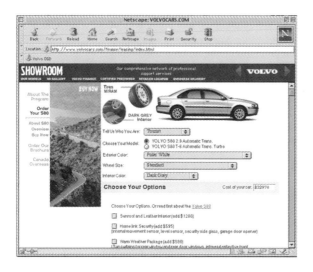

>> *Courtesy of Volvo Corporation.*

"Interactive TV is the next step for Volvo," according to Frank D'Angelo, director of interactive services at Volvo's U.S. advertising agency, MVBMS. D'Angelo adds, "Imagine a prospective customer watching TV and an advertisement for a Volvo comes on, but it gives the viewer the choice of which ad they would like to watch. Some viewers may select our all-wheel-drive vehicle, and other viewers will select our convertible."

Interactivity is a delicate dance between technology and information. Its purpose is to engage the user and to create a memorable brand experience with what the Web is capable of doing. Other companies and brands whose sites give users an interactive brand experience include America Online (www.aol.com), BMW (www.bmwusa.com), the Body Shop (www.bodyshop.com), Delias (www.delias.com), Dis-

EXHIBIT 8.6

Form and Function Intersect on Volvo's Website

>> *Courtesy of Volvo Corporation.*

ney (www.disney.com), Epicurious (www.epicurious.com), the Gap (www.gap.com), Hewlett-Packard (www.hp.com), IBM (www.ibm .com), Intel (www.intel.com), iVillage (www.ivillage.com), Lego (www .lego.com), Levi's (www.levis.com), Martha Stewart (www.martha stewart.com), Maybelline (www.maybelline.com), Nike (www.nike .com), Pillsbury (www.pillsbury.com), Swatch (www.swatch.com), and Texaco (www.texaco.com).

Virtual Retailing

Virtual retail applications are gaining popularity as the types and numbers of products available on the Internet expand. Books and music can be sold using text and sound. Clothing and accessories, cars, some electronics, furniture, and beauty and other products need more than text and sound to sell online. Interactivity and virtual reality may help marketers communicate brand messaging and positioning in order to differentiate brands from their competitors in the crowded online marketplace. Even with the obvious bandwidth limitations, some good examples of virtual retailing already exist:

- *Garden.com*—Garden.com is an extensive e-commerce, content, and community site for gardening. It is a very sticky site that has leveraged the unique characteristics of gardening aficionados, virtual retailing, personalization, content, and community, all wrapped up in one website. Garden.com provides a Garden Planner application that allows customers to design a garden online and then buy the plants in the design. For the 1999 holiday season, Garden.com allowed users to design their own wreath online. A customer could place bows and other decorations on the wreath, then buy one made to those specifications.

- *The Body Shop*—The Body Shop (www.bodyshop.com) website features a virtual makeover in which visitors can try different makeup styles on models while listening to signature music. The makeover includes lessons on makeup application.

- *Lands' End*—The website for clothing retailer Lands' End (www.landsend.com) has a feature called Your Personal Model. As the customer completes a questionnaire, this application builds a virtual model based on physical dimensions, hair color, and face shape. The system then suggests outfits, in the appropriate sizes and styles for the model, and the customer can try them on the virtual model and purchase them. Also, a style guide advises customers on the best clothing style for the physical characteristics they have provided about themselves. Two other interactive applications involve more of a human touch. One of these is Lands' End Live, a special button that shoppers click on to talk directly with a customer service representative. Clicking on Lands' End Live initiates either a call over a second phone line or a live online text chat. The second feature, called Shop with a Friend, allows two shoppers to browse the website together, at the same time, and chat online or talk by phone while looking at the same Web shopping session within the Web browser.

- *Herman Miller*—Herman Miller, a leading manufacturer of office furniture, created the Herman Miller Store on the Web (www.hmstore.com). The store features the Room Planner, an interactive design tool that allows users to plan an office that contains their own furniture along with Herman Miller furniture they might consider adding.

The inability to try before they buy makes online customers a bit hesitant to purchase anything online. But as virtual applications are made more widely available, online shopping will become part of every person's life.

Personalized Brand Experience

One-to-one marketing has been around for a few years. The concept came to the marketing community slightly before the Internet came to marketers. When the Web became commercially available, marketers immediately saw its potential for conducting one-to-one marketing. Web personalization has been a popular topic because it can maximize the monetary value of each customer to sellers while maximizing the value of the company to the customer. The basic premise of one-to-one Web marketing is that if customers invest much time personalizing their Web experience, they develop a vested interest in the site—create switching costs. Once someone has registered for a site and/or purchased from a site, the website can recognize the customer by name, preference information, and site behavior (site visits or site purchases). According to a survey by the U.K. firm Fletcher Research, 68 percent of Web users who personalized a site made a purchase online, whereas 28 percent of users who didn't personalize made a purchase online.

>> What Personalization Does

On the Web, personalization looks a lot like certain human interactions:

- Personalization is a conversation. Personalization can mimic the conversation a person has in a personal selling situation. A personalization system includes a lot of dialogue. This personalization conversation should take place over time. Each visit is an opportunity to add the next layer of depth in further understanding the customer.

- Personalization is a concierge. Anyone who has stayed in a nice hotel has had the benefit of the personal service given by the concierge. A Web personalization system should behave like a personal concierge or assistant who finds solutions that are most relevant and will satisfy the customer.

- Personalization is collaboration. Customers must collaborate with the website, and some personalization systems use collaborative filtering technology to personalize recommendations based on other customers with like interests. This technology gives personalization a feeling of serendipity.

Web personalization can facilitate customer relationships via product guides, decision guides, interactive information that can be stored by the customer for future reference, cross-selling or upselling, personalized e-mail reminders, and other technologies. With any of these, the core element for personalization is the customer profile, which is built over the duration of the customer-brand relationship. As noted earlier, personalization profiles typically contain a mix of user-declared data and behavioral information.

Web personalization opens up the door for the personalization of the actual offerings themselves. Early on the Web, online buyers could receive personal recommendations for music CDs to purchase on a site. Now customers can build their own CDs with a personalized music selection via the Net. The Web has served as a catalyst for many companies to become more one-to-one in their approach to marketing, selling, and service. The next stage for websites will be to bring personalization deeper into the organization at every point of contact with the customer.

>> Personalization Success Stories

Among the companies that have used personalization to build brand loyalty are online retailer Amazon.com, Dell Computer, toy maker Mattel (with its website for Barbie dolls), American Airlines, and Home Depot. In the first half of 1998, repeat buyers accounted for 60 percent of Amazon.com's revenue, and key factor in getting customers to return has been personalization. Since many of the products Amazon.com carries are fungible, personalization has given customers a reason to become loyal. Amazon.com has implemented personalization features in a very integrated way with personalized cross-selling based on prior customer purchases. Amazon.com was the innovator of the one-click ordering feature. The site's 1-Click and Gift-Click features conveniently store credit card and address information so customers can select an item and purchase from the product page, skipping the shopping cart process, by clicking on a single button. Amazon.com also uses collaborative filtering to make personalized recommendations based on the buying patterns of customers who have made similar purchase decisions. A newer feature, Purchase Circles, recommends products based on other customers' purchases by geography, companies, government, education, or other criteria.

Dell Computer has powerful personalized features for consumer, home office, and business customers. Customers can configure their own computer, including the personalized selection of memory amount, hard drive size, modem type, Internet service provider (if needed), software, monitor, service warranties, accessories, printer, speakers, scanner, power protection, and digital camera. Once a customer orders a product, he or she can monitor order status all the way through the process, including when the order is processed, when the computer is being assembled, and when it ships—including package status if it is in transit or delivered. Dell's Premier Pages service allows business to create a personalized Dell website, including preselected and customized product offerings and pricing according to the businesses' specifications. Business customers have secure access to preapproved product configurations, manufacturing status of systems on order, and order-history reporting to track purchases.

Mattel's website for the famous Barbie doll (www.barbie.com) allows users to personalize and purchase a Barbie doll. With a feature called My Design, the customer can personalize the Barbie doll based on skin, eye, lip, and hair color as well as hair style and fashion.

American Airlines (www.aa.com) undertook a huge effort to get its more than thirty-one million AAdvantage frequent-flier accounts online. The site stores travel profiles of AAdvantage members, including home airport, destinations, favorite destination types, hotel and car rental preferences, class of service, seating preference, payment preference, and Net SAAver fare e-mail notification. The website also allows customers to choose their seat when they book a flight online. In contrast to this situation, a traditional travel agent recently responded to an inquiry by saying the agency did not keep records on prior trips of a client. The Web can't replace human interaction, but it has already shown that traditional retailers and service providers must either improve personalized account management or lose to the Web.

A traditional retailer that has used the Internet to improve its personalization is Home Depot, the world's largest home improvement retailer. On the Home Depot website, customers can store how-to projects in their own My Projects profile. The My Projects feature also allows customers to sign up for a customized e-mail service that features information on the types of home-improvement projects they are interested in. In addition, the Home Depot website offers a store finder and home improvement calculators for estimates on carpet, paint, and other products.

These companies are succeeding not merely because of their personalization technology. By itself, the technology won't make the endeavor successful. Success will come from inside the minds of marketers and customers. Personalization for its own sake is expensive. Intimately investigating how and why customers buy is critical to the process of building personalized communications. Web personalization should be thought of as a valuable service being provided to site visitors. Also, since personalization requires customers to share personal information, protecting the user's privacy is essential to his or her trust and participation.

E-Mail and Desktop Branding

E-mail is the top activity for online users. By the end of 1999, there were at least 569 million e-mail boxes in the world, according to a study by Messaging Online. That study estimated that about two-thirds of U.S. workers and one-fourth of U.S. households use e-mail. In other countries, usage is lower but growing even faster. According to Pew Research, 85 percent of Internet users use e-mail, and 21 percent are on an e-mailing list. At the same time, people do not like getting unsolicited e-mail, or spam. According to Georgia Tech's the GVU survey of Web users, over 90 percent of respondents disagreed strongly or somewhat with the phrase "I like receiving mass electronic mailings."

To reconcile e-mail use with dislike of spam, marketers should remember that their e-mail, just like the other information they offer online, should be indispensable to the recipient. Letting customers opt in to the e-mail rather than opt out is one indication that the user is interested in receiving and, more importantly, responding to the e-mail. Used in this way, e-mail is a powerful pull mechanism for a brand to keep the dialogue going with its customers. Brand marketers should therefore entice customers to sign up to receive a periodic e-mail message.

Most websites offer an e-mail newsletter or notification service, so Web users have to choose which ones to receive and read during their precious time. To convince Web users to opt in, marketers therefore have to offer something of value. An easy way to remember the qualities of a successful e-mail campaign is to think of the letters *ROI*. As illustrated in Exhibit 8.7, these letters stand for e-mail Relevance, Opt-in, and Incentive. Thus, to get a good ROI on e-mail, marketers must make sure it is relevant to the interests of the recipient in terms of content, targeting, or personalized content. "Opt-in" means letting customers choose to add themselves to the e-mail list (versus opt-out, where the customers must take themselves off the e-mail list that the site automatically put them on). Giving customers incentive can mean that the information contained in the e-mail is motivating enough for

EXHIBIT 8.7

Building Blocks of E-Mail ROI

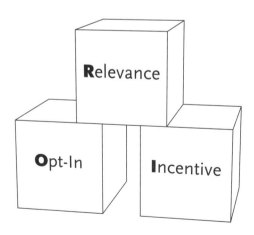

customers to receive and respond to the e-mail. Incentive can also take the form of rewards or special offers contained in the e-mail. Some incentive or reward e-mail programs achieve up to 50 percent response rates, generally because the user elected to receive the e-mail, it provides useful and relevant information, and it offers incentives. Such e-mail has been very effective at strengthening brand communications as well as realizing direct-response benefits.

E-mail is considered a "push" method, meaning the communications are pushed out to customers in order to attract them to the website or brand. Another push method is desktop branding, described in Chapter 7. Its applications include push software, special branded Web browsers and pop-up windows, desktop tickers, task bars, Post-it Software Notes plug-ins, and other push mechanisms. These can deliver results similar to those of e-mail news and notifications. The Pillsbury Company, whose many well-known food brands include Pillsbury, Häagen-Dazs, Old El Paso, Green Giant, and Progresso, uses desktop branding. Visitors of the Pillsbury website can download a Post-it Notes plug-in, which stays on the desktop screen, alerts the customer with a daily recipe sent to the desktop, and accesses the Pillsbury Recipe Search website. *USA Today* has a special deskTOPnews feature—a small pop-up browser window that features the latest news headlines. Also, many websites encourage site visitors to make the brand's website the default home page for the browser.

"Membership Has Its Privileges"

Membership and rewards programs have long been popular among traditional brand marketers. On the Web, these programs have grown very quickly. They are hugely popular among both customers and brands marketers. In a study conducted to learn user opinions of online loyalty programs, NFO Interactive found that over half of online U.S. consumers would buy more online if there were incentive or point schemes, and almost half would return to sites regularly if the site offered a loyalty program. The most popular loyalty incentives among the respondents were product or gifts, airline miles, gift certificates, and cash. The study also found that loyalty programs were most popular among users thirty-five years old or younger.

The personalization and database capabilities of the Web, along with the ability to integrate e-mail into the program, make the Web a perfect venue for managing loyalty programs. CompuBank and 1-800-Flowers.com offer airline miles for bank transactions and purchases, respectively, through the ClickRewards program. CBS Sportsline is offering its SportsLine Rewards program, which gives users one point for every page viewed, to be redeemed on merchandise and other rewards. Customers willing to pay $39.95 per year can get additional SportsLine Rewards benefits, such as double Web page points. Brands can create their own membership programs or participate in third-party loyalty programs such as MyPoints.com, NetCentives, ClickRewards, and CyberGold.

Another capability of Web technology is to provide rewards that encourage existing customers or members to recommend the company or brand to their friends, families, and colleagues. Websites and e-mail can facilitate a refer-a-friend program that rewards existing customers or members who recommend the service to others. Some companies put hyperlinks within e-mail so that it can be forwarded to another person, who simply clicks on the link and is taken to a special Web page. When that friend, family member, or colleague becomes a member, the original member gets a special discount, promotion, or merchandise credit. This model, also known as viral marketing, leverages the Internet's networked communications. This wired word-of-mouth advertising has the added benefit of low marketing costs.

Branding the Community

Traditional brands have always sought to create affinity for the brand. Word-of-mouth referrals help to build affinity, trust, and loyalty. The Internet is a community, and community participation is widespread. For instance, the IntelliQuest WWITS study found that 40 percent of online users participate in chat rooms or forums. Companies have already leveraged the Web to foster community relationships through the use of chat, bulletin board systems, and discussion lists. In keeping with the community spirit, the accepted approach has been to support and facilitate the community without overt commercialism. The resulting customer-generated content is extremely powerful, because customers consider it as coming from people like themselves, so they accept it more readily than a commercial pitch.

An example of a branded online community is the discussion forum on the History Channel's website (see Exhibit 8.8), which is an extension of its TV brand. According to Doug Rice, chief creative officer of Luminant Worldwide Corporation, which created the History Channel website, "There is a strong relationship between the History Channel TV programming and the discussion groups on the website. We would see an increase in Web traffic in the discussion area for a

EXHIBIT 8.8

History Channel Discussion Area

>> *Courtesy of A&E Television Networks, Interactive 8, now part of Luminant Worldwide Corporation.*

discussion subject that was related to what was being shown on TV at the same time."

REI's Learn and Share community at www.rei.com has features that go beyond online chat. Site visitors can share their favorite outdoor trips on a discussion list. Going a step further, the community area includes another discussion list matching up people who want to go camping or hiking, cycling, climbing, paddling, or participate in snow sports. Visitors to REI's website can also share their favorite trip photos and logs, tips, recipes, books, and websites with other online community participants.

Communities also can reside in business-to-business websites. The Hewlett-Packard website features a community within the Information Exchange portion of its Small Business Center (http://www .hp.com/sbso/exchange/index.html). Here customers can post and read questions and answers from customers in the same situation. The brand can benefit from its association with the community. Also, customers will come back repeatedly as well as stay on the website a lot longer than at sites that only sell products, and this stickiness further helps the brand exposure and preference.

Many other websites successfully relate to online communities. They include ivillage.com, aol.com, about.com, discovery.com, ances try.com, mtv.com, gorp.com, and thetrip.com.

Total Customer Experience (TCE)

The brand relationship doesn't stop at the website interface. It flows through all interactions between customer and brand. This is just like the goal of the total customer experience (TCE) in the traditional branding environment.

Some dot-com companies have struggled a bit with TCE because many lack experience with operations, fulfillment, and customer service. Fundamentally, compared to traditional channels, any website has a key disadvantage: building trust. Users are already skeptical of the security and stability of e-commerce sites. As detailed previously, websites can build trust through fulfillment features such as protection of personal information, tracking, recourse, return policy, and simplicity of process. For traditional retailers going online, the challenge is to integrate the Web with retail and other operations. Most companies that have a website and physical stores are allowing customers to return products purchased at the website to a store. In this and other ways, websites should keep the customer in the loop during the entire purchasing and service processes.

For a few years, the Web was filled with early adopters willing to put up with its hiccups. Now that the Web audience is looking more like the general population, the expectations and standards are changing. Websites need to attend to the processes that address existing customer's needs as much as acquiring new customers. As Scott Cook, founder and CEO of Intuit, told attendees at a Conference Board/Bain & Company conference about loyalty, "Really, we have hundreds of thousands of salespeople. They're our customers. And if you can't please your current customers, you don't deserve any new ones."

Basically, a website is a representative of the company—just like salespeople, customer representatives, and company spokespeople. Websites communicate with individual customers primarily through e-mail. However, many companies have been slow and clumsy in responding to customers' e-mail. Other companies are making progress at integrating e-mail and chat into the Web service process. Ideally, the standard response times on the Web should follow the standard response times practiced in traditional retail and call centers, or even stores—whichever is fastest! Since e-commerce sites operate in the same way as catalog companies, other benchmarks are useful for these websites to consider, according to Maxwell Sroge, a well-known catalog industry consultant:

- Fulfill 92 to 96 percent of orders within two or three days. Inform the customer if an item isn't available, and suggest a substitute or place a back order.
- Achieve a 2 percent return rate on average. (Some industries, including apparel, have higher return rates.)
- Among traditional catalog retailers, 20 percent of sales include additional items as a result from cross-selling by a telephone representative.

These benchmarks contribute to creating a successful TCE.

Websites are becoming more creative in enhancing customer interactions. They are adopting technologies such as real-time account tracking and management, e-mail confirmations and notifications, real-time chat (text and voice) with company representatives, and Web-to-call-center integration.

TOP-OF-MIND THOUGHTS

Many marketers interviewed for this book said the Internet is well suited for establishing brand preference and loyalty. Personalization, interactivity, communities, e-mail communications, virtual applications, and other techniques can facilitate the building of brand loyalty. No other marketing and sales medium, outside of the personal selling relationship, has these capabilities.

>> Loyal customers are committed customers. Such customers bring along other customers, who are also potentially loyal. Once begun, the loyalty effects continue to build momentum.

>> The brand *is* the experience on the website. The experience is the brand. In the Interactive Age, the brand is no longer a name, badge, or thing. It is a dialogue or interaction between the customer and the brand.

>> The future of the website is total customer experience (TCE). The company must not just own the users' experience on the site, the experience should flow across all communications, media, and channels in an integrated, holistic way.

CHAPTER 9

[Branding's Tech Future]

>> THE GREAT THING IN THIS WORLD IS NOT SO MUCH
WHERE WE ARE, BUT IN WHAT DIRECTION WE ARE MOVING.>>

-- OLIVER WENDELL HOLMES

Internet technology is shaping the future of brand marketing. While marketers are still trying to figure out the Web as a marketing vehicle, along come new opportunities like interactive TV and the proliferation of Internet devices small enough to fit into a person's pocket. On the horizon are integration of online and offline media and channels, increased use of cookies to leverage the Web's targeting power, and high-speed Internet access among households. Broadband Internet access from the home will relax the creative constraints of the current Web medium.

Brands have a bright future with access to technologies that can help meet branding objectives. Consumers and business customers can access Web content such as news and music, Web advertising, classified advertising, and information-based tools, including package delivery tracking from UPS, personalized online trading, and personal online auction tracking. However, gratuitous and premature use of Web technology for marketing has already proved unsuccessful and frustrating for both customers and marketers. The keen marketer will be the one who keeps a watchful eye on his or her marketplace to effectively time the introduction of Web technology for online brand marketing, such as interactive applications, virtual reality, video, audio, and technology not available yet.

Port-a-Brand

The Internet reached fifty million people in just five years—faster than any other medium. Already, the technology wizards have taken the Internet beyond the personal computer. According to International Data Corporation (IDC), about 94 percent of access to the Internet is from the PC today, but access by PC will drop to 64 percent by 2002. This decline represents a shift to portable Internet access devices such as Internet set-top boxes, Web phones, palm-sized computers, Net gaming devices, and more. Dataquest estimates that twenty-one million handheld computers (including brands like Palm and Windows CE) will ship in 2003. These devices may accelerate the adoption of the Internet, widening the appeal of the Web and making it commonplace for companies and consumers.

>> Appliances

Just as brand marketers are gaining more creative freedom beyond the standard Web banner with more and varied online advertising formats, new devices are coming along that whittle down the brand messaging into tidbits sent to pocket-sized devices. Snippets of brand messages can be sent to pagers, cell phones, personal digital assistants (PDAs), and other handheld devices. Here is a sample of the variety of information appliances that already can make the brand message portable:

<< Palm-Sized Computers or PDAs >> Palm Computing and Microsoft Windows CE are just a couple of the many palm-sized computers and similar devices on the market. These portable computers can be synchronized with a user's PC to download information, including Internet information and advertising. Some models, like the Palm VII, are wireless and can download a small bit of Net information from content publishers and e-commerce companies.

<< *Cell Phones, Web Phones, and Pagers* >> According to Cap Gemini America and Corechange estimates, the percentage of Internet users using cell phones to access wireless data will grow from 3 percent to 78 percent from April 2000 to April 2001. Some cellular phones, telephones, and pagers feature display screens. These phones allow for wireless Internet connections to download information and advertising. Providers of this technology include Sprint (see Exhi-

EXHIBIT 9.1

The Sprint Web Phone

>> *Courtesy of Dennis Bancroft.*

bit 9.1), Nokia, Qualcomm, AT&T PocketNet, InfoGear iPhone, and
PageNet.

<< *Content Devices* >>   Other Internet content devices can be hooked
up to a computer or the Internet so that users can download music,
books, and news. These content devices take several forms:

- *Audio and music players*—Portable music and audio players can
  be hooked up to the Internet, allowing songs and audio books to
  be downloaded to the players. Audible.com provides spoken
  audio content (e.g., audio books, news, and magazines) to
  handheld devices, including its own MobilePlayer product.
  Diamond Multimedia's Rio portable digital audio player allows
  users to download music and other audio (poetry, short stories,
  news, education) from the Internet via RioPort.com.

- *E-books*—An e-book is a book-sized computer with a display and
  software that lets users download books and other types of
  published content. Users can download the books, news, and
  magazines using a PC connection to the Internet or via a direct
  e-book connection to the Internet. For example, Nuvomedia's
  Rocket eBook downloads text from book and content publishers.
  The SoftBook Reader from Softbook Press is also an electronic
  reader that allows users to download books and content from
  publications such as *Time, Fortune, Money,* and the *New York
  Times.*

- *Tablets*—Another variation of portable Internet devices is a wireless device with which users can connect to the Internet at home
  without being wired to the PC. Qubit Technology (www.qubit.net)
  has created a "laptop" information appliance that is another
  variation of the e-book theme in that it is a magazine-sized
  tablet-like device that allows the user to surf the Web and send or
  receive e-mail. The user can use Qubit while sitting on the couch
  a few yards away from the Qubit cradle—much like using a
  cordless telephone.

<< *Set-Top Devices and Internet Devices* >> Set-top boxes are non-PC devices that let users access the Internet with an Internet connection and their television. Microsoft's WebTV is one such device. CMI Worldwide (www.cmiworldwide.com) created the iCEBOX, which is four appliances in one, including "one-touch Internet dial-up." It features a specially designed Web portal that provides news and allows users to order groceries. The iCEBOX appliance is installed in the kitchen and includes TV, CD player, VCR, e-mail, and Web access—and is also ready for home appliance networking.

<< *Internet Kiosks* >> Now seen in airports, malls, doctor's offices, cyber cafés, and other public places, Internet kiosks give marketers a way to reach their market in a targeted way. For example, an Internet kiosk placed in a doctor's office can contain pharmaceutical advertising targeted to time, place, and context. A kiosk located in a sports bar might carry advertising related to sports news, apparel, or other topics of interest to the bar's patrons.

>> *Applications*

Users of these portable and distributed Internet devices will be able to access weather reports, maps, news, stock quotes, personal calendars, games, and online shopping. For instance, Amazon.com's feature called Amazon.com Anywhere (www.amazon.com/anywhere) offers product and auction searching (with the top three results displayed) and secure 1-Click ordering.

If the Web is at a nascent stage, then marketing via Web-enabled portable wireless appliances is at an even earlier stage. Brands are just starting to enable their content and marketing for Internet devices. AvantGo (http://avantgo.com/channels/), a software application for Microsoft Windows CE and Palm Computing platforms, allows users of handheld devices to download favorite content featuring major dot-com and traditional content providers such as Bloomberg, Frommers, Hollywood.com, MySimon Pocket Shopper, Weather Channel, and Stock Smart. Exhibit 9.2 shows how Web content is displayed on a handheld device.

The Promise of Broadband

In spite of the hype surrounding the growth in the use of high-speed broadband Internet access, the current state of Internet access for home users is narrowband. The adoption of high-speed access by U.S. households will take a few more years. According to Forrester Research, sixteen million U.S. households will have broadband access to the Internet by 2002. The Gartner Group estimates that of the forty-six million Internet access lines in use by 2003, 63 percent will still have analog modems.

Higher-speed access gives brand marketers more creative options to include ever richer ads that behave more like television advertisements—full of dynamic sound and visuals—but also employ interactivity. In the meantime, advertisers are already using rich media such as streaming audio and video to present sound and images in banner advertising. IBM's HotMedia allows advertisers to create rich-media banners where the first frame of the ad banner (at five to eight kilobytes) is downloaded quickly, and the rest of the advertising elements are downloaded while the customer is viewing or interacting with the banner ad. Unicast uses a special nonintrusive technique of down-

EXHIBIT 9.2

AvantGo Software Showing Web Content on Microsoft Windows CE Screen

>> Courtesy of AvantGo Inc., the Authority in Managing Mobile Information.

loading Superstitial ads in the background and then presenting the ads after downloading is complete. Some ad technology and service providers detect the user's connection speed in order to send the advertisement that is most efficient and effective for the download speed. For example, a user with a 28.8 Kbps modem would receive a more streamlined advertisement than someone with broadband Internet access, who might receive full audio, animation, interactive, and transaction elements within the advertisement.

Broadband delivers on the promise that online advertising will be more effective for advertisers and more accepted by Web users. Studies by Excite@Home found that recall and click-through rates for broadband rich-media ads were significantly higher than for standard banner advertising. In general, rich-media ads in either environment—broadband or narrowband—provide a higher average click-through rate than the generic static Web banner or animated GIF banner. However, rich-media ads cost more to produce, so further research is needed to find whether the incremental cost is outweighed by the incremental return on investment. Fortunately, the tracking capability of the Web allows marketers to determine this.

A Smarter Idiot Box

Television has been a passive medium ever since its creation. People watch TV shows and commercials while sitting quietly on the couch, or they half-listen while cleaning the kitchen, working on the computer, or performing other home activities. The interactivity of traditional TV has been limited to a viewer using the remote control to change channels when commercials come on, or ordering pay-per-view movies.

This style of use is changing as interactive TV allows the TV audience to participate in some of the activities that can be performed on a computer, such as surfing, shopping, and even selecting an advertisement to watch. Interactive TV had a false start in the early 1990s, but with improvements in Internet connectivity, the dream is becoming a reality. In 1999 there were already more than a million Microsoft

WebTV users. Significant penetration of interactive TV will be in a few more years—sixty-seven million users by 2003, according to Data-monitor. Interactive TV provides many online activities, including shopping, chat, and instant messages. Brand marketers will be able to create advertisements targeted to different TV audience segments using viewer demographics as simple as gender and geographic location. A leading pizza delivery brand might broadcast a commercial that lets the viewer place an order with the local store while watching the advertisement.

Integration of Online and Offline Media

Until recently, the Web and websites have been digital islands apart from other media or channels. In fact, to shorten cycle times, many companies created separate operating units to develop websites. According to a mid-1999 Jupiter Communications report, 75 percent of advertisers always or often integrated campaigns across media, but 70 percent were *not* using cross-media audience reporting or measurements, and 57 percent never or rarely compared online and offline media performance. However, marketers have quickly appreciated that integration is essential to the growth and adoption of the online channel. In the Jupiter Communications study, 89 percent of advertisers said they planned to increase integration efforts in the next year.

One example of integrating online and offline marketing efforts is the use of couponing—either direct-mail promotion and coupons that can be redeemed online or online coupons that can be redeemed offline at the bricks-and-mortar retail locations. To increase toy purchases during the 1999 holiday season, Amazon.com mailed $10-off coupons for toy purchases. On each coupon was printed a unique redemption code. The coupon holder could go to the Amazon.com website to redeem the discount coupon with his or her online toy purchase. The Charleston, South Carolina, *Post and Courier* daily newspaper allows readers to scan articles with special barcodes that contain website addresses. They can then visit the sites referred to in the articles by connecting a hand-held scanner to their computers. Imagine the advertising opportunities!

Other efforts integrate online and offline shopping. Many traditional retailers have created online store locators that use maps to help online shoppers find the store nearest them. Traditional retailers like REI allow customers who make purchases on their website to return most items to local stores. Clixnmortar.com has created FastFrog.com, which allows teen shoppers to buy online and offline in a synchronized manner. Teens can check out a ZapStick (high-tech scanner) at the mall and go to participating retailers and "zap" (scan bar code on item) items they want at the mall. The resulting purchase data are automatically synchronized with the teens' Shopper Hopper lists on the website.

Of course, integration of offline and online media is currently a complex task. For online advertising, the challenge comes from bandwidth constraints and, thus, creative constraints. Integrating the Web into an ad campaign can call for some complex coordination of media and timing. Online advertising has made enough progress to allow offline messages to be presented consistently online, not only with static visuals, but with sound and music used in the offline TV and radio commercials. Nike recently created a media campaign where the TV commercial begins on TV and ends on the website.

Another challenge is database integration. The Web is great at building deep customer profiles for one-to-one marketing and service. But if a customer who has ordered and built a personal profile on the Web walks into the retail store, store personnel or kiosks probably will not recognize the customer. Even if the in-store retail systems can identify the person, the retail representative may not be able to look up the in-depth profile. However, the future of Web-to-retail database integration is not that far off. Databases have become very cost-effective in terms of storage and analysis. Internet connectivity also is becoming cheaper. It won't be too long before the website, call center, and retail outlet work in concert.

Don't Get a Hand Caught in the Cookie Jar

Cookies are both beauty and beast. Marketers love cookies. Web users have yet to truly realize the benefits of cookies. They mistrust the use of cookies by marketers. Users believe that marketers obtain too much personal information using cookies. To protect the privacy of Web users, ad-serving companies have embraced anonymous profiling. For the masses to adopt the Internet into their daily lives, website owners will have to be more up-front about privacy and the use of cookies.

To review, a cookie is a message sent to a Web browser by the Web server and stored in a text file. Each time the browser requests a Web page from the server, the cookie is sent back to the Web server that gave the browser a cookie. Cookies identify the computer and/or the unique user of the computer. Cookies thus allow for personalization, targeting, and tracking. For example, Amazon.com will recognize a returning customer and will make recommendations based on the customer's prior purchases. The personalization is based on a unique user profile built from data like prior website usage (clickstream tracking of website visits and page clicks), as well as the data a user enters when he or she registers on the website as a member or establishes a customer account.

Marketers like to use cookies because they provide a way to track the user's activity on a site or target an online advertisement for better results. For users, cookies can be a huge benefit if marketers are good at communicating the benefits of the cookies and do not abuse the privilege. Cookies remember the user so he or she can receive information and product recommendations that are personalized to his or her preferences. With cookies, a registered user of a website doesn't necessarily have to log on during every visit to the site, because the user is automatically recognized via the cookie file. Cookies can thus make online surfing and buying very convenient and personal.

Cookies are making online advertising a better targeting vehicle. The cookies help to build a user profile based on behavioral data (Web usage and interaction tracking), demographic data, and interest data inferred from the types of sites visited by the user. Some of the online ad solution providers that offer profile-based targeting include Engage Technologies, DoubleClick, and Excite@Home with MatchLogic.

Cookies are also useful as measurement tools. Advertisers can track the person who clicked on an ad all the way through the sale on the website. This enables advertisers to calculate ROI—cost per lead, cost per sale, customer acquisition costs, and more. Cookies also allow advertisers to know whether a user was served the online ad (and viewed it) and even whether a user viewed the ad, didn't immediately click through, but came to the website at a later date to browse or buy. In other words, advertisers can track a delayed response to advertising. Cookies certainly are very powerful—if they are not abused by marketers, and if privacy protection is in the front of the marketer's mind, just as privacy is on the top of the online consumer's mind.

Following a debate about Internet profiling in the November 1999 hearings of the Federal Trade Commission, the FTC issued a warning to the online advertising industry: Websites that claim they do not collect information from customers yet allow advertisers to obtain profile information from the customers while they are on that site are violating consumer protection laws by collecting information from customers without their knowledge or permission. In other words, the problem occurs when a Web user is on a website that promises not to collect personal information but does collect profiling information about someone who is on the site and/or interacts with an online ad. The question that will be answered in the future is, At what point does data about a user's website activity become personally identifiable? Most third-party ad servers and networks that use profile-based targeting state that they are building anonymous profiles. The FTC's position is that over time the profile will contain so much data that it becomes too personal. Until this difference is settled, marketing and industry associations are working with the FTC to formulate self-regulatory standards regarding notification of Web surfers of the profiling activity of third-party ad servers.

TOP-OF-MIND THOUGHTS

On the Internet, no one can guess what is coming, because no one has ever been there before. The best any marketer can do is look ahead a few short months and try to keep up with the fast-moving technology. Over the next few years, brand marketers must be willing to experiment with the technology and expect that the outcome may be different than anticipated.

>> Portable Net devices bring the brand close to the customer. Cell phones, wireless handheld computers, pagers, and laptop Net tablets bring the Internet to the customer, no matter where the customer is. Because users are no longer tethered to a computer, they can receive marketing and selling messages anywhere. Users can even place orders on these mini Web devices.

>> Interactive TV is going to be huge.

>> Cookies can work if marketers go about using them right. Microtargeting advertisements and serving up personalized Web services, information, and advertising can really produce tangible ROIs for brand efforts beyond what marketers could achieve with traditional methods.

[**Case Studies**]

United Parcel Service: Delivering the Twenty-First-Century Brand

www.ups.com

United Parcel Service (UPS) is just about as old as the practice of branding itself. UPS made it through the twentieth century with its name and its brown corporate identity intact. However, the company has reinvented itself along the way—from bicycle messenger to digital-information deliverer. UPS is continuing to stretch its brand to succeed on the Internet and to survive in this millennium. As UPS moves from delivering packages by human power to delivering information by digital power, it hasn't sacrificed the brand's essence over more than nine decades.

>> *History*

UPS began as the American Messenger Company in Seattle, Washington, a private message and delivery service founded in 1907 by nineteen-year-old Jim Casey. In 1929, the company began offering package delivery by airplane from the West Coast to Texas. A short time later, the company changed its name to United Parcel Service, and all of its vehicles were painted the famous Pullman brown still seen on vehicles and uniforms today. UPS continued to expand its reach nationwide, and in 1988 the company received authorization to operate its own airline.

In December 1994, UPS launched its first website, www.ups.com. UPS launched additional websites in 1998, including UPS and the Community (community.ups.com), UPS and E-Commerce (www.ec .ups.com), and UPS Document Exchange (exchange.ups.com). UPS has also created websites for public relations efforts, including the UPS Panda Express (pandaexpress.ups.com). Today UPS operates in more than 200 countries and delivers more than 13 million packages to more than 1.8 million customers daily. The company's website receives more than a million package-tracking requests per day. According to the company, in 1999 the website received about 2 to 3 percent of all daily Internet traffic. In 2000 UPS was named America's Most Admired transportation company by *Fortune* magazine for the seventeenth consecutive year.

>> *Brand Attributes*

The UPS brand has the following core brand characteristics:

- *Quality, reliable service*—UPS is known as a reliable delivery service. Its expert logistics and sophisticated package tracking have set the standard for delivery services. The UPS logistics group has even served as a consultant to other companies.

- *Technological innovator*—UPS spends more than $1 billion on information technology every year. The UPS website is full of innovative e-commerce and Web-based tools that customers can easily use to track packages or add package tracking to their own e-commerce website. According to UPS, the company plans to be the global facilitator of commerce in the next century—moving goods, information, and funds.

- *Fast and flexible*—The company's tag line demonstrates the attributes of speed and flexibility: "UPS. Moving at the speed of business."

>> *The UPS Online Brand Experience*

According to Tom Daly, the online national brand manager of UPS, "The goal of our website is to ensure that it performs in a way that is consistent with the UPS brand." Features that demonstrate the UPS brand on the website include screen design and flow, utility, and download speeds. UPS is well known for package tracking, and customers can efficiently track packages from the UPS website. The company also allows other websites to include UPS tracking. UPS offers companies additional tools for managing e-commerce. Tools such as UPS-branded package tracking and cost calculators on other websites should help make UPS as ubiquitous on the Web as it is in the offline world. "Each time another website's customer uses UPS tracking, it is a branding opportunity for us," says Daly.

UPS has created other websites to communicate its brand positioning and promise through public relations demonstrating the company's expert capabilities as the largest provider of express package delivery. In 1998 UPS created a website for Keiko, the whale that was featured in the movie *Free Willy*. UPS had played a central role in moving the whale from Mexico City to his new home in Oregon. Web visitors could track the location of Keiko during his journey, just as customers can track their own packages. Similarly, in 1999 UPS shipped another care package: two giant pandas traveling from China to Zoo Atlanta. Visitors to the UPS Panda Express website, shown in Exhibit A.1, could meet and track the pandas, Lun-Lun and Yang-Yang. The website also took the opportunity to showcase UPS expertise in logistics and shipping. This website allowed UPS to connect with customers via their emotional connection with the animals, making the UPS brand very approachable.

Besides using the Web to support package delivery, UPS introduced the UPS Document Exchange in 1998. With Document Exchange, customers have an alternative to sending documents in hard-copy (paper) format via express delivery; instead, a customer can send a document in a secure, encrypted electronic format via the Internet. E-mail has become one of the most popular ways to send documents via the Internet. Companies have embraced e-mail because it is faster and cheaper. Thus, UPS has embraced Internet technology, rather than shying away from it.

In a speech to the International Mass Retailers Conference, Jim Kelly, chairman and CEO of United Parcel Service, said, "We can either build brand power by differentiating our products through quality service, innovation, and even new lines of business, or we can prepare to compete on price alone. We have no intention of becoming a price-shopped commodity player. This is equivalent of killing your brand as far as I'm concerned." Although UPS has changed dramatically over almost a century, the brand has remained consistent yet flexible in order to adapt to a changing marketplace—moving from low-technology transportation of packages to high-technology transfer of documents and monetary funds. The UPS website has been the

EXHIBIT A.1
_____

UPS Panda Express Website
_____

>> *Courtesy of United Parcel Service Corporate Public Relations.*

bridge connecting these changes. This is what executives at UPS call "brand elasticity"—being able to stretch the brand.

>> Take It from UPS

"Brand is of paramount importance," says Tom Daly, online national brand manager at UPS. This is a unique philosophy, considering how UPS as a company is driven by technology. UPS.com is an extension of the service our customers have come to know. Our job is to make it a favorable experience, meeting the same expectations our customers have experienced in the real world. We have brought dependability, trust, knowledge, and personal service to the website."

Fatbrain.com: Smarter than Its Name Suggests

www.fatbrain.com

The biggest challenge for any company is picking the right brand name—because the name of the brand is everything. The brand name embodies and conveys the brand promise and personality. For fatbrain.com, selecting a name was a gut-wrenching experience that tested the company and its customers. The experience was quite risky, according to CEO Chris MacAskill, but sometimes the greatest rewards come from the greatest risks.

>> History

Like many dot-coms, fatbrain.com started out in a cofounder's garage. With the name Cbooks, the company was founded in June 1995. Two years later, the founders bought Computer Literacy, a small chain of bricks-and-mortar computer bookstores in Silicon Valley, and went online under the name Computerliteracy.com. The company's mission is to be "THE place for professionals seeking information resources that contribute to career enhancement."

In March 1999, Computer Literacy changed its name to fatbrain.com. Under that name, the company has expanded its product offerings from computer books to science, math, and business books and training products. Besides selling books to the retail market, fatbrain.com works with corporations to set up a cobranded bookstore on the companies' intranets. In August 1999, fatbrain.com introduced eMatter, a secure digital publishing service that authors and publishers can use to publish short documents and entire books.

>> Brand Attributes

The fatbrain.com brand has the following core characteristics:

- *Focused on helping the professional*—The fatbrain.com website provides many features that help professionals, including a targeted selection of books and training products, precision search engine, custom recommendations from customer service, online reviews, detailed information about books, staff recommendations, minisites for special-interest groups, and FINDitNOW, the customized company intranet bookstores.

- *Smart and geeky*—The fatbrain.com product selection reflects this brand attribute by focusing solely on professional titles for computers, Internet, business, science, and math, rather than making the company a mass retailer of every type of book. The company's tag line, "Because great minds think a lot," demonstrates the smart and geeky brand attribute. Thus, fatbrain.com is all about growing the large intellect.

- *Irreverent and friendly*—Much of the style of fatbrain.com's website, especially the copy, reflects this characteristic. For example, fatbrain.com engineers have their own recommendations for computer book titles, which are presented in favorites lists alongside photos of the engineers. Within the Engineers' Favorites section, the following text expresses fatbrain.com's refusal to take itself too seriously: "We've got computer books coming out of our ears. So why do we use these? 'Cause they work!"

>> Brand-Marketing Program

Like many dot-com start-ups, fatbrain.com is reshuffling its media mix. In 1998, 82 percent of the company's budget was online. In 1999, more than two-thirds of the budget shifted to offline marketing activities such as magazine advertising (see, for example, Exhibit A.2). In the future, fatbrain.com plans to increase its offline presence further, possibly using television, radio, and outdoor advertising. The company's experience so far has been that magazine advertisements are most effective for branding and banner ads are least effective.

Some online cobranding partnerships have done much to build fatbrain.com's brand awareness. The most successful cobranding relationships have been those that were the most integrated—presenting books on websites that complemented the products the partner site was selling. Cobranding has worked extremely well when it has involved complete integration right down to an integrated shopping cart that allows the Web customer to order products from both fatbrain.com and the cobranding partner at the same time.

For fatbrain.com, the website establishes brand loyalty better than traditional branding vehicles do, because the relationship with the customer has more depth. The company gives customers an inside look at the company as much as possible, so customers can really experience fatbrain.com. The website makes it easy for a customer to interact with company representatives, and the company's culture and personality permeate the website to reach the customer.

Ultimately, in terms of brand-marketing results, the best performer has been fatbrain.com's own customer e-mail list. The company also uses opt-in e-mail marketing lists, but they don't perform as

EXHIBIT A.2

Fatbrain.com Magazine Ad

>> *Courtesy of fatbrain.com.*

well as fatbrain.com's own e-mail list. To build its customer database and e-mail list, fatbrain.com uses sweepstakes and other promotions.

<< *What's in a Name?* >> The name *is* the brand. It represents everything about the brand, including brand personality, promise, and positioning. Creating a new name is difficult. It is very personal, and companies must try to get the right name the first time. It is more difficult to change a brand name. Brands have to get customers to unlearn the old name and learn a new name, which is not only difficult, but expensive. However, Computer Literacy undertook such a change because several events suggested its original name wasn't an advantage.

To succeed online, the company needed a name that Web users would remember, know how to spell, and like. Observing browsing behavior, the company found that when users typed *computer* and *literacy* into their search engines, links to Computer Literacy's website were buried amidst hundreds of thousands of references. Worsening the problem, many of the users had difficulty spelling (ironically) *literacy*. Certainly, CEO MacAskill could appreciate that this was a problem, and the importance of standing out in a crowd was reinforced when he heard Amazon.com founder Jeff Bezos speak at a conference. Bezos commented that readers' ratings of books affected their sales; books that received the highest or lowest ratings outsold books rated in the middle—"proving once again that the only real problem in life is to be ignored."

Computer Literacy definitely did not want to be ignored. Rather, it wanted a name that Web users would notice and click on. From CNET (www.cnet.com), the company learned that when an Internet brand such as Outpost.com was placed alongside a bricks-and-mortar brand like CompUSA, the Internet brand got overwhelmingly more click-throughs. CNET users are primarily early Net adopters and technophiles, like Computer Literacy's own target market. Thus, CNET's experience that customers prefer dot-com brands seemed to apply to Computer Literacy. Clearly, the company needed a dot-com name.

With these insights, the company could set goals for its new name: It should be eight characters or less, so customers could type it in quickly. Also, the name must be memorable and evoke emotions and imagery. Thinking of such a name was difficult, to say the least. Many names were proposed. Focus groups like most of the names, but none yielded excitement. Meanwhile, Deborah Bohn, the company's director of editorial, was doing a little research of her own, trying to find names that weren't already taken (which is quite difficult for anyone registering a domain on the Internet these days). She thought up a unique domain name, "fatbrain.com." And the name met one goal: focus groups, company employees, and partners all had strong emotional reactions—mostly negative emotional reactions. But the high degree of emotion convinced Paul Parkin from Interbrand, the company helping find a new name, that this was *the* name for the company.

MacAskill asked other dot-com companies such as Yahoo!, Motley Fool (fool.com), and FogDog about their experience with brand naming. All of these companies said that people hated the company names at first. So Computer Literacy ran a third focus group. Participants hated fatbrain.com less than in previous focus groups, but the scores remained negative. Still, encouraged by other dot-coms' experiences, the company launched fatbrain.com. The launch received great press—positive news coverage from everyone from CNN to the *Wall Street Journal*. Best of all, the stock price doubled.

Today, some customers buy from fatbrain.com just because of the name. When asked whether the fatbrain.com name has caused the company's personality to come out further, MacAskill replied, "Most definitely."

<< *Getting Inside Companies' Heads* >> Besides the requisite affiliate marketing program, fatbrain.com has a strategy that is unusual for an online book retailer. The company partners with corporations to set up a cobranded internal online bookstore, customized to each company's needs. This intranet bookstore service is called FINDitNOW. (See Exhibit A.3 for a sample Web page.) The service is completely in line with fatbrain.com's positioning and also recognizes that the busi-

ness-to-business book market offers significant differentiation from the crowded online book market, as well as a significant growth opportunity.

With this strategy, establishing brand trust is crucial. A corporation has to really trust a brand and company in order to let the brand operate on its secure corporate intranet. Not surprisingly, the name change presented a challenge to this service. Companies were comfortable with a conservative noncontroversial name like Computer Literacy, whereas fatbrain.com is far from sounding formal and corporate. However, despite fatbrain.com's informal name, its FINDitNOW intranet bookstore service is being used by many large corporations, including Hewlett-Packard, Xerox PARC, Cisco Systems, Sun Microsystems, and Bank of America.

<< *If You Don't Mind, We'll Do eMatter* >> Just as fatbrain.com created a new model for the process of buying business books and training products, the company is creating a whole new model for book

EXHIBIT A.3

Demo of Fatbrain.com's Cobranded Intranet Bookstores

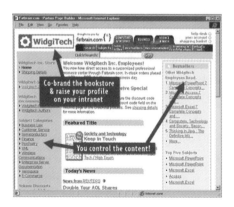

>> *Courtesy of fatbrain.com.*

publishing using the Internet. Its service, called eMatter, does not just digitally publish books for publishers. It is more of a community-oriented service that brings together buyers and sellers of valuable content. Think of it as a meeting of the minds. Authors can self-publish their works, corporations can publish their own materials and documentation, and magazine publishers can make content available online, to name just a few options. Short runs, sample chapters, short works, out-of-print titles, and other works can be made available.

This type of service will change the face of publishing. With companies like fatbrain.com driving the change, the Internet is about creating new models, not just creating new spins on the same old things.

>> *Take It from Fatbrain.com*

About fatbrain.com's name, CEO MacAskill says, "When it comes to the Internet, the naming process is not the conventional method of creating a name that is descriptive. For us, it was creating a name that would make an emotional connection, that would be memorable and distinct." He adds a caution that especially applies to Internet-only companies: "Dot-com companies that don't have retail presence have to get noticed, since they don't have a storefront on every corner. Online it is about getting noticed; otherwise, you will be ignored."

Virgin Atlantic Airways: Shaglantic, "Yeah, Baby!"

www.virgin-atlantic.com

Virgin Atlantic Airways was one of the first airlines on the Web, a move that was consistent with the brand's attribute of being innovative. The airline has been able to leverage the Internet medium's targeting capabilities and interactive nature. Virgin Atlantic, born from entertainment, uses entertaining Web features and marketing campaigns to further its online presence. One of Virgin Atlantic's key promotions in 1999 was a campaign that coincided with the release of the very popular pop-culture movie *Austin Powers: The Spy Who*

Shagged Me. A related contest and events created all kinds of media buzz that contributed to Virgin Atlantic's success.

>> History

Virgin Atlantic Airways was created in 1994 by Richard Branson, an exuberant U.K. entrepreneur, as an extension of the Virgin record company brand Branson had started in the early 1970s. His original strategy for the airline was to create a passenger service from London to New York. Now Virgin Atlantic flies out of London's Heathrow and Gatwick airports to fourteen destinations all over the world.

Virgin Atlantic embodies the entertainment and service personality of its parent company, the Virgin Group, by delivering the best in-flight experience a traveler can have. This view of service experience comes from Branson himself.

Virgin Atlantic was one of the first airlines with a website, which was launched in 1996. The company released its second-generation website in June 1999.

>> Brand Attributes

The Virgin Atlantic brand has these core characteristics:

- *Entertaining and fun*—Virgin Atlantic stands out in its approach to flying in that it focuses on the actual flying experience, instead of just moving people from one destination to another. Travelers are entertained with the latest movie releases, television, radio, computer games, *Hot Air* magazine, and/or the animated Sky Map, which shows travelers what country they are flying over at any time during the flight. Virgin Atlantic also has entertainment dedicated to child travelers—notably, a K-iD backpack filled with goodies and kid-friendly food such as burgers and french fries. Travelers who fly Premier Class can expect a chauffeur-driven limousine, haircut, manicure, and massage.

- *Hip and innovative*—Coming from its entertainment roots, Virgin Atlantic is hip—which means the company is aware of the latest developments and trends, including the desire for informality. Also drawing on its Virgin roots, the airline has been an innovator. It consistently reinvents travel and service. Virgin Atlantic features the newest planes in the industry, which have personal video screens at every seat, movies on demand, music on demand, video games, and telephones. What other company's CEO travels around the world in a hot-air balloon? That is pretty hip—and daring.

- *Niche air travel service*—Virgin Atlantic serves very specific markets with a specially positioned travel product. The airline has transatlantic flights to London from eight U.S. airports. From London, Virgin Atlantic serves South Africa, Greece, Japan, Hong Kong, the Caribbean, and Shanghai.

>> Brand-Marketing Program

Virgin Atlantic's marketing programs for the transatlantic flight service are highly targeted, since the airline serves only seven gateway airports: New York, Los Angeles, San Francisco, Miami, Orlando, Boston, and Washington, D.C. The primary goal for Virgin Atlantic's website is to generate online revenue—specifically, flight bookings. Marketing efforts related to the website are designed to promote the brand and generate traffic and response.

Until recently, 90 percent of the company's marketing budget was dedicated to offline marketing efforts. To promote the airline and the website, Virgin Atlantic uses traditional media, including radio, direct mail, public relations, outdoor promotions and contests, events, and sports. According to Sarah Buxton, formerly director of marketing for Virgin Atlantic Airways and now director of marketing at Virgin Entertainment Group, the most effective marketing activities for Virgin Atlantic have been events, promotions, and publicity. Buxton says Virgin Atlantic believes in programs that are highly integrated: "Integration is fundamental for us. It's all about using online to deliver the brand experience that our offline brand stands for. Online is essentially a media vehicle and we integrate it just as we would integrate all vehicles in our media mix." Integration extends to measurement tools. Virgin Atlantic uses an annual brand-tracking study across all media to determine overall brand awareness.

Virgin Atlantic is planning to shift its budget to include 25 percent online. Buxton explains why: "The Web has been an excellent vehicle for promoting the Virgin Atlantic brand, since it is a true niche product. Since we compete with airlines with very large marketing budgets, we were able to use the Web to reach potential customers cost-effectively and create a perception of size and power online." The airline uses many online marketing activities, including banner ads, site sponsorships, other online advertising formats, promotions and contests, e-mail lists, e-mail newsletters, and affiliate programs. The company has found that banner ads and content sponsorships in travel and entertainment sections of websites have worked well for generating brand awareness online. For enhancing brand loyalty online, what has worked is giving customers access to the frequent-flier program on the website, along with making special offers to online customers.

<< *The Virgin Atlantic Experience: In Flight and Online* >> The Virgin Atlantic website contains features to deliver the brand experience online. "Since Virgin started out as an entertainment brand and we provide an entertaining in-flight experience, our website needs to reflect this attribute," states Buxton. In addition to flight schedules and frequent-flier account management, the website includes interactive features to give a consistent brand experience online. For example, website visitors can see a 360-degree view of Virgin Atlantic planes and the Virgin Clubhouse lounges around the world.

>> *Austin Powers Campaign*

When New Line Cinema released the second Austin Powers movie, *The Spy Who Shagged Me,* Virgin Atlantic capitalized on the event to promote its flights to London, home of the Austin Powers character (see www.austinpowers.com). Like the Virgin Atlantic brand, this popular movie about an English spy and his travels and antics embodies a spirit of entertainment and fun. Many elements of the promotional campaign built upon one another to generate "enormous equivalency through press exposure," in the words of Virgin Atlantic's Buxton. In other words, the publicity brought about a lot of so-called free advertising.

The campaign was a giveaway of 1,000 free trips to London from the U.S. during a ten-hour period. Its goals were to create brand awareness through publicity and to capture data for the company's prospect database. The campaign included several elements:

- *Event promotion website*—At the website (www.virginshaglantic .com, shown in Exhibit A.4) contest participants played a game of chance to try to win one of the 1,000 tickets.

- *Newspaper ads*—The ads, in papers for all of the gateway cities, announced the online event at the promotional website.

- *Outdoor advertising*—The billboards, such as the one in Exhibit A.5, appeared in the gateway cities.

- *Major public relations effort*—News releases about the promotion generated significant print and broadcast exposure, which drove traffic to the website.

- *Event marketing*—A key event was the release of a 747 jet painted with the Austin Powers character. Mike Meyers, who played a few of the characters in the movie, including Austin Powers, was present with Richard Branson for the christening of the newly painted jet in Los Angeles one month before the movie debut. Everyone who flew on this plane received Austin Powers masks and other promotional items.

- *Interactive Austin campaign*—This e-mail campaign, by New Line Cinema, included an interactive Richard Branson character. Interactive Austin was an episodic adventure communicated via e-mail.

- *Additional tie-in campaign elements*

The ten-hour campaign generated significant publicity that resulted in twenty million website hits and 100,000 site registrants within the duration of the campaign. Among the contest winners, 99 percent purchased companion tickets at a time of the year when the airline normally expects a lull in demand.

Well-coordinated events proved powerful for increasing the brand awareness of Virgin Atlantic Airways within its geographic and demographic target markets. The Austin Powers promotion was a great fit with the personality of the airline.

EXHIBIT A.4

Promotional Website for the "Virgin Shaglantic" Campaign

>> Courtesy of Virgin Atlantic Airways.

>> *Take It from Virgin Atlantic Airways*

Buxton speaks from experience when she says, "Online demands that you really provide entertainment and value to the customer in your branding effort, or you simply won't get noticed. In the online environment, the brand is effectively your 'talent.' You have to use it to get people to choose to interact with you."

EXHIBIT A.5

Billboard Advertising for the "Virgin Shaglantic" Campaign

>> *Courtesy of Virgin Atlantic Airways.*

[**Resource Guide**]

A whole host of resources is available on the Internet and in print. Here is a select list of resources used in the development of this book. Visit the book's website, **www.brandingbook.com**, for a monthly editorial and convenient links to these and other resources.

>> *Internet Population, Usage, and Demographics*

Computer Industry Almanac—*www.c-i-a.com*
CyberAtlas—*www.cyberatlas.com*
Cyber Dialogue—*www.cyberdialogue.com*
GVU WWW Surveys—*www.gvu.gatech.edu/user_surveys*
Harris Interactive—*www.harrisinteractive.com*
Headcount—*www.headcount.com*
IDC Research—*www.idc.com*
IntelliQuest—*www.intelliquest.com*
Media Metrix—*www.mediametrix.com*
NFO Interactive—*www.nfoi.com*
Nielsen//NetRatings—*www.nielsen-netratings.com*
NUA Internet Surveys—*www.nua.ie/surveys/*

>> *Brand Marketing and Advertising*

Ad Talk—*www.adtalk.com*

Advertising Age—www.adage.com

Advertising Media Internet Center—*www.amic.com*

Advertising World—*advweb.cocomm.utexas.edu/world/*

Adweek—www.adweek.com

Association of National Advertisers—*www.ana.net*

Business Marketing—*www.businessmarketing.com*

Direct Marketing Association—*www.the-dma.org*

Marketing (U.K.)—www.marketing.haynet.com

Media Central—*www.mediacentral.com*

>> *Online Marketing and Advertising*

@d:tech—*www.ad-tech.com*

Adknowledge—*www.adknowledge.com*

Ad Resource—*adres.internet.com*

Back Channel—*www.aaaa.org/bc*

BrandEra.com—*www.brandera.com*

CASIE—*www.casie.org*

Channel Seven—*www.channelseven.com*

Cheskin Research—*www.cheskin.com*

ClickZ.com—*www.clickz.com*

Digitrends—*www.digitrends.net*

eMarketer—*www.emarketer.com*

FAST (Future of Advertising Stakeholders)—*www.fastinfo.org*

IBM HotMedia—*www.ibm.com/hotmedia*

Iconocast—*www.iconocast.com*

Internet Advertising Bureau (IAB)—*www.iab.net*

Internet Advertising Report—*www.internetnews.com/IAR/*

Internet Advertising Resource Guide—*www.admedia.org*

Internet Marketing News—*www.imarketingnews.com*

IPSOS-ASI Interactive—*www.testing1234.com/extranet/*

MB Interactive—*www.mbinteractive.com*

NetMarketing—*www.netb2b.com*

Web Marketing Info Center—*www.wilsonweb.com/webmarket*

>> *E-Business, E-Commerce, and Web Design*

ActivMedia—*www.activmedia.com*

Business 2.0—*www.business2.com*

Business Week eBiz—*www.businessweek.com/ebiz/*

CIO WebBusiness—*webbusiness.cio.com*

eLab (Project 2000)—*www2000.ogsm.vanderbilt.edu*

Forrester Research—*www.forrester.com*

The Industry Standard—*www.thestandard.com*

Interactive Week—*www.interactiveweek.com*

Internet Indicators—*www.internetindicators.com*

Jakob Nielsen's Useit.com—*www.useit.com*

Jupiter Communications—*www.jup.com*

New Media—*www.newmedia.com*

One-to-One Web Marketing—*www.1to1web.com*

Personalization.com—*www.personalization.com*

Usable Web—*www.usableweb.com*

>> *Other*

Electronic Privacy Information Center—*www.epic.org*

Federal Trade Commission (U.S.)—*www.ftc.gov*

Hobbes Internet Timeline—*info.isoc.org/guest/zakon/Internet /History/HIT.html*

Online Privacy Alliance—*www.privacyalliance.org*

[Bibliography and Recommended Readings]

Articles, Papers, Newsletters, and Reports

ActivMedia. "Website Success: Strategies, Benchmarks and Best Practices."
ActivMedia Inc., 1999.

AdKnowledge. "AdKnowledge eAnalytics Online Advertising Report."
AdKnowledge, Inc., Third Quarter 1999.

Briggs, R. "Abolish Clickthrough—Now!" *Digitrends*, Fall 1999, 83–86.

Burrows, P., A. Reinhardt, and H. Green. "Beyond the PC." *Business Week*,
March 8, 1999, 79–88.

Cheskin Research. "The eCommerce Trust Study." Cheskin Research and
Studio Archetype/Sapient, January 1999.

———. "Sound and Brand: The Impact of Sound on the Web," Cheskin
Research and Beatnik, Inc., March 1999.

———. "Teens and the Future of the Web." Cheskin Research and
Cyberteens.com, August 1999.

Davis, J. "A New Way of Branding." *Business 2.0*, November 1998, 75–86.

eMarketer. "The eAdvertising Report." eMarketer, April 1999.

Excite@Home. "Rich Media I Advertising," Excite@Home and Intel
Corporation, March 1999.

———. "Rich Media II Advertising." Excite@Home and Intel Corporation,
August 1999.

Hamm, S. "Masters of the Web Universe." *Business Week e.biz*, September 27,
1999, EB21–EB68.

Hof, R. "The New Era of Bright Hopes and Terrible Fears." *Business Week,* October 4, 1999.

———. "Now It's Your Web." *Business Week,* October 5, 1998, 164–178.

IntelliQuest. "eBranding Insights." Austin, Tex.: IntelliQuest, Inc., First Quarter 1999.

———. "WWITS: Worldwide Internet/Online Tracking Service." Austin, Tex.: IntelliQuest, Inc. Second Quarter 1999.

Internet Advertising Bureau (IAB) and PriceWaterhouseCoopers, "IAB Internet Advertising Revenue Report." IAB, First Quarter 1999.

Keller, K. L., M. Lindsay, B. Wansink, and J. Karolefski. "The Century of Brands." *Brand Marketing,* Spring 1999, 3–83.

Kirsner, S. "The Customer Experience." *Fast Company,* Fall 1999, 12–21.

Mandell, M. J. "The Internet Economy: The World's Next Growth Engine." *Business Week,* October 4, 1999, 74.

Masten, D. "Silence of the Brands." *Business 2.0,* November 1999, 216–224.

McQuivey, J. L. "The Net Powered Generation." Forrester Research, August 1999.

Millard, E. "Spool of Thought." *Business 2.0,* October 1999, 219-221.

Mooney, K. "The Experienced Customer." *Fast Company,* Fall 1999, 24–29.

Nail, J., with J. Aldort, C. Charron, and T. Grimsditch. "Driving Site Traffic." Forrester Research, April 1999.

Nail, J., with J. Aldort and B. Bass. "The New Brand Experience." Forrester Research, September 1998.

Neuborne, E., and R. D. Hof. "Branding on the Net." *Business Week,* November 9, 1998, 74–86.

Nickell, J. A. "Marketing Makeover." *Business 2.0,* October 1999, 91–92.

Peppers, D., and M. Rogers. "The State of One to One Online." Stamford, Conn.: Peppers and Rogers Group, April 1999.

Rayport, J. F., and J. J. Sviokla. "Managing in the Marketplace." *Harvard Business Review,* November–December 1994, 141–150.

Sealey, P. "Brand Building in the 21st Century." *The Advertiser,* October/November 1999, 32–36.

———. "How E-Commerce Will Trump Brand Management." *Harvard Business Review,* July–August 1999, 3–7.

Shern, S. M. "Global Online Retailing." Ernst & Young, January 2000, 11–23.

Shern, S. M., and F. Crawford. "The Second Annual Ernst & Young Internet Shopping Study." Ernst & Young, 1999.

Ward, S., L. Light, and J. Goldstine. "What High-Tech Managers Need to Know About Brands." *Harvard Business Review,* July–August 1999, 85–95.

Webster, R. "Web Site Management & Internet Advertising Trends," 3d ed. Association of National Advertisers, 1999.

Books

Aaker, D. A. *Building Strong Brands*. New York: Free Press, 1996.
———. *Managing Brand Equity*. New York: Free Press, 1991.
Allen, A., D. Kania, and B. Yaeckel. *Internet World Guide to One-To-One Web Marketing*. New York: John Wiley & Sons, 1998.
Clemente, P. *The State of the Net*, New York: McGraw-Hill, 1998.
Fox, S. *Mirror Makers*. New York: Vintage Books, 1985.
Godin, S. *Permission Marketing*, New York: Simon & Schuste, 1999.
Hagel, J., and A. G. Armstrong. *Net Gain*, Boston: Harvard Business School Press, 1997.
McKenna, R. *Real Time*. Boston: Harvard Business School Press, 1997.
Meeker, M. *The Internet Advertising Report*. New York: Harper Business, 1997.
Morgan, A. *Eating the Big Fish*. New York: John Wiley & Sons, 1999.
Pine, B. J., and J. H. Gilmore. *The Experience Economy*. Boston: Harvard Business School Press, 1999.
Reichheld, F. *The Loyalty Effect*. Boston: Harvard Business School Press, 1996.
Smith, J. W., and A. Curlman. *Rocking the Ages*. New York: Harper Business, 1997.
Tapscott, D. *Growing Up Digital*. New York: McGraw-Hill, 1998.
Upshaw, L. B. *Building Brand Identity*. New York: John Wiley & Sons, 1995.

Websites

Buskin, J. "Online Persuaders." *Wall Street Journal*, Interactive, www.wsj.com, July 12, 1999.
Cranor, L. F., J. Reagle, and M. S. Ackerman. "Beyond Concern: Understanding Net Users' Attitudes About Online Privacy." AT&T Labs—Research, website, www.research.att.com/projects/privacystudy, April 1999.
CyberAtlas, "US Internet Users Going Wireless." www.cyberatlas.com, April 17, 2000.
Georgia Tech Graphic, Visualization and Usability (GVU) Center. www.cc.gatech.edu/gvu/user_surveys, April 1997–October 1998.

Goode, E. "The Online Customer? Tough, Impatient and Gone in a Blink of an Eye." www.nytimes.com, September 22, 1999.

Levine, R., C. Locke, D. Searls, and D. Weinberger. The Cluetrain Manifesto. www.cluetrain.com, 1999.

Media History Project. www.mediahistory.com.

Messaging Online, "E-Mail Continues to Take over the World." www.messagingonline.com, April 2000.

Miller, M. "Looking Back." *PC Magazine*, www.zdnet.com/pcmag/special/anniversary/back/lkintro.htm, 1996.

U.S. Department of Commerce/National Telecommunications and Information Administration (NTIA). "Falling Through the Net: Defining the Digital Divide." www.ntia.doc.gov/ntiahome/digitaldivide, July 1999.

Index

The American Marketing Association is the world's largest and most comprehensive professional association of marketers. With over 45,000 members, the AMA has more than 500 chapters throughout North America. The AMA sponsors 25 major conferences per year, covering topics ranging from the latest trends in customer satisfaction measurement to business-to-business and service marketing, attitude research and sales promotion, and publishes nine major marketing publications.

For further information on the American Marketing Association call toll free at 800-AMA-1150.

Or write to:

The American Marketing Association
311 South Wacker Drive
Suite 5800
Chicago, IL 60606-2266
Fax: 800-950-0872
URL: http://www.ama.org